D1565638

GOETHE'S MODERNISMS

ASTRIDA ORLE TANTILLO

continuum

2010

The Continuum International Publishing Group Inc
80 Maiden Lane, New York, NY 10038

The Continuum International Publishing Group Ltd
The Tower Building, 11 York Road, London SE1 7NX

www.continuumbooks.com

"Damned to Heaven: The Tragedy of *Faust* Revisited." Originally published in *Monatshefte* 99.4 (Winter 2007): 454–68. © 2007 by the Board of Regents of the University of Wisconsin System. Reproduced courtesy of the University of Wisconsin Press.

"The Subjective Eye: Goethe's *Farbenlehre* and *Faust*." Originally published in *The Enlightened Eye: Goethe and Visual Culture*. Eds. Evelyn Moore and Patricia Simpson. Amsterdam: Editions Rodopi, 2007. 265–77. © 2007 Editions Rodopi. Reproduced courtesy of Editions Rodopi.

"The Catholicism of Werther." Originally published in the *German Quarterly* 81 (2008): 408–23. © 2008 by the *German Quarterly*. Reproduced courtesy of *German Quarterly*.

Cover image of Goethe's Color Circle courtesy of the Frankfurter Goethe-Haus — Freies Deutsches Hochstift. Photograph by David Hall.

Library of Congress Cataloging-in-Publication Data
A catalog record for this book is available from the Library of Congress.

ISBN: 978-1-4411-8832-8 (hardcover)
         978-1-4411-2020-5 (paperback)

Typeset by Pindar NZ, Auckland, New Zealand
Printed in the United States of America

For Steve

CONTENTS

ABBREVIATIONS AND GOETHE EDITIONS

Unless otherwise noted, quotations from Goethe's works are taken from the *Sämtliche Werke* (Ed. Hendrik Birus, *et al.* 40 vols. Frankfurt: Deutscher Klassiker Verlag, 1985–) and are abbreviated in the text as "FA." All translations from Goethe's works, unless otherwise noted, are taken from *Goethe's Collected Works* (12 vols. New York: Suhrkamp, 1983–89).

ACKNOWLEDGEMENTS

I would very much like to thank my editor at Continuum, Haaris Naqvi, who was enthusiastic and supportive of the project from the beginning. Many people have helped me to write this book. I am grateful to my graduate students from the "Goethe and the Modern World" seminar and to the participants from the 2008 Eighteenth-Century Workshop at the Newberry Library, especially to Dorothea von Mücke and Angela Borchert. My gratitude extends to Msgr R. Michael Schmitz for his instruction in the intellectual tradition of Catholicism. I am very thankful for the help and support of my colleagues and friends, Bill Bridges, Jerry Graff, Agnes Herget, Daryl Koehn, Susan Levine, Imke Meyer, Susanne Rott, Heidi Schlipphacke, and John T. Scott. I also wish to thank the graphic designer, Andrea Federle-Bucsi, for her enthusiasm for my project and the wonderful cover that emerged. My research assistant, Vera Pollina, did an amazing job on all aspects of the project, and I am thankful for the care and seriousness with which she approached the task. I would, however, most like to thank my husband, Steve, who has helped me on every aspect and at every phase of the book and without whom it never would have been completed.

Finally, I am grateful to Rodopi, *Monatshefte*, and the *German Quarterly* for the permission to reuse portions and earlier versions of my work.

INTRODUCTION

This book argues that by studying the works of Johann Wolfgang von Goethe (1749–1832), we can gain insights into the foundational principles of American society and its shortcomings. Perhaps most importantly, this study also reveals him to be one of modernity's profoundest critics. His works have exerted a pivotal influence on the development of modern Western society, and this influence has spread far and wide, shaping not only aesthetic issues, but a myriad of cultural and intellectual ones as well.[1]

Several nineteenth-century figures already recognized Goethe as a modern *par excellence* and wrote of his multifaceted influence in Europe as well as in America. His novels, scientific works, and poetry were read and admired and touted by supporters on both continents as endorsing democracy, evolution, and a heightened notion of individualism. The influential Jesuit priest and literary critic, Alexander Baumgartner (1841–1910), tried to struggle against this trend. While admiring the artistry of Goethe's poetry, Baumgartner worried about his power as an "idol" of modernity and asked whether Goethe's works should be viewed with suspicion, i.e., as "the Trojan horse" that threatened to undermine traditional values and society as a whole. Others, like Ralph Waldo Emerson (1803–82), embraced Goethe as the quintessential modern: "all before [Goethe] are ancients, and all who have read him are modern" (242). Emerson, unlike Baumgartner, encouraged others to follow Goethe's suit. Surprisingly, given Goethe's own bourgeois background and at times aristocratic leanings, important Marxists, including Karl Marx (1818–83), Friedrich Engels (1820–95), and Georg Lukács (1885–1971), see Goethe's works as promoting a progressive stage in world history. This book takes up such interpretive tensions and contends that Goethe's works introduced and promulgated central concepts of modernity, including individualism, bourgeois values,

---

[1] Goethe still has marketing pull: Scott paper towels, Celestial Seasonings Tea, and Yoga to the People have all used his words to help sell their products.

1

capitalism, secularism, and faith in scientific progress. At the same time, however, it also argues that Goethe himself warned against aspects of these same concepts — the very ones that his most strident proponents have associated with him.

In a recent biography, *Love, Life, Goethe,* John Armstrong argues that we can learn a great deal by studying Goethe's life. The scope of what we can learn, for Armstrong, however, remains largely on the small, household, and individual scale. In the end, he wishes to make of Goethe a guru of the everyday — a kind of Martha Stewart meets Dr Phil. According to this author, if we read Goethe's works and study his life, we will gain "hints on how to live. Keeping the house clean, arranging kitchen cupboards and balancing the books, all have their real dignity illuminated by Goethe's loving regard" (16). I would agree with Armstrong that Goethe has a great deal to teach us, but I argue that his lessons are on a much grander scale than organizing cupboards and often contradict the message of self-indulgence that Armstrong wrests from Goethe's life.[2] Goethe's works treat extensively those aspects of society where tensions and fissures arise. In science, should we value the benefits to society to the extent that we become willing to sacrifice individuals for the greater good of all? How should we weigh gains in our physical well-being against losses in the arts and education? What happens to art in a technologically advanced society? Can democracies, with their strong sense of majority rule, become oppressive forces in themselves? Do they enervate one's spirituality and destroy a sense of community by empowering the individual too much? What happens to educational systems when we care more about self-esteem than knowledge?

These are the sorts of questions that Goethe's works explore and will be the ones at the center of this book. His age, like our own, was one in which technology was quickly changing all aspects of life and culture; fundamentalist beliefs came into direct conflict with secular ones; and groups fiercely debated pedagogical methodology. Each chapter of this book presents an interpretation of literary texts and then demonstrates their connection to a contemporary issue, namely 1) the ascendancy of science and technology and their close connection to new economic theories (*The Tragedy of Faust*); 2) the cultural success of religious Evangelicalism and its consequences (*The Sorrows of Young Werther*); and 3) the pros and cons of progressive, student-centered education (the *Wilhelm Meister* novels).

---

[2] For a more extensive analysis of Armstrong's book, see my review of it.

A natural question that may arise for a reader is why I have decided to focus on the repercussions of Goethe's thinking for contemporary American culture rather than upon Europe or the West as a whole. In part, the answer can be found within Goethe's writings. He was both entranced and repulsed by aspects of what America promised, and in his own works, he reflects upon the future possibilities in America. In the *Wilhelm Meister* novels, some characters go to America because of the vast potential of commerce and economic development. They are excited about trying to form a new kind of government and community. Others, however, return disenchanted because America lacks culture and does not value the beautiful. The America within these pages existed, of course, only in Goethe's imagination, but I have been struck with the variety of similarities between Alexis de Tocqueville's (1805–59) 1831 eyewitness accounts and predictions and Goethe's slightly earlier speculations on the potential and the problems of the United States, and I draw some comparisons between the works of these two men throughout this book. America captured Goethe's imagination because it represented a breeding ground for what was new, and he predicted that it would lead the way to change society radically. For the issues addressed in this book, he was largely right: America embraced capitalism to a greater extent than Europe; emotion-based religion and secular spiritualism play much larger roles in American life than in Europe, which primarily treats religion as a cultural artifact; and progressive education has been a dominant force in America for about a hundred years, whereas Europe has only recently begun to explore more student-focused options. France's educational system, for example, still remains incredibly centralized and prescribed.

By turning to Goethe's immense influence — which over the years has been both endorsed and repudiated by the left and the right — we can gain acute insights into some of the more divisive issues of our time. His texts provide a fruitful source of inquiry because he refuses to divide ideas and trends into black and white categories, but forces us to examine opposing ideas and multiple perspectives before reaching a conclusion. His aesthetic corpus thus simultaneously presents at least two possible, albeit radically opposed, responses to the vicissitudes of the modern world: a liberal response that promotes faith in progress, secularism, and individualism, and a conservative one that views change with suspicion, suffers a sense of loss, and seeks to maintain traditional values. Indeed, I use the plural term "modernisms" in the title of this book to emphasize that Goethe's main philosophical approach, whether in his literary, scientific, or critical works, is one of dynamism that precludes simplistic points of view. Any decision, any political or cultural stance, has a cost associated with it, and, before forging a new path, we need to stop to consider what the consequences might be.

GOETHE'S DYNAMIC PHILOSOPHY: THE PRINCIPLE OF COMPENSATION

What is striking about many of Goethe's texts, and certainly about those addressed in this book, is that readers have been arguing over their most basic aspects ever since their publication. Although many have seen his works as endorsing modernity and liberal values, others have argued the opposite. It would not be surprising that critics disagree about books. What is surprising in this case is that they vehemently disagree about even their main messages and themes. Is *Faust* a paean to modern science or a cautionary tale against it? Does *Werther* condemn or valorize the growing power of individualism and its consequent influence upon religion? Should education be centered on experience or books — the student or the teacher?

These disagreements point to the heart of the matter regarding Goethe's texts and their complexity. The Goethe scholar Jane Brown is correct in her hesitation to label Goethe either a conservative or a modern, arguing: "But it was never possible for Goethe to see anything out of the larger context — neither the present nor the future could make any sense for him apart from their relation to the past" ("When is" 42). Goethe's works have had such staying power precisely because they have mirrored the complexity and contentiousness of modern issues. This propensity does not mean that they present, as many scholars of the last two to three decades would have it (e.g., Bennett, Miller, etc.), a postmodern perspective, i.e., one without some set of principles for evaluation. Rather, Goethe's works portray a world that revolves around dynamic gains and losses. His works, therefore, are enlightening to us because they assume that there are positive and negative outcomes to our actions no matter what they might be: while there may be better and worse solutions, there are no absolutely good and bad ones. By examining modernity in this way, we are better able to see not only how it is that we have arrived where we are, but also how to analyze the effects of the decisions that we are facing today. Within Goethe's works, whenever there is a loosening of strictures or traditions, whether political, aesthetic, pedagogical, or religious, there is a subsequent loss of some kind. Similarly, whatever advances he portrays, whether in technology or in the recognition of the importance of the individual, he examines those human spheres that are threatened as a result of these advances. It is telling that the great nineteenth-century scientist, Hermann von Helmholtz (1821–94), saw the principle of conservation of energy at work in Goethe's *Faust*.

Goethe himself referred to this type of dynamic principle as compensation and saw it as one of the most basic principles of natural and human behavior. In short, nothing can be added — e.g., a specialized feature of an animal, growth in political power — without something being taken away — e.g., a diminished appendage, a loss of some aspect of one's humanity. In many ways, this principle of compensation will become the guiding thread throughout this book. First, it provides the dynamic structure with which to understand Goethe's complex works, and second, it is a useful tool to analyze the contemporary issues that so divide us today. This principle, moreover, helps to explain why Goethe can be viewed in such opposing ways. His works portray and balance against each other different perspectives in an attempt to show the advantages and disadvantages to each.

As I have argued in more detail in my book, *The Will to Create*, Goethe was a natural philosopher in that he looked toward nature in order to understand human life. For him, nature as a whole was an entity that both followed rules and constantly created new ones. His compensation principle was one among several that he applied equally to his morphological studies as to his anthropological and literary ones. It therefore illustrates both how he understood the functioning of the natural world as well as how it could be applied to analyze various aspects of human society. Within his essays on comparative anatomy, he gives many examples of this principle. He thinks of animals as having been given a particular budget which they can expend upon their features. For example, if we compare the closely related snake and lizard, this principle would assert that snakes have a long body at the expense of having feet, whereas lizards have legs at the expense of body length. As he explains in the poem, "Metamorphosis of Animals":

So, if you see that a creature possesses a certain advantage,
Put the question at once: What is the fault that afflicts it
Elsewhere? — and seek to discover the defect, always inquiring;
Then at once you will find the key to the world of formation.

This principle becomes quite interesting when applied to the human sphere. The poet here argues that we can analyze the actions and endeavors of human beings in the same way we analyze the body types of animals. In questions regarding politics, morality, or aesthetics, the principle of compensation becomes our guide:

> May this beautiful concept of power and limit, of random
> Venture and law, freedom and measure, of order in motion,
> Defect and benefit, bring you high pleasure; gently instructive,
> Thus, the sacred Muse in her teaching tells you of harmonies.
> Moral philosophers never attained to a concept sublimer
> Nor did men of affairs, nor artists imagining; rulers,
> Worthy of power, enjoy their crowns on this account only. (1: 163)[3]

Like the specific features of animal forms, human endeavors have certain costs and limitations. If we seek to excel in a certain area, it will have costs in others. Whether in the realm of politics or aesthetics, Goethe examines the world according to give and take, or a dynamic version of the conservation of energy formula. In order to analyze the ultimate success or failure of an organism, a work of art, or a political structure, we need to examine not only what has been gained, but also what has been lost. A mole, for example, is extraordinarily well suited for digging, but this ability comes at the cost of its being able to see and move freely above ground. A poet who tries to incorporate political messages into his poetry loses artistic freedom and suffers as a poet (*Eckermann* March 1832).

Just as the compensation principle can describe stunted animal formations, so too does Goethe use it to describe stunted human personalities. Human beings can have "lopsided" characters because one trait dominates over others. We, however, have it within our power to change ourselves:

> We are well enough aware that some skill, some ability, usually predominates in the
> character of each human being. This leads necessarily to one-sided thinking since

---

[3] Siehst du also dem einen Geschöpf besonderen Vorzug
Irgend gegönnt, so frage nur gleich, wo leidet es etwa
Mangel anderswo, und suche mit forschendem Geiste,
Finden wirst du sogleich zu aller Bildung den Schlüssel . . .
Dieser schöne Begriff von Macht und Schranken, von Willkür
Und Gesetz, von Freiheit und Maß, von beweglicher Ordnung,
Vorzug und Mangel erfreue dich hoch; die heilige Muse
Bringt harmonisch ihn dir, mit sanftem Zwange belehrend.
Keinen höhern Begriff erringt der sittliche Denker,
Keinen der tätige Mann, der dichtende Künstler; der Herrscher,
Der verdient es zu sein, erfreut nur durch ihn sich der Krone. (FA 1, 2: 499–500)

man knows the world only through himself, and thus has the naive arrogance to believe that the world is constructed by him and for his sake. It follows that he puts his special skills in the foreground, while seeking to reject those he lacks, to banish them from his own totality. As a correction, he needs to develop all the manifestations of human character — *sensuality* and *reason, imagination* and *common sense* — into a coherent whole, no matter which quality predominates in him. If he fails to do so, he will labor on under his painful limitations without ever understanding why he has so many stubborn enemies, why he sometimes meets even himself as an enemy. ("Ernst Stiedenroth," 12: 45–6, emphasis in original) [4]

As a first step to making this change, human beings need to be aware of their own imbalances. They must be able to apply the theory of compensation to themselves. Notably, in the discussion above, the balancing of contrary impulses is the goal. Reason is just as important as the passions. So, too, creative endeavors are valued as highly as practical ones. In each of these pairings, the individual is told to strive toward balance. Second, it is important to note that, although the relationships among the parts are fluid and dynamic, there is still nevertheless an ideal that one should strive to achieve: a balance of the various components that make up human character. In other words, one's personality is dynamic, but actual goals exist toward which one ought to strive.

According to Goethe's perspective, although nature was bound by many rules that would often cause it to follow certain regular principles, it was much more interesting in those instances where the rules were broken or overstepped — when nature broke free and created new ones. Goethe explained evolutionary change according to the willed changes, the formative impulses of specific organisms: such organisms decide to change their "allocation" of resources. As he explains in a scientific essay:

---

[4] Recht gut wissen wir, daß in einzelnen menschlichen Naturen gewöhnlich ein Übergewicht irgend eines Vermögens, einer Fähigkeit sich hervortut und daß daraus Einseitigkeiten der Vorstellungsart notwendig entspringen, indem der Mensch die Welt nur durch sich kennt und also, naiv anmaßlich, die Welt durch ihn und um seinetwillen aufgebaut glaubt. Daher kommt denn daß er seine Haupt-Fähigkeiten an die Spitze des Ganzen setzt und was an ihm das Mindere sich findet, ganz und gar ableugnen und aus seiner eignen Totalität hinausstoßen möchte. Wer nicht überzeugt ist, daß er alle Manifestationen des menschlichen Wesens, *Sinnlichkeit* und *Vernunft, Einbildungskraft* und *Verstand*, zu einer entschiedenen Einheit ausbilden müsse, welche von diesen Eigenschaften auch bei ihm die vorwaltende sei, der wird sich in einer unerfreulichen Beschränkung immerfort abquälen und niemals begreifen, warum er so viele hartnäckige Gegner hat, und warum er sich selbst sogar manchmal als augenblicklicher Gegner aufstößt. (FA 1, 24: 615, emphasis in original)

> We will find that a limit is set to nature's structural range, but the number of parts
> and their modifications allow for the form to be changed *ad infinitum* . . . we will
> find that many varieties of form arise because one part or the other outweighs the
> rest in importance. Thus, for example, the neck and extremities are favored in the
> giraffe at the expense of the body, but the reverse is the case in the mole . . . nothing
> can be added to one part without subtracting from another, and vice versa.
>
> These are the bounds of animal nature; within these bounds the formative
> force seems to act in the most wonderful, almost capricious way, but is never able
> to break out of the circle or leap over it. The formative impulse is given hegemony
> over a limited but well-supplied kingdom. Governing principles have been laid
> down for the realm where this impulse will distribute its riches, but to a certain
> extent it is free to give to each what it will. If it wants to let one have more, it may
> do so, but not without taking from another. Thus nature can never fall into debt,
> much less go bankrupt. (12: 120–1)[5]

This principle, then, has two important functions. It highlights that
every change has a related cost, so anything that seems advantageous
comes at the cost of some kind of disadvantage. Second, the very
principle demonstrates two contradictory elements at play. Depending
upon the perspective, the world can either be seen as free (as when an
animal changes its form through a creative impulse) or as determined
(because of the costs and limits of those changes).

By using compensation as a kind of guiding principle, we can begin
to unravel the complexity of Goethe's literary works and the insights
that they have for us. His works thus examine a multitude of perspectives as well as the points of transition among them. One can therefore
understand why his works have given cause to such fierce debates —
both sides, whether conservative or liberal, can find evidence to support

---

[5] So finden wir, daß der Bildungskreis der Natur zwar eingeschränkt ist, dabei jedoch,
wegen der Menge der Teile und wegen der vielfachen Modifikabilität, die Veränderungen der
Gestalt ins Unendliche möglich werden . . . So sind, zum Beispiel, Hals und Extremitäten auf
Kosten des Körpers bei der Giraffe begünstigt, dahingegen beim Maulwurf das Umgekehrte
statt findet. Bei dieser Betrachtung tritt uns nun gleich das Gesetz entgegen: daß keinem Teil
etwas zugelegt werden könne, ohne daß einem andern dagegen etwas abgezogen werde, und
umgekehrt. Hier sind die Schranken der tierischen Natur, in welchen sich die bildende Kraft
auf die wunderbarste und beinahe auf die willkürlichste Weise zu bewegen scheint, ohne
daß sie im mindesten fähig wäre den Kreis zu durchbrechen oder ihn zu überspringen. Der
Bildungstrieb ist hier in einem zwar beschränkten, aber doch wohl eingerichteten Reiche
zum Beherrscher gesetzt. Die Rubriken seines Etats, in welche sein Aufwand zu verteilen ist,
sind ihm vorgeschrieben, was er auf jedes wenden will, steht ihm, bis auf einen gewissen Grad,
frei. Will er der einen mehr zuwenden, so ist er nicht ganz gehindert, allein er ist genötigt an
einer andern sogleich etwas fehlen zu lassen; und so kann die Natur sich niemals verschulden,
oder wohl gar bankrott werden. (FA 1, 24: 233–4)

their points of view, just as both sides can find central points with which to take issue. Conservatives of Goethe's time harshly criticized the morality of his literary works, declaring that he pandered to the low tastes of the people. Conservatives of the late nineteenth and twentieth century, in contrast, saw him as an icon that could help lead Germany and the West out of an age of darkness. The liberals of Goethe's time ignored him as a political irrelevancy, while those of the late twentieth century claimed that he, as a proponent of high classical standards, was partially responsible for the Holocaust. In short, over the years, he has been accused of being an elitist by the more populist groups and a leveler by the more conservative ones. "Faustian" has come to mean both a selling of one's soul and the tremendous promise of economic and technological growth.

What is most important for the purposes of this book is that the principle of compensation itself reflects the central aspects that are at stake in understanding the conflicts between conservatives and liberals. If we briefly, and in an admittedly very general way, canvass this issue, we can see how Goethe's theory of compensation has elements of both liberal and conservative principles. For Goethe, just as nature is both determined (rule bound) and free (creative and at times able to break free of rules), so too can one view society as being both determined by universal standards (the traditional conservative position) and free (the more liberal, value-based view). Only by incorporating and balancing both views can we have a complete view of society as well as an understanding of what we lose or gain at any transitional juncture.

STANDARDS, VALUES, AND CONTEMPORARY POLITICS: ARISTOTLE AND ROUSSEAU

Since the time of Aristotle (384–322 BC), many traditional conservatives have believed in universal standards that can be recognized through the application of one's rational abilities.[6] They assert that standards, especially ones involving justice but not limited to this virtue, are timeless and universal in that the same standards ought to apply everywhere and at anytime. This is not to mean, however, that the standards are

---

[6] In what follows, I use "conservative" and "liberal" according to certain philosophical traditions. The overview is admittedly broad, but seeks to capture some of the main points of contention between those who follow a "standards" approach, i.e., the conservatives, versus those who follow a "values" approach, i.e., the liberals.

mathematical or mechanical. One is not reduced to applying the same formulas in all instances. Rather, by using the power of reason — as long as it has been properly trained with the requisite experience — one can uncover the right and wrong ways of doing things in particular instances. Reason is king. Conservatives thus can argue that there is a right way and a wrong way of doing things and that the concepts of good and bad really exist. In order to discover the right path, one has to rely primarily upon reason and not the emotions.

For these conservatives, Aristotle's definitions of virtue and Plato's (428/427–348/347 BC) search for the ideal good (the beautiful, the just, the noble, etc.) are defining features. Both philosophers establish strict hierarchies where the rational part of one's soul is to be lord and master (literally) over all other parts of the soul. Aristotle tells us that it is as natural for reason to rule over the irrational as it is for parents to rule over their children. For Aristotle, it is a matter of fitness. Those who are more capable ought to rule and determine the lives of those who are not. He is firmly committed to the notion that those who are smarter, stronger, and better leaders ought to be given more power in a polity (*Politics*, Book I).

One can therefore see why politics and religion are often so closely intertwined with this group. Laws should not be subject to change, because the principles of good and evil, of right and wrong, of just and unjust do not change. These groups have traditionally turned to examples in nature to back their claims, whether they argue against the suitability of women for certain jobs or the efforts to sanction only heterosexual unions: women are naturally weaker, and nature's *telos* or end is to reproduce. The principle of hierarchy is closely related to this line of argument. Accordingly, some people are born with more talents, more intelligence, more natural abilities than others, and society ought to be formed in a way that would acknowledge such differences and seek to enable those with more abilities to flourish. Justice is perhaps one of the most important overriding principles for this group. One should harshly punish anyone who violates the standards, and one should reward people according to their merits. Classroom pedagogies are similarly firmly rooted in teacher-centered models. Teachers clearly know more than their students, so they should be disseminating knowledge in a hierarchical, largely one-directional way. For example, in an English composition class, grammar and spelling rules would be of central importance. We have seen the drive toward standardized tests in our schools in the *No Child Left Behind Act* (NCLB) as a means of evaluating students as well as their teachers. One can also easily see how such perspectives can be taken to extremes. George W. Bush's Secretary of Education, Margaret Spellings, would have liked to have seen these same types of standardized tests forced upon all aspects of higher education; she believed that by doing so, we could compare colleges as readily as we can compare cup-holders in cars.[7]

Many liberals, in contrast, do not believe in universal standards, but in changing ones. If reason is the most important part of the conservative value system, then the passions, especially compassion and empathy, take center stage with the liberals. The neo-conservative Irving Kristol, for example, believes that "politicized compassion constitutes the very heart and soul of the Democratic Party," while Clifford Orwin traces Bill Clinton's ability to "feel" our pain back to J. J. Rousseau's (1712–78) philosophy. Liberals do not believe in timeless and universal standards, but in ever-shifting ones. Different societies as well as different time periods will create their own, equally valid systems. Even scientific objectivity comes into question because the particular perspective or agenda of a particular scientist working within a particular time will color the "objective" results of his or her scientific experiments. One could perhaps say that the liberal philosophical tradition has two branches: the cut-throat one of expediency (Niccolò Machiavelli 1469–1527 and Thomas Hobbes 1588–1679) and the more sentimental one of compassion (Rousseau). In the first instance, if standards do not indeed exist, then one is foolish to strive after some non-existent good, especially within the political realm. Life is nasty, brutish, and short, and therefore one ought to use whatever power one can to gain control and maintain power. In the process, one is to reject any moral system that does not ultimately serve one's own good. To paraphrase Machiavelli, it is more important to seem good than to be good.

Rousseau presents a kinder and gentler face of liberalism. For him, language is not simply the embodiment of reason as it was for the ancient Greeks. (The Greek word *logos* means both reason and speech.) Instead, Rousseau emphasizes that language arises because of human passions. Accordingly, "one does not begin by reasoning, but by feeling" (Rousseau, *Languages* 11). In his *Second Discourse*, Rousseau tells

---

[7] In speaking of the need for greater transparency in comparing universities, Secretary Spellings used the following analogy: "We live in the 'Information Age.' If you want to buy a new car you go online and compare a full range of models, makes, and pricing options. And when you're done you'll know everything from how well each car holds its value down to wheel size and number of cup-holders." Secretary Spellings' Prepared Remarks at the National Press Club: An Action Plan for Higher Education. September 26, 2006. <http://www.ed.gov/news/speeches/2006/09/09262006.html>.

an evolutionary tale where human beings begin by living in a largely solitary state that is not much distinguished from that of other animals. Only gradually, and with the passing of time, do human beings learn to form ties with others. Each stage of human development, accordingly, has its own laws and appropriate standards of behavior. Human beings are perfectible, and hence the laws need to change as human beings do. One of the most important human developments, and the one which enabled the growth of society, was the ability to feel pity and compassion: "Pity is what, in the state of nature, takes the place of laws, mores, and virtue, with the advantage that no one is tempted to disobey its sweet voice. Pity is what will prevent every robust savage from robbing a weak child or an infirm old man of his hard-earned substance" (55). Pity and not reason is the basis for the existence of any virtues. Rousseau then takes the Golden Rule (Do unto others as you would have them do unto you) and gives it a twist that is in essence a nod to Machiavelli, but with much more compassionate underpinnings: "Do what is good for you with as little harm as possible to others" (55).

For this tradition, then, laws are not natural, but they are relative not only within different time periods but within different societies. Values are emphasized rather than principles, and as a consequence, adherents seek to respect values different than their own. To the extent possible, they seek to understand people's behaviors within the larger contexts of their lives and social structures. Instead of justice, compassion is at the center of their philosophy. Before rendering a judgment upon criminals, for example, one needs to understand their background. Were they raped or abused as children? Did they come from broken homes? Laws are not absolute, nor are people to be judged dispassionately according to them. Rather, one needs to seek to understand lawbreakers before rendering punishment.

As part of the respect for the value systems of others, liberals do not believe that one should force anyone to comply with the rules of others. People, for example, should be able to be free from the religious influences and symbolisms of others and able to pursue their sexual and family lives as they wish, as long as they do not harm others. Moreover, because standards are not acknowledged, any sort of hierarchy developed around them is to be discounted as well. They propose a democratic view of the world where everyone in every field should be considered equal. For example, there is a belief that all young people should have the opportunity to go to college, even if they are developmentally disabled and incapable of doing the work, because no one should be denied the experience.[8] Liberal classroom pedagogies are rooted in self-expression rather than in precision, where the student rather than the teacher is at the center of instruction. Work is more collaborative in such a classroom. Students are given more group work, for example, so they can teach themselves. The predominant approach in this country to college composition courses perhaps best illustrates the philosophy and characteristics of the liberal, student-centered approach. The most important aspect is for students to be able to write about their feelings rather than to know how correctly to express them on a page, especially since students have a "right" to their own language, i.e., teachers are instructed not to correct the grammatical errors of their students as this would be to impose the standard of the educated elite upon them. They should instead be taught to embrace their own way of speaking.[9]

It is easy to see why the battles between these two groups are so fierce and seemingly irreconcilable. At stake are the most central aspects of culture and society. Are we better off with a conservative view of the world, where established political hierarchies, religious strictures, and strict educational norms prevail, or with a more liberal one, where the masses determine politics, individuals are more free to determine the direction (or not) of their spirituality, and students have a greater role in determining their own educational programs? The culture wars of the 1980s, wars that in many ways continue to be fought today, addressed many of these same issues. Books like Allan Bloom's *Closing of the American Mind* (1987) sought to show how contemporary culture had gone astray. Such books tend to be extremely reactionary. Society has gone to hell in a hand basket because of the changes that have occurred through the import of modern values. The only way to return to better days is to go back to earlier values. Thus, according to Bloom, pre-pubescents and teenagers had been so desensitized by early erotic exposures via Bo Derek, Michael Jackson, and Mick Jagger, *et al.* that they were no longer capable of directing their erotic energies toward serious thought and inquiry. Only by returning to the Socratic method of inquiry, where *eros* could be channeled to higher goals, could society regain its proper footing. Such works tend to attack one side

[8] See, for example, Leslie Kaufman's 'Just a Normal Girl' in *The New York Times Education Life* (November 5, 2006).
[9] See, for example, the National Council of Teachers of English policy statement that students have a "right to their own language," i.e., one should not force Standard English on students who speak other forms of it. <http://www.ncte.org/library/NCTEFiles/Groups/CCCC/NewSRTOL.pdf>.

and believe the solutions reside in their camp alone. They also tend to downplay or discredit the societal gains of the new, more liberal agenda, whether the advances for women and minorities or the growth in the percentages of students attending college. Compassion itself is often condemned as a danger to society.

The left, however, has been equally blind to the societal deficits that have emerged from its point of view. Although since the presidential election of 2004 one has seen a growth in the liberal attempt to embrace conservative values of religion and family, Hillary Clinton's 1996 book, *It Takes a Village*, serves to exemplify the contrasts between a conservative and liberal approach still at the heart of the breach. Clinton advocates a very different worldview than Bloom's, one which very much argues against going back to the "good old days" (13–5). In her book, she argues against certain standards. Rather than evaluate individuals according to measurable standards of excellence, whether of music or intellect, she argues that one needs to value each individual equally. Everyone, for example, should be allowed to sing in a choir whether tone deaf or not (51–68, 98). It is about allowing everyone to participate in everything. Where conservatives believe that people should be held accountable for their actions, one of Clinton's mottoes bespeaks the liberal policy of compassion. She takes the following epigram from Alice Keliher for one of her chapters: "If I could say just one thing to a parent, it would be simply that a child needs someone who believes in him no matter what he does" (33). The corollary of such unconditional love is a dark one. Parents are discouraged from disciplining children and teaching them proper behavior. Why should they, if no matter what children do we are to approve of them?

READING GOETHE FOR TODAY

If we now return to Goethe's principle of compensation, we can see how it negotiates between both approaches. It represents a nuanced way of understanding the world precisely because it includes both worldviews in interpreting it. It acknowledges that some things are unchangeable and others are changeable. What makes the theory so provocative for studying concerns of our time is that no matter whether one believes in fixed or changing principles, one nevertheless has to examine the end results behind the decisions that are made by either group. What are the benefits and what the losses behind the change in religious sensibilities? In scientific protocols? In educational pedagogies?

What aspects of each ought to remain constant?

Because Goethe's works examine both perspectives and the consequences associated with each, they present us with a complex analysis of modernity. This is especially true because the topics that his major literary works center upon are the ones at the heart of our lives: technology and the economy, religion, and education. An examination of his works, moreover, will show that in many ways he predicted the direction that society would take. He foresaw the rise of democracy, capitalism, secularism, progressive education, and the power that technology would wield.

First and foremost, as discussed above, he did not believe in absolute answers. One could not solve one problem without creating others. The solution to a problem today may not work tomorrow if situations have significantly changed. This is not to say that for Goethe there were no solutions or that people should not make specific attempts to better particular situations. Indeed, when all is said and done, Goethe believed quite strongly that certain aspects of society should be preserved and certain paths ought to be selected. However, in order to reach such a conclusion, he proposed that one had to examine every situation from a variety of perspectives before deciding which path to take. While the ultimate goal is to strike the right balance in order to come up with the best solution for a given circumstance, one must fully understand the strengths and weaknesses of each side. And even when one decided upon a path, one had to be conscious of what the costs of that decision were, as there will always be costs.

The "right solution" could very well depend upon the particular time and place or particular character. In this, Goethe's philosophy is related to Aristotle's concept of correct behavior. Aristotle believes that one cannot set formulas for moral behavior beyond saying that one should act in the right way, at the right time while taking into account one's own personality. His famous "mean" is not an absolute concept: "Virtue then is a settled disposition of the mind determining the choice of actions and emotions, consisting essentially in the observance of the mean relative to us" (*Nicomachean Ethics* 1107a 1–5). Aristotle does not give us commandments, but seeks to train our minds to evaluate individual circumstances against our own particular traits so that, with education, we can act correctly in disparate situations.

Goethe's works provide us with many case studies, where we can analyze how different personality types act within certain circumstances. Although Goethe's understanding of ethics as enunciated above may have Aristotelian roots, his philosophy of human and natural striving is quite different from the conservative notions of Aristotle. For Goethe, the ultimate goals for striving, human or otherwise, were always subject to change. In his scientific works, he propounded a theory of evolution that explained changes in species according to the inner drive of organisms. In this, his philosophy resembles that of Rousseau, in that the status quo is constantly in flux. Rousseau's *Second Discourse* postulates that human beings are perfectible, i.e., that their characteristics and characters are subject to change: "the faculty of self-perfection, a faculty which, with the aid of circumstances, successively develops all the others, and resides among us as much in the species as in the individual" (45). Although Rousseau questions the ultimate desirability of progress for the happiness of humankind, he nevertheless believes that human beings — our needs and desires — have substantially changed over time, and that these changes have been accompanied by related ones in all aspects of human life, including trade, division of labor, family units, and forms of governments.

Whereas Rousseau refuses to speculate about evolution because "comparative anatomy has as yet made too little progress" (38), Goethe's own work on comparative anatomy led precisely to an understanding of evolution that influenced animal and human forms as well as human institutions. For animals, this meant adapting to new environments or challenges, and for people this meant adapting one's mode of being to the times and circumstances. Chapter 1 will explore the issue of human progress against the backdrop of modern science and technology. It thus tracks the meaning of progress and change through Goethe's most famous character, Faust. Faust is already quite modern because, unlike the earlier portrayals of this character, Goethe's Faust does not sell his soul to the devil primarily for knowledge, but for life experiences. His story is equally about the soul as it is about the body. Faust begins the play as a medieval hack: a man who is caught up in tradition and lives in a stuffy and closed world. The devil enables him to leave this world behind, and his journey includes trading witchcraft for capitalism and alchemy for technology. (Marshall Berman goes so far as to characterize this play as a tragedy of the modern day real estate developer.) Of course, this journey is fraught with problems, as his love affair with Gretchen (which leads to matricide and infanticide) and his murderous acts attest. Most notably for our own times, the entire story of Faust's technological mastery has as its backdrop a financial collapse. The devil prints up paper money to solve a credit crisis, but this only leads to greater problems for the empire, from inflation to a war fought with dirty weapons.

Chapter 2, by examining Goethe's most popular novel, *The Sorrows of Young Werther*, argues not only how deeply Goethe has been misunderstood as wholeheartedly supporting liberal values, but also how closely related contemporary, conservative Evangelical movements ultimately are to these very values. The majority of readers have viewed this novel as an endorsement of heightened, emotional individualism. As a consequence, many critics have argued that Goethe sided with the liberal and democratic aspects of his protagonist. The readers, according to this argument, were to sympathize with the novel's protagonist because of his efforts to challenge hierarchical societal norms and expectations and were then to be sad when Werther failed in these endeavors. For such readers, Werther is a noble character, driven mad by the strictures of society. Chapter 2, however, argues for a multifaceted reading of the text that highlights the role of Evangelicalism in America today. In many ways, the religious experience of Goethe's Germany and of contemporary America is quite similar. Both can be characterized by Evangelical Protestantism, i.e., a kind of Protestantism that focuses equally upon biblical literalism and one's personal, emotional relationship to God. A close reading of the novel demonstrates Goethe's ironic stance toward the young protagonist, a Bible-quoting man who eventually rejects all sources of mediation between himself and God. Werther's story, however, presents a much more complex case in which an extreme example of modern individualism is subtly contrasted against an older, more communally ordered tradition. Thus, rather than being a whole-hearted endorsement of modernity, Werther's inability to cope with the newer ways highlights what has been lost in the older traditions.

Chapter 3 continues this examination by turning to the influence of democratic principles upon issues of modern education. Within his two *Wilhelm Meister* novels (*Wilhelm Meister's Apprenticeship* and *Wilhelm Meister's Journeyman Years*), Goethe explores a variety of pedagogical theories, from student-centered to teacher-centered, from socialist to capitalist, and from religious to secular. While each theory is given a spokesperson who advocates for his or her own perspective, in the end, a hybrid educational theory arises: one that rejects aspects of student-centered learning while embracing others, and one that questions the success of the new capitalist endeavors unless its participants are liberally educated. The novel thus repudiates an important aspect of contemporary educational theory (placing the student in the controlling seat of learning), while simultaneously condemning the conservative approach of standardized testing. Or, to state the case from the more affirmative side: democracy, in valuing the contributions of individuals, promises great strides in promoting education as long as it is committed to certain timeless values as well.

It is important to note that Goethe's theory of compensation is neither nihilistic nor self-negating. Such distinctions are important because it is not that Goethe believes that all options are equal. Just because he advocates examining issues from a variety of perspectives does not mean that the reader becomes involved in an endless ping-pong game often played by postmodernist theorists. Rather, his texts teach us that if we are to make the best decisions, we must analyze issues from many different perspectives. Once we make that decision, however, we must always be aware that it will have some costs. In my analysis of Goethe's texts, I will show how they sustain multiple readings, including ones that go against the grain of most scholars in order to demonstrate Goethe's insistence on multiplicity of views — on a wide range of possible modernisms. I will also argue, however, that Goethe is very clear about the gains and losses of these points of view and that some solutions result in more important losses than others. Thus, I will argue that from Faust's perspective it is a very bad thing for him to go to heaven, while Werther is not, in the end, the poster-child for modern individualism. So too, while it is a good thing that more people have the benefits of education, there are profound dangers involved when they come to believe that they are empowered to educate themselves or that one size of an educational approach fits all.

As we now turn to Goethe's literary texts, we can begin to see how his works have both shaped what we have come to be and how they simultaneously provide a means of thinking about how we can do better.

Chapter 1

FAUST, CAPITALISM, AND TECHNOLOGY

To my mind, the greatest evil of our time, which allows nothing to come to frui-
tion, is that each moment consumes its predecessor, each day is squandered in
the next, and so we live perpetually from hand to mouth, without ever producing
anything. Do we not already have newspapers for each part of the day! Some
clever soul could probably insert one or two more. The result is that everyone's
deeds, actions, scribblings, indeed, all intentions, are dragged before the public.
No one is permitted to rejoice or sorrow except to entertain all the rest; and so
everything leaps from house to house, from town to town, from empire to empire,
and finally from continent to continent.

As little as the steam engines can be throttled can anything similar be done
in the moral realm. The liveliness of commerce, the continual rustle of paper
money, the increase in debts to pay off other debts — all these are frightful
elements that the young man of the present confronts. He is fortunate if he is
endowed with a moderate, peaceable disposition that neither makes excessive
demands on the world nor allows itself to be determined by it. (10: 298)[1]

---

[1] These maxims are found both in *Wilhelm Meister's Journeyman Years* as well as in the
"Maxims and Reflections." They are quoted below from the "Maxims":
  "Für das größte Unheil unserer Zeit, die nichts reif werden läßt, muß ich halten, daß
man im nächsten Augenblick den vorhergehenden verspeis't, den Tag im Tage verthut, und
so immer aus der Hand in den Mund lebt, ohne irgend etwas vor sich zu bringen. Haben wir
doch schon Blätter für sämmtliche Tageszeiten! ein guter Kopf könnte wohl noch eins und
das andere interpoliren. Dadurch wird alles was ein jeder thut, treibt, dichtet, ja was er vor
hat, in's Oeffentliche geschleppt. Niemand darf sich freuen oder leiden als zum Zeitvertreib
der übrigen; und so springt's von Haus zu Haus, von Stadt zu Stadt, von Reich zu Reich, und
zuletzt von Welttheil zu Welttheil, alles velociferisch."
  "So wenig nun die Dampfmaschinen zu dämpfen sind, so wenig ist dieß auch im
Sittlichen möglich; die Lebhaftigkeit des Handels, das Durchrauschen des Papiergelds,
das Anschwellen der Schulden, um Schulden zu bezahlen, das alles sind die ungeheuern
Elemente, auf die gegenwärtig ein junger Mann gesetzt ist. Wohl ihm, wenn er von der Natur
mit mäßigem, ruhigem Sinne begabt ist, um weder unverhältnißmäßige Forderungen an

A country is in turmoil. Foreign wars are faring poorly and are costing more than expected. Citizens spend more than they earn. Sources of wealth have so dried up that payrolls are not being met and loans are being called in. Interest payments threaten to consume "what future years must yet produce" (4870–1). So begins Part II of Johann Wolfgang von Goethe's *magnum opus, Faust.*

Readers generally focus upon Part I, the love story between Faust, a scientist/scholar who sells his soul to the devil to seek physical and intellectual gratification, and Gretchen, the pure and simple young girl whom he seduces, impregnates, and abandons. This storyline has captured the imagination of writers, composers, and artists from the time of its publication to today.[2] When Part I ends, Gretchen is about

die Welt zu machen, noch auch von ihr sich bestimmen zu lassen." (FA 1, 13: 133–4; Nos. 2.19.3 to 2.19.4)

[2] It is impossible to catalog the literary works that have a significant connection to Goethe's *Faust*, but among the most noteworthy are Lord Byron's *Manfred* (1817), Alexander Pushkin's *Scenes from Faust* (1826), Ivan Turgenev's *Faust: A Story in Nine Letters* (1856), Klaus Mann's *Mephisto* (1936), Boris Pasternak's *Doctor Zhivago* (1957) and Mikhail Bulgakov's *The Master and Margarita* (1940). Turgenev was said to know by heart the whole of *Faust* Part I (Kostovski 14), Pasternak at one time planned to subtitle *Doctor Zhivago:* "An Attempt at a Russian *Faust*" (Livingstone 14) and Pushkin called *Faust* "the *Iliad* of Modern Life" (Lukács 157). Numerous musical pieces have been based upon or have found their inspiration from Goethe's play and run the gamut from Richard Wagner's *Faust Overture* (1840) to Robert Schumann's *Scenes from Goethe's Faust* (1843–53) to Sergej Rachmaninov's piano sonata op. 28, No. 1: *After Reading Faust* (1920) to Randy Newman's (of the *Short People* fame) *Faust* musical (1995). Even Broadway's *Damned Yankees* is a child of the Faust legend. The Faust theme is also well represented in operas, whether Hector Berlioz's *The Damnation of Faust* (1846), Arrigo Boito's *Mefistofele* (1868), or Charles Gounod's *Faust et Marguerite* (1859). The Gounod opera was so popular that for decades the New York opera season opened with a performance of it. Edith Wharton's *The Age of Innocence* (1920) begins with her characters in attendance at this opera, and the opera also plays a role in the dramatic climax of Gaston Leroux's *The Phantom of the Opera* (1909–10). *Faust* has inspired countless films as well, including ones directed by F. M. Murnau (1926) and Jan Svankmajer (1994) to the more pop version of *Bedazzled* of 1967 and its remake of 2000. It was furthermore the main inspiration behind William Kentridge's and Lesego Rampolokeng's 1995 puppet play, *Faustus in Africa.*

Nor has the influence of this play been limited to the realm of arts and letters. The famed German physicist Hermann von Helmholtz (1821–94) turned to *Faust* as a means to argue for Goethe's prescience as a scientist. Not only does Helmholtz compare Faust's search for the causes of things to the project of the modern physicist, but Helmholtz quite literally reads parts of Goethe's *Faust* as a scientific manifesto that proclaims the principle of conservation of energy. Albert Einstein, for one, was quite taken by Helmholtz's argument and encouraged anyone interested in scientific perspectives to read it (1917, in Mandelkow 3: 523–4). Recently, Gino Segrè has written the history of quantum mechanics through the lens of *Faust.* He does so, first, because the world's most important physicists staged a parody of this play to conclude their 1932 meeting in Copenhagen; second, because *Faust* was part of their cultural milieu in general (the physicists from various countries knew both the play and that it was the hundredth anniversary of Goethe's death); and third, and most importantly for the purposes of this chapter, many of its themes and characters resonated with contemporary

to be executed for infanticide, but refuses to run away with her former lover when the opportunity presents itself because of his associations with the devil. A voice from above proclaims her saved from her sins, and Faust departs with the devil.

Part II of the play is rarely read or performed, yet it is here that we fully witness Goethe's vision of the modern world and here that we see a mirror of many of our economic circumstances of today. When a kingdom does not have enough money to handle its excessive spending and bad debts, the devil, Mephistopheles (or Mephisto), proposes that the emperor print paper money — and lots of it. This money is not tied to any value, gold or otherwise, but to a vague promise of future wealth and future taxes on that wealth. When the country's chancellor criticizes this scheme, he is berated for only trusting in the value of tangible goods, a notion that is considered quaintly old-fashioned. The emperor listens to the devil, and the printed paper money initially works like magic: credit is freed up, debts are paid off, small businesses boom, and the kingdom thrives.

Unfortunately, this "bailout" does not have a happy ending. When we next see the kingdom, it is in civil war and about to collapse. The devil's "rescue plan" did not include any measures to reign in spending, and as a result, the emperor and his people continued to pursue their pleasures without restraint, fiscal or otherwise. The kingdom becomes destabilized through inflation and property disputes. People eventually turn on the emperor for the very principles they themselves once endorsed and try to overthrow him. With the help of the devil's mercenaries and the aid of "dirty weapons," the emperor regains his kingdom, but at a high cost. It is the end of its dominance, and he himself gives up a great deal of his individual powers. Things do not end much better for his people, who will have to labor without pay in essence to pay off the emperor's debts to the devil.

The threats to the people of this kingdom, however, go beyond monetary problems. The budget here serves as an overall metaphor for several of our own competing concerns. In Faust's story — in the trajectory that takes us from watching him at first struggle against the pull of modernity to finally embracing it and becoming its champion — one can see the literal and metaphorical costs associated with the decisions he makes. In terms of Goethe's principle of compensation, whatever gains that Faust makes need to be weighed against the losses that are

science. In the Copenhagen parody, for instance, Niels Bohr replaces the Lord, Wolfgang Pauli the devil, Mephistopheles, and Paul Ehrenfest the hero, Faust.

sustained. In the first three acts of Part II, Faust values beauty and the arts as goods in themselves. By Act IV, he endorses economic principles of wealth maximization that today we associate with the Chicago School of Economics. Up until Act IV, Faust focuses his attention on Helen of Troy: first in conjuring her ghost to perform in a masque, then in finding the "living being" in ancient Greece and bringing her back to life; and finally in having a child with her. Faust still loves nature, beauty, and poetry during this phase. Indeed, his child with Helen, Euphorion, overtly embodies Lord Byron and the heightened sensibilities of Romantic poetry. The child, however, is doomed, and once he dies, so too dies Faust's concern with the liberal arts. His great and final dream seems banal. In a completely modern twist, Faust wields the devil's power to reclaim land from the sea and create new living and work space for millions. He wishes to use the devil's technology to be a real estate developer (Berman). The path toward this dream is anything but banal. The action is played out against the backdrop of scientific and technological advances. A scientist creates life in a test tube, but once created, this form cannot be contained or controlled by its creator. Throughout the play, we see the seamy side of scientific advances: capitalist-backed technology excuses the murder of a few for the benefit of the many; the arts must be sacrificed so that science can move forward without the distraction of or concerns about nature's beauty; and the desire for power replaces the desire for understanding. In short, ethics is replaced by expediency, humanities by the sciences, and contemplation by acquisitive knowledge. These cold-hearted exploits in the best tradition of modern capitalism are seemingly justified both by Faust's redemption and by the increase in well-being for millions of people.

Given the rudimentary state of scientific knowledge and capitalism in Goethe's day, it is remarkable how well he was able to predict the close alliance among science, trade, and politics: advances in technology and the growth of trade lead to new political principles and structures. Interpreting Goethe's stance toward these developments, however, is rather more difficult. How are we to understand the author's attitude toward his protagonist and his actions? Is Faust a proto-capitalist, and if so, is this a good thing or bad? Does Faust represent the modern scientist with his ceaseless, amoral questioning, and if so, does the play's conclusion valorize or condemn this image? Are we to believe that this poet of nature and radical opponent of Newtonianism endorses the Faustian view of the future or merely that he sees it as inevitable? Many of the readers of *Faust* believe that the play backs the new, capitalist-driven, scientific, world order. After all, Faust according to all traditions should go to hell. He made a pact with the devil, seduced and destroyed the innocent, young Gretchen, cavorted with witches, fought a dirty war, and killed a lovely couple, Baucis and Philemon, known since antiquity for their love for each other and their gracious hospitality. Goethe's Faust, however, does not go to hell. Why, after all, if Goethe did not at least agree in large part with his protagonist, would he send his hero to heaven? What can be learned about our own economic and intellectual conditions by applying a principle of compensation to an analysis of *Faust*?

DYNAMIC PERSPECTIVES AND *FAUST*

In the very beginning of Part I, Faust is presented as the best of human beings. The Lord in the Prolog particularly praises him because his dissatisfaction keeps him active. This undoubtedly seems strange. Why should dissatisfaction — or put more baldly, unhappiness — be something desirable in human beings? The Lord explains:

> Human activity slackens all too easily,
> and people soon are prone to rest on any terms;
> that's why I like to give them the companion
> who functions as a prod and does a job as devil. (340–3)[3]

The Lord here is not the Christian God who demands moral rectitude and goodness. Rather, the Lord of Goethe's play places the highest value on human striving. The Lord explains how the devil, in this particular case, Mephistopheles, serves God's purposes. Human beings, left to their own devices, would be lazy. The Lord, however, expects greater things of humankind, but realizes that they often need help in order to achieve greatness. The devil's job is to keep them active and striving toward grand accomplishments.[4] By plaguing human beings, i.e., by constantly making them unhappy, the devil is able to goad them into action. Happiness is seen as soporific and disabling. The

---

[3] Des Menschen Tätigkeit kann allzuleicht erschlaffen,
  Er liebt sich bald die unbedingte Ruh;
  Drum geb' ich gern ihm den Gesellen zu,
  Der reizt und wirkt, und muß, als Teufel, schaffen. (340–3)
[4] For an in-depth discussion of Mephisto's relationship to creativity, see McCarthy (191–9).

devil is not therefore an evil being, although his intentions are not beneficent. He becomes God's instrument. Mephisto, like the devil in Job, believes that he will be able to tempt the Lord's most exemplary man. The wager here, however, is not about cursing God as it is in the Bible, but whether the devil will be able to trick Faust into a moment of happiness, i.e., stasis. This theme, as we will see below, is taken up again in the wager that Mephisto then strikes with Faust.

It is important to note at the onset that it is not any sort of activity that is praised by God. It is not busyness, but rather a higher kind of directed activity that leads one to accomplish greater things than had ever been achieved before. God permits, even encourages Faust to err, as long as his actions are characterized by onward striving: finding new experiences and new sources of knowledge, even when personally painful. Throughout most of the two parts of the play, Faust wants to experience the highest highs and the lowest lows and strives to do so by a study of nature, art, and science on the one hand and sexual pleasure (his seduction of Gretchen and Helen) on the other. He does not become obsessively driven by his schemes of land reclamation until one half of his soul stops striving. Only with the death of his child (who in the play symbolizes poetry), and the departure of Helen of Troy (who symbolizes both absolute beauty and sensuality), does Faust focus on his capitalist schemes. In other words, within the play, the drive toward capitalism occurs once one has given up on the arts, aesthetics, and nature. Faust's actions from this point on reflect a more narrow and constricted sphere, and one which the play, as I argue, asks us to question. In terms of the principle of compensation, his acquisitive nature gains power at the cost of his appreciation for art and nature.

Faust, in his early analysis of his own character, echoes the Lord's assessment. Faust realizes that he wants to experience both intellectual and physical pleasures and that the contradictory nature of these desires will lead to a lifetime of dissatisfaction. At the moment that one desire is on the brink of being satisfied, the other creeps in to remind him of its demands, leading to a perpetual seesaw of one extreme to the other. Faust very famously describes this conflict as a battle of two souls:

> Two souls, alas! reside within my breast,
> and each is eager for a separation:
> in throes of coarse desire, one grips
> the earth with all its senses;

the other struggles from the dust
to rise to high ancestral spheres. (1112–17)[5]

This notion of a dynamic, polar struggle between two opposing forces is central to understanding Goethe's works in general and is closely affiliated with his principle of compensation. If compensation traces the gains and losses as organisms or individuals balance competing desires, then polarity goes to the source of that division. One polar side exists in close connection and balance with the other. Much of the narrative of both parts of *Faust* can be traced back to polar conflicts: the entire play is premised on a bet between the devil and God, Faust describes the agony of his own existence as being due to the two conflicting souls within his breast, Mephisto defines himself as that which desires to do evil but accomplishes instead the good, and the final words of the play involving the eternal feminine have long encouraged reading the whole as the struggle between masculine striving and feminine love.[6] It is impossible to overestimate the importance of polarities in Goethe's oeuvre. By turning to Goethe's discussion of polarity in non-literary texts, we can gain a better understanding of them in *Faust*. Indeed, in a scientific essay where Goethe describes his principle of polarity, "two souls" can be found among a list of examples:

We and the objects (Wir und die Gegenstände)

Light and darkness (Licht und Finsternis)

Body and soul (Leib und Seele)

Two souls (Zwei Seelen)

Spirit and matter (Geist und Materie)

---

[5] Zwei Seelen wohnen, ach! in meiner Brust,
  Die eine will sich von der andern trennen;
  Die eine hält, in derber Liebeslust,
  Sich an die Welt, mit klammernden Organen;
  Die andre hebt gewaltsam sich vom Dust
  Zu den Gefilden hoher Ahnen. (1112–17)
[6] In her discussion of Act V of Part II, Brown also focuses upon the dialectical character of the ending: "The first half of the act seems to reject all of the positions the play has hitherto sought to affirm — the classical tradition, beauty, creative magic, activity — and to embrace what it earlier avoided — the traditional models of tragedy and traditional ethics. In the second half of the act a sudden reversal in tone releases all of these concerns into a finale that exploits the full exuberance of the operatic stage. The extent to which this finale is understood as triumphant or bitter, genuine or ironic, dishonest or weak, will depend very much on how one reads the rest of the fifth act" (*Faust* 231). However, whereas Brown argues for moments of synthesis, I focus upon the moments of tension between the two polar sides — on the need to move constantly from one perspective to the next.

God and the world (Gott und die Welt)

Thought and extension (Gedanke und Ausdehnung)

Ideal and real (Ideales und Reales)

Sensuality and reason (Sinnlichkeit und Vernunft)

Fantasy and understanding (Phantasie und Verstand)

Being and desire (Sein und Sehnsucht)

Two halves of the body (Zwei Körperhälften)

Right and left (Rechts und Links)

Breathing (Atemholen)

Physical experience (Physische Erfahrung):

Magnet. (12: 155)[7]

On the surface, this list may seem to be about separations and divisions and not about the balancing of dynamic tensions and interactions. Metaphysical and physical worlds seem to be neatly divided, as do the subject from the object. Goethe, however, emphasizes a different aspect of the relationship of these pairs. For him, the primary relationship is a dynamic one that illustrates the indivisibility of one side from the other. Inhaling is meaningless without exhaling, just as the body is meaningless without the soul or light without darkness. Each side of the polar pair exists only insofar as it is contrasted and related to the other side. In this sense, the magnet becomes a metaphor for the relationship of all of the pairs: two opposites coexist within one entity. To look at a magnet from only the perspective of one of its poles would be to miss its very essence.

In terms of the action of *Faust*, polarities also serve to illuminate a central aspect of the bet that Faust makes with the devil. Faust will lose should he ever desire a moment or literally the glance of the eye (Augenblick) to stand still. Goethe, in his scientific work, *The Theory of Colors*, spends a great deal of time examining the polar functionings of the eye. The retina, for example, expands and contracts in order to see objects. Like the magnet above, it contains within itself both opposing abilities. If in seeing, the retina is, as Goethe argues, simultaneously in opposing states,[8] then to "see" the meaning of *Faust* also requires the ability to view it in two opposing ways. One must incorporate both poles to have a whole. It is therefore no coincidence that the terms of the bet between Faust and Mephisto revolve around a moment in time that is

---

[7] FA 1, 25: 142–3.

[8] Die Netzhaut befindet sich bei dem, was wir sehen heißen, zu gleicher Zeit in verschiedenen, ja in entgegengesetzten Zuständen. (#13)

defined by the eye's activity. Most disagreements about the play's basic elements (e.g., whether God cheats Mephisto, whether Mephisto or Faust wins their bet, whether Faust is an exemplary character, whether his final land reclamation project represents a utopia, or whether the play as a whole is moral or immoral) reside quite literally within the eye of the beholder — within the question of perspective or the glance of the eye (Augen/blick). Indeed, the play is structured to encourage opposing views as a means of seeing the whole picture. To see only one side of the whole comes to symbolize the stasis (or death) that Faust embraces once he takes up his capitalist plan at the expense of nature and the arts. In terms of the principle of compensation, the polar pairs represent a budget. To privilege one side over the other comes at a cost. To understand the situation in its entirety, one would have to examine the perspectives of each side to see the gains and losses of each.

The play itself provides many clues that we ought to read it according to a dynamic dualism. Throughout most of the play, Faust is driven to strive because of his dissatisfaction. As soon as one soul reaches a level of satisfaction (as when the earthly one is tempted by Gretchen's simple world or Helen of Troy's worldly sensuality), it is immediately countered by its opposing mate (as when it drives Faust to understand nature or conquer the waters). Mephisto further notes that although reason elevates human beings above the animals, it also at times makes human beings worse than any animal (tierischer als jedes Tier zu sein, 287).[9] The same force, thus, is responsible for our greatest elevation and our greatest degradation. Similarly, the devil, too, is not outrightly an "evil" force. As mentioned above, Mephisto explains to Faust that he is "A part of that force/ which, always willing evil always produces good" (1335–6),[10] and "a part of the Part that first was all,/ part of the Darkness that gave birth to Light" (1349–50).[11] Mephisto's destructive evilness creates goodness just as the darkness that is a part of him leads to the creation of light. The polarities are inextricable, and if there are benefits associated with the dominance of one side of the pair, then one must also look to analyze the inevitable downsides.

What, then, do these polarities mean for an interpretation of the

---

[9] This view is a familiar one throughout Western culture, whether in Aristotle's observation in the *Politics* that a human being is the most perfect animal, but if he "has not excellence, he is the most unholy and the most savage of animals" (1253a 30–5) to the observation in Shakespeare's Sonnet #94 that "Lilies that fester smell far worse than weeds."

[10] Ein Teil von jener Kraft,/ Die stets das Böse will und stets das Gute schafft. (1335–6)

[11] . . . ein Teil des Teils, der Anfangs alles war,/ Ein Teil der Finsternis, die sich das Licht gebar. (1349–50)

play? They encourage the reader not to see only one side, but to weigh
one interpretation against another. Goethe calls his play a tragedy, but
its ending mirrors Dante's *Divine Comedy*. The play ends happily if we
examine it from God's perspective but ends unhappily for Mephisto.
If Mephisto accomplishes good by doing evil, what do God and his
angels accomplish by doing good?[12] In a real sense, Faust is saved only
because God cheats. Mephisto, by rights and terms of the bet, ought
to have gained control of Faust's soul. Instead, he ends up like Job,
covered in boils caused by the petals of heavenly roses (11809). Hell
may be governed by rules of contract and precedent (1413), but heaven
does not appear to be. In the end, it is the angels' posteriors that
determine the outcome. The naked backsides of the heavenly, "pure"
cherubs prove too much of a distraction to the devil, and Faust's soul
slips through his fingers.

Perhaps most provocatively, only one of Faust's two souls, as I argue
below, eventually makes it to heaven. If, however, Faust needs two
souls to strive and to be active, what could this separation mean? In
the beginning of the play, God explains that "Men err as long as they
keep striving" (327).[13] Striving and error appear to go hand in hand.
The heavenly assumption of one of Faust's souls may very well mean
that it will no longer err, but will Faust's immortal existence continue to
strive?[14] Or, to put the same point in another way, Gretchen and Faust
have completely exchanged roles. On earth, Faust was the active agent
(the seducer), Gretchen the passive one (the seduced). In heaven,
she now is active and he passive: she intercedes for him (12069–75),
she will be teaching him (belehren, 12092), he will be following her
(12093), and the feminine in general seems to determine the direction
of activity (12110).

One could similarly go through many aspects of the play to see
how opposing views are simultaneously represented. Does the good of
private individuals (Baucis and Philemon) trump the greater good of

[12] For another example of how inversions of principles operate in the play, see Brown, who
in her analysis of Act IV draws parallels between Faust's temptation and Christ's. The logic of
this scene is turned upside down from the biblical one: "Faust can only be saved by accepting all temptations. To reject temptation would be Christian, and hence Mephistophelean"
(*Faust* 221).

[13] Es irrt der Mensch solang' er strebt. (327)

[14] I use the term "assumption" rather than ascension because the two terms have quite
different theological meanings. Christ ascended into heaven, i.e., he achieved this movement
with the strength of his own powers. The Virgin Mary, in contrast, was assumed into heaven;
i.e., she did not go to heaven on her accord but with divine assistance. It is quite clear from
the passages of the text that Faust's souls need assistance at every step of the way.

society (a larger, thriving community)? Does Faust's rejection of magic and regret at his pact at the end of his life wipe out his earlier deeds? One of the strengths of the play is that it forces the reader into these various positions and gives justification for both sides. The play does not support just one perspective on its main issues, but provides at least two for us to consider before making up our minds about which is the better course of action. It also teaches us to look for the disadvantages of each decision. It therefore encourages the same kind of dynamism that Goethe wrote about in the eye and that he saw throughout all of nature. One perspective immediately calls forth its opposite and vice versa. Or, to put this sentiment in Goethe's own words in a letter to Zelter (June 1, 1831), *Faust* was to be "an obvious puzzle" (ein offenbares Rätsel) that would "continually entertain human beings and give them something to worry about" (die Menschen fort und fort ergötze und ihnen zu schaffen mache).

FAUST AS A TRAGEDY

In the pages that follow, I propose an interpretation that has not yet been given to the play; namely, that the play is a tragedy because Faust goes to heaven. This perspective, one that takes into account the devil's and Faust's earthly soul, as well as the nature of Faust's abilities, will provide a necessary balance to prior interpretations that have focused upon the positive aspect of Faust's assumption. Once we have taken this perspective and balanced it against more canonical ones, I believe that we will be in a better position to understand Goethe's analysis of our own cultural, social, and technological modernisms, both positive and negative. Ultimately, Goethe's explicit choice of the genre of tragedy (he titles his work, *The Tragedy of Faust*) provides an important clue to his assessment of modern scientific and technological endeavors.

When I use the word "tragedy," I do so in the "better" Aristotelian sense. While Aristotle contends that tragedies did not have to have unhappy endings, he argues that the better ones do. I argue that the play can be read as having an unhappy ending from several different perspectives. The tragedy, however, is not a moral one in the Christian sense. It is not that an evil, non-repentant man goes to heaven, thereby breaking a traditional, Christian moral codex. Instead, Goethe's dynamic principles of action replace a Christian moral code within the play, and Faust's final end is tragic in that he is rendered incapable of further activity. In this sense, the play signals its ultramodernity: a scientific,

naturalistic understanding of the world replaces a religious one.[15]
Productive activity replaces moral rectitude as the goal of human
striving. The God of the Prolog who praises human activity speaks not
as the Judeo-Christian, commandment-giving being, but rather as the
personification of nature's forces. Faust's assumption into heaven at
the end of the play thus spells his "doom" because there he will be
"condemned" to an eternity of stasis. Even the way the wager is set up
between Faust and Mephisto is indicative of the importance of ceaseless
activity.

The terms of the bet between Faust and Mephistopheles in Goethe's
version are quite different than earlier Faust traditions. For example,
in Marlowe's *Doctor Faustus* the contract between the devil and the
protagonist is for a fixed period of 24 years. During that time, the devil
is to do Faust's bidding, but afterward, he takes Faust's soul to hell. In
Goethe's version, the contract is an open-ended one. Faust will only
"lose" the bet and die, if he ever becomes self-satisfied:

> If I should ever say to any moment (Augenblick):
> Tarry, remain! — you are so fair!
> then you may lay your fetters on me,
> then I will gladly be destroyed!
> Then they can toll the passing bell,
> your obligations then be ended —
> the clock may stop, its hand may fall,
> and time at last for me be over! (1699–1706)[16]

In many ways, Faust banks on his own unhappiness. Because he never
believes that he will be able to be satisfied, the terms of the bet are
appealing. He will obtain the devil as his servant for eternity:

---

[15] For a related perspective, see McCarthy, for whom the central relationship in this
ultramodern view is that between energy and matter. When matter decays, energy is released
back into the ecology of the whole to take form in some other way at some point somewhere.
McCarthy, however, argues that Faust will return to earth to continue some form of activity,
and "the cycle will begin again. While not the self-same, it will be self-similar" (229).

[16] Werd' ich zum Augenblicke sagen:
Verweile doch! du bist so schön!
Dann magst du mich in Fesseln schlagen,
Dann will ich gern zu Grunde gehn!
Dann mag die Totenglocke schallen,
Dann bist du deines Dienstes frei,
Die Uhr mag stehn, der Zeiger fallen,
Es sei die Zeit für mich vorbei. (1699–1706)

If ever you [Mephisto], with lies and flattery,

can lull me into self-complacency

or dupe me with a life of pleasure,

may that day be the last for me! (1694–7)[17]

Faust believes that his divided nature will make a moment of self-satisfaction impossible, and that he will live forever. He sees his own life in terms of a constant back and forth, just as Goethe describes the movement of the retina of the eye as going from one state to another. Faust overtly recognizes that should a static moment ever occur, it would signal, if not actually be, the definition of death. Striving and life itself are premised on a dynamic tension. The cessation of the tension between the two souls means the cessation of interacting with the world. Yet, Faust does lose the bet in some way (because he dies), and notably, he dies at the very moment that he predicts his own future state of self-complacency.

By returning again to the list of polarities above, another aspect is important for the context of Goethe's play. The list and the explanation that accompanies it focus upon issues of creation. The structure of the universe is based upon polar tension. Things come into being and interact only to the extent that they coexist with their polar opposites. Within this essay, Goethe speaks of the "economy" or "thriftiness" (Sparsamkeit) of nature. It creates everything through a couple of principles that in turn dynamically interact with each other as well (FA 1, 25: 143). According to Goethe's theories, polarities on their own only create simple, unevolved entities. In order for polarities to create complex ones, they need to combine with the principle of *Steigerung* (a term that roughly means heightening, deepening, or intensification). Together, these two principles create something new, higher, unexpected (FA 1, 25: 143). *Steigerung* is closely connected with the concept of striving within *Faust*. Goethe explains that *Steigerung* is being in a state of ever-striving ascent (immerstrebendem Aufsteigen, FA 1, 25: 81). In the Prolog of *Faust*, God praises the striving of human beings, even if it means that they will err in the process. Within Goethe's scientific works, the striving of natural entities leads to procreation as well as the production of beautiful objects.

[17] Kannst du mich schmeichelnd je belügen,
   Daß ich mir selbst gefallen mag,
   Kannst du mich mit Genuß betrügen,
   Das sei für mich der letzte Tag! (1694–7)

One can best see how *Steigerung* acts in concert with polarities in Goethe's "Metamorphosis of Plants." Although this essay is a botanical treatise, it is also simultaneously about human beings and their development.[18] Here, Goethe postulates that every organ of a plant (calyx, corolla, stamens, etc.) is actually a modified version of the organ of the leaf. (For example, in the shape and form of the calyx of a plant one can often readily see its similarity in appearance to the leaf, or in the tulip one often sees the transition from the green of the leaf to the coloring of the flower petals.) This "proto-organ" of the leaf, however, is only able to change and metamorphose to the extent that it strives toward a more complex existence. Here again, Goethe's principle of compensation comes into play. According to Goethe, the leaf transforms into more complex organs of the plant by following a process of alternating polar phases of expansion and contraction. Every expansive stage (e.g., the formation of the corolla) is followed by a contracted stage (e.g., the formation of sexual organs).[19] Once the plant reaches a stage of expansion, such as the growth of large petals, the next stage, as the theory of compensation teaches us, is effected, and is one characterized by contraction: the smaller, albeit more complex forms of the sexual organs.

The striving of a plant to reach its highest stage is achieved by the interplay of one polar stage (expansion) against another (contraction). Polar tensions drive the plant, as they do Faust, onward. In his account of the leaf's development, Goethe focuses upon nature's inner drive to become more specialized and articulated (#50). For some plants, they reach their pinnacle in reproduction, for other plants, in glorious, fragrant, but infertile blossoms (#7). In both cases, plants must strive to overcome, through polarities, their previous and more jejune state. Not all plants reach this articulated stage. With excessive nourishment, the plant remains at a more crude stage (roher) of development, and

[18] For a more detailed discussion of this essay, see my *Will to Create* 64–78.

[19] We first noted an expansion from the seed to the fullest development of the stem leaf; then we say the calyx appears through a contraction, the flower leaves through an expansion from the seed to the fullest development of the stem leaf; and the reproductive parts through a contraction ... the greatest expansion [occurs] in the fruit, and the greatest concentration in the seed. In these six steps nature steadfastly does its eternal work of propagating vegetation by two genders (#73). Vom Samen bis zu der höchsten Entwickelung des Stengelblattes, bemerkten wir zuerst eine Ausdehnung, darauf sahen wir durch eine Zusammenziehung den Kelch entstehen, die Blumenblätter durch eine Ausdehnung, die Geschlechtsteile abermals durch eine Zusammenziehung; und wir werden nun bald die größte Ausdehnung in der Frucht, und die größte Konzentration in dem Samen gewahr werden. In diesen sechs Schritten vollendet die Natur unaufhaltsam das ewige Werk der Fortpflanzung der Vegetabilien durch zwei Geschlechter. (#73)

flowering is impossible (#30). Such a plant does not progress toward its goal (Ziel) and remains in an immature, less refined stage (#38). Nature as a whole, however, does not like the possibility of growth in endless stages, but would prefer to hasten toward its goal (#106). Thus, although nature allows for stagnation, it prefers its organisms to strive and progress. Plants, like the human beings described in the Prolog, lose their ability to strive and create if they are sated and not challenged. This theme of satisfaction thwarting natural striving is common throughout Goethe's natural works. Even an oak tree, Goethe notes, cannot be beautiful if it has been overnourished (FA 2, 12: 599).

At the end of the play, Faust dies precisely at the moment that he anticipates the satisfaction of a static moment. He (mistakenly) believes himself to be on the verge of his life's greatest goal and further believes that therefore his name will live on in light of his achievements. He is willing to rest on his laurels and as a consequence withdraws from the world of activity. In this, Faust is completely fooled by Mephisto. The digging he hears is for his own grave and not for the completion of the land reclamation project. He also thinks that he has conquered and controlled one of the world's most powerful forces, the ocean, but Mephisto foresees a day when the levies will break, and the land will disappear. It is, however, Faust's prediction of a future, teeming and thriving community that leads to his downfall. Though that community has not yet been established, Faust is so confident that everything will go according to his plan that he is willing to enjoy that static moment now:

> then, to the moment (Augenblick), I could say:
> tarry a while, you are so fair —
> the traces of my days on earth
> will survive into eternity! —
> Envisioning those heights of happiness,
> I now enjoy my highest moment (Augenblick). (11581–6)[20]

Faust's desire for time to stand still signals his death. His particular perspective or eye's view (Augenblick) of his own project leads to the

---

[20] Zum Augenblicke dürft' ich sagen:
   Verweile doch, Du bist so schön!
   Es kann die Spur von meinen Erdetagen
   Nicht in Äonen untergehen. —
   Im Vorgefühl von solchem hohen Glück
   Genieß ich jetzt den höchsten Augenblick. (11581–6)

moment (Augenblick) of his death. Significantly, at this point Faust is blind, so it becomes especially ironic that he is misled by the moment/ glance of the eye. In being willing to stand still, Faust is no longer capable of the polar striving that would keep him active on earth. Unlike the seeing eye that cannot be at rest, Faust's blinded eye (meta-phorically and literally) leads him to his moment of death.

   Faust has lost his ability to play one polar force against another to insure striving and further development. Although the majority of scholars argue that Faust wins the bet and the devil loses,[21] Goethe him-self wrote in a letter to Schubarth (November 3, 1820) that Mephisto *half* wins the bet. He half wins, I would argue, because although he does not get Faust's soul, Faust still loses. The scholars who argue that Faust wins contend that he defeats the devil on a technicality. According to the bet, Faust will lose if he ever desires a particular moment to stand still: "If I should ever say to any moment (Augenblick):/ Tarry, remain! — you are so fair" (1699–1700).[22] Faust, however, does not ever make this statement in its declarative form, but in a future subjunctive one: "then, to the moment [Augenblick], I could say:/ tarry a while, you are so fair" (11581–2).[23] The technicality is not enough to "save" Faust from his "condemnation" to heaven because his stated intention is enough to lose the bet.

   The original terms of the bet are more complicated than just desir-ing a moment to stand still, but are in fact threefold. Faust would lose if 1) he would no longer desire to act (Werd' ich beruhigt je mich auf ein Faulbett legen: 1692); 2) the devil is able to trick him so that he is satisfied with himself (Kannst du mich schmeichelnd je belügen,/ Daß ich mir selbst gefallen mag, 1695); and 3) he desires a moment to stand still (1699–1700). All three of these conditions are met within his final speeches. It is clear that Faust views his land reclamation project as his great and final achievement (11501–10). He further sees its completion as the culmination of his career (Höchsterrungene, 11563). In other words, once the project is done, he would have no desire to continue to work, but would lose his desire to act (the first condition of the bet). Faust, however, has also lost the second condition of the bet. The devil has tricked him into feeling satisfied. Faust is musing about the future possibilities because he falsely believes that his project is being completed as he speaks. Mephisto has misled him into a state

---

[21] See, for example, Klett 67, Eibl 276, and Hoelzel 2.
[22] Werd' ich zum Augenblicke sagen:/ Verweile doch! du bist so schön! (1699–1700)
[23] Zum Augenblicke dürft' ich sagen:/ Verweile doch, Du bist so schön! (11581–2)

of self-satisfaction. Finally, although Faust restates the formula in the future subjunctive, he is confident enough that the moment will occur that he is willing to enjoy it right now: "Envisioning those heights of happiness, I now enjoy my highest moment" (11585–6).[24] Faust, thus, does enjoy the pleasure of a moment that he desires to stand still and loses the third condition of the bet.

After his death, Faust is deprived of yet another means of continuing his polar striving. The angels strip him of one of his two souls and hence eliminate the tension between the two that kept him active. The angels who are carrying his remains complain of their dirty burden and await the time at which "eternal love" will separate the earthly from the heavenly.[25] As the angels observe of Faust's earthly soul:

> This remainder of earth,
> it's distasteful to bear it
> even cremated,
> it would still be impure.
> When a strong spirit
> has taken the elements
> and made them its own,
> angels can't separate
> two natures conjoined
> in one single entity —
> only Eternal Love
> can disunite them. (11954–65)[26]

---

[24] Im Vorgefühl von solchem hohen Glück/ Genieß ich jetzt den höchsten Augenblick. (11585–6)

[25] Although Atkins questions whether it is "desirable that such a separation [of the two souls] take place," he, in the end, argues that Faust's soul is not separated from its earthly part, and that "real heavenly existence as defined by the Angels is not seriously posited here" ("Irony" 288). Atkins wishes to argue that the place in which Faust finds himself is not that different from his former earthly one, and hence that Faust will still be able to strive. It is unclear, however, why Atkins believes that Faust's being does not get separated. Even apart from the angels' predictions about the separation, one of the last words about Faust's existence, from Gretchen's mouth, describes how Faust's earthly ties are being cast off (12080–90).

[26] Uns bleibt ein Erdenrest
    Zu tragen peinlich,
    Und wär' er von Asbest
    Er ist nicht reinlich.
    Wenn starke Geisteskraft
    Die Elemente
    An sich herangerafft,
    Kein Engel trennte
    Geeinte Zwienatur

That which most characterized Faust and explained the basis of his striving (his two souls) is destroyed.[27] Of course, the angels themselves see this as a process of purification, but if we are to believe God's words in the Prolog, human beings are at their best when they strive, and God even praises Mephisto for his role in insuring human activity (336–41). Moreover, if Mephisto defines himself as that which desires to do evil but winds up doing good (1335–6), one must wonder what it might mean about the angels that they desire to do good. The angels, unlike God, see Mephisto only as a bad influence (11934–5) and therefore do not recognize the need for contradiction and opposition in human striving.

Strikingly, the celestial beings praise Faust for being active precisely at the moment in which he is being *passively carried* (stage instructions between 11824 and 11825 and between 11933 and 11934). The angels in this scene proclaim "for him whose striving never ceases/ we can provide redemption" (11936–7).[28] Yet, Faust here becomes completely passive. He is being carried and is therefore no longer

> Der innigen Beiden,
> Die ewige Liebe nur
> Vermags zu scheiden. (11954–65)

See also lines 12085–94.

[27] As Swales notes, the tension between Faust's two souls is not only about striving, but also about the "dynamic elation and eroding despair." And although one is tempted to place emphasis upon the element of despair, Swales notes that we should not "undervalue the moments of delight, for they too . . . are part of the perennial endowment of humanity" ("The Character" 39). Faust's dualism allows for both great happiness and great despair. That one of Faust's two souls appears devalued in heaven further places into question whether going to heaven is an unqualified good. For a different perspective on the conflict of Faust's two souls, see Van der Laan, who looks to them as a basis to argue that "*Faust* presents us with the incoherent individual whose inner division prevents moral decision and action" (455). McCarthy has argued that the separation of the souls is necessary in order to continue the cycle of life: the two souls separate only temporarily but are destined to reunite and begin the life cycle anew (223).

[28] Wer immer strebend sich bemüht/ Den können wir erlösen (11936–7). Although much has been made of the fact that in one draft, Goethe wrote of the angels carrying Faust's "Entelechie" (Schöne 800; Trunz 730–2), I would argue that it is significant that Goethe changed the term to Faust's immortal part (Unsterbliches) in the final version. Faust may live on in heaven, i.e., have some form of immortality, but what type of existence that will be is questionable. Even if, however, one grants Goethe's intention for the use of the term within the text, it does not necessarily imply a purely positive reading. For Goethe, entelechy was a term that connoted a kind of life energy that continued even after an individual had passed away. That energy, however, could take on different forms. For example, in a conversation with Eckermann (March 11, 1828), he described individuals with both inferior or weak (gering) and powerful (mächtig) entelechies. In his scientific works, he further spoke of lamed or thwarted entelechies (FA 1, 24: 464–5).

active, and thus according to the angels' own words, not worthy of being saved. The last and probably most famous lines of the play further emphasize the passive nature of Faust's final journey. He is being pulled or drawn up by the Eternal Feminine and is not raising himself or acting on his own accord. Even the Blessed Boys (babies who have died at birth) have greater agency than Faust for they are able to raise themselves to the higher spheres, speak, and move about with free will (11918–19, 11925–9). Faust in contrast has been completely silenced. He seems to be the only character in heaven who does not speak. And although the Blessed Boys believe that he will teach them (12083), the very next verse informs us that Faust will be the one being taught (12092).

That Faust loses half of himself in heaven is a signal that he can no longer strive and be active in this, the next phase of his existence. Heaven represents but one half, the spiritual side, of existence. If we return to the polar list of Goethe's essay above, God coexists with the world just as body coexists with the soul or the two souls together. Faust's heavenly manifestation is an incomplete one when compared to his earthly existence. By being deprived of one of his two souls, he no longer can strive or be active. In many, if not in all, of the pairs above, it is the interaction between the two that defines each side of the pair.

In a conversation with Eckermann (February 4, 1829), Goethe explains that he believes in his own immortality as long as he remains active until the end: to such beings, nature is obligated to grant immortality. Goethe states: "To me, the eternal existence of my soul is proved from my idea of activity; if I work on incessantly until my death, nature is bound to give me another form of existence when the present one can no longer sustain my spirit" (233).[29] Because Faust did not continue in his own ceaseless activity until the end, his activity does not continue into the next world. In becoming self-satisfied, he no longer engages with the world. Faust does not rejoin nature in his death; rather he is spirited away from nature into a different realm: the inactivity of heaven. His satisfaction at being a real estate developer has cost him a soul and with it an active life in the afterworld.

---

[29] Die Überzeugung unserer Fortdauer entspringt mir aus dem Begriff der Tätigkeit; denn wenn ich bis an mein Ende rastlos wirke, so ist die Natur verpflichtet, mir eine andere Form des Daseins anzuweisen, wenn die jetzige meinem Geist nicht ferner auszuhalten vermag (FA 2, 12: 301). Goethe describes such a notion of the afterlife on other occasions as well. See, for example, his similar sentiments in a conversation with Falk, January 25, 1813.

FAUST'S LOSS OF SOUL

Where did Faust go wrong? When does this man of active striving take the wrong turn? I believe that we can trace Faust's demise to his changing relationship with nature. Only after he abandons his appreciation of nature (and along with it poetry and art) does he become capable of damning self-satisfaction. Although scholars disagree whether Faust ought to be viewed positively or negatively, many are in agreement that he represents aspects of the modern scientist.[30] Goethe's stance toward modern science is well known, especially his diatribes against Isaac Newton. Goethe, in virulent attacks that led some to even doubt his sanity, accused Newton of everything from dishonesty to passing off deception as science.[31]

Goethe thought Newton was wrong in his approach, not only because his theories did not stress the interactive dynamism of nature but also because Goethe was afraid that mathematical formulas and complicated experiments would replace the observation of the actual phenomena in nature. He believed that nature's dynamism could only really be understood in the larger context: the whole was always greater than the sum of the parts. For him, science's ultimate laboratory was nature itself, and those things that could not easily be explained or mathematically defined were at the heart of nature. Throughout his *Theory of Colors*, Goethe argues that Newton's reliance upon mathematical principles caused him to miss what was crucial in the visible phenomena of the experiment. Newtonian science inappropriately, in Goethe's mind, subordinates nature and its phenomena to abstract scientific principles.[32] Anything that distanced the scientist from the phenomenon of nature, whether the use of a mathematical formula to generalize properties or the use of a microscope to divide into parts what ought to be viewed as a whole, was something that Goethe fought

[30] See, for example, Spengler, who most famously argues that Faust is symbolic of modern Western human beings in general (1: 354) and contrasts that which is "Faustian" against that which is "Classical." Specifically, he focuses upon the Faustian as related to "Galilean dynamics" (1: 183) and argues that the "specific tendency of all Western mechanics is toward an intellectual conquest by measurement, and it is therefore obliged to look for the essence of the phenomenon in a system of constant elements that are susceptible of full and inclusive appreciation by measurement" (1: 377). See also McCarthy, who turns to chaos and complexity theory to explicate the role of activity and change in *Faust*.

[31] *Farbenlehre*, Polemischer Teil §45; FA 1, 23: 314.

[32] Newton, in his central experiment, missed "seeing" the colored shadows that made one colored square appear higher than the other. For a detailed discussion of the differences between Goethe and Newton, see Sepper's insightful book, *Goethe Contra Newton*.

against in his own scientific works. Formulas could very well help us to control nature, but what, asked Goethe, would happen to our understanding of nature's vital and creative forces if we turned toward formulas and instruments rather than to nature itself?

Faust, in the end, becomes a scientist of the Newtonian, Cartesian ilk: someone who is more interested in conquering and controlling nature than in understanding it. Faust the technocrat emerges once Faust has lost his sense of beauty. Moreover, his feelings of self-satisfaction that ultimately spell his doom are linked to this modern stance. Whereas Goethe's own science was Romantic, in the sense that he viewed human beings as an integral part of nature, Faust is like a modern scientist, who sees himself and his creations as being superior to nature.[33]

Faust, of course, does not begin the play despising nature, but in desperately desiring to understand it. His first speeches in Part I reflect his frustration in his inability to understand nature. In his very first monolog, he rejects most of his learning as useless and turns to magic to understand the natural world around him (382–3). To this end, he summons the Earth Spirit, only to be rejected by him.[34] Faust is completely dejected because he worries that he will never understand the creative powers of nature (619–21). He therefore no longer believes he is created in God's image, because he fears that he will neither understand nor be able to take part in its creative processes:

Nature, mysterious in day's clear light,

lets none remove her veil,

and what she won't discover to your understanding

you can't exhort from her with levers and with screws.

(672–5; cf. 623–33; 652)[35]

In these lines, Faust seems nothing like a modern scientist. Where the fathers of modern science, Bacon and Descartes, quite literally advocate putting the screws on nature to get it to reveal its secrets, the Faust of Part I rejects such notions. Nature will remain an enigma

---

[33] For a discussion of the Romantic elements in Goethe's science, see Richards' *The Romantic Conception of Life.*

[34] For an excellent and extensive analysis of the Earth Spirit, see McCarthy (188–91). He shows the complexity of this being and traces its connection to Pietism, Paracelsus, Bruno, and Pentecostal imagery.

[35] Geheimnisvoll am lichten Tag

Läßt sich Natur des Schleiers nicht berauben,

Und was sie deinem Geist nicht offenbaren mag,

Das zwingst du ihr nicht ab mit Hebeln und mit Schrauben. (672–5)

to him, and this thought plunges him into a suicidal depression. His rejection of nature, however, is momentary. Although the Easter bells initially deter his suicide, his religious thoughts almost immediately turn into meditations on nature (775 ff.). Time and again, in spite of his inability to capture the Earth Spirit, Faust's most moving speeches involve such reflections on nature. In Part I, his brief escape to the wood and cave allows him to reflect upon nature's beauty, and, in the process, to rediscover aspects of himself and lament his partnership with Mephisto (3220–50). Similarly, in the beginning of Part II, Faust believes himself to have found new strength and energy from nature's restorative powers (4680–94).

Faust's relationship to nature changes drastically from the beginning to the end of the play, and in this change one can begin to see how he will come to lose one of his two souls. He no longer cares about the enigmatic or even creative aspects of nature, nor does he have any desire to understand it. If Act III, with Faust's union with Helen of Troy, symbolizes the quest for absolute beauty and Romantic poetry that arises from it, then Act IV demonstrates what happens once the poetry has died. By Act IV, his relationship to nature is about control and possession. One can tell how far removed he is from his own self by comparing his reaction to church bells. In the beginning of Part I, hearing the bells brings him away from the brink of suicide and into a mood that allows him to revel in the beauties of nature. By Act V of Part II, church bells remind him only of a small bit of land that he does not own. Once he destroys this sanctuary and the trees that surround it, he does not mourn the nature lost, but contemplates the building of a tower that will be better than the trees: the tower will be higher and allow him to survey better the expanse of his land. He no longer judges nature according to its power or beauty, but what use it can have for him, and what power he can have over it.

Faust's moment of greatest hubris occurs when he reveals to Mephisto his great dream: controlling the vast powers of the ocean for his own purposes. Ignoring the incredible fecundity of the ocean, he views it as "sterile" (Unfruchtbar) and "purposeless" (Zwecklose). Again here, one is struck by the vastly different view of the water in Act II of Part II. There, not only is it the source of all life, but it is also represented as teeming with gods, goddesses, and nymphs. Homunculus, the lab-created presence that exists as intellect only, goes to the sea in order to gain a complete life, body and soul. He is advised to go there because the water is seen as the source of all life, and there he joins with a goddess that represents love and fecundity. The contrast to Faust's view of the sea in Act IV is therefore quite striking. Faust is driven to despair by the perceived wastefulness of the unbridled energy of the waves. The oceans, however, seem wasteful primarily because Faust does not control them:

> The surging sea creeps into every corner,
> barren itself and spreading barrenness,
> expands and grows and rolls, and covers
> a long expanse of ugly desolation.
> Imbued with strength, wave after wave holds power
> but then withdraws, and nothing's been accomplished —
> a sight to drive me to despair,
> this aimless strength of elemental forces!
> This has inspired me to venture to new heights,
> to wage war here against these forces and subdue them. (10212–21)[36]

Gone is his earlier notion that nature cannot be forced with screws and levers. He has selected one of nature's most powerful and sublime aspects and declared war upon it (10221). It no longer matters whether he understands the power of the oceans, as long as he can harness them for his own purposes.

In desiring to conquer (besiegen) the oceans, Faust perhaps is seeking to avenge himself on the Earth Spirit that rejected him in Part I. The Earth Spirit, in defining itself to Faust, focuses upon its weaving, polar force of creative activity. It frames that creativity within language that characterizes the very bodies of water that Faust seeks to control:

> In the tides of life, in action's storm,
> I surge and ebb,
> move to and fro!
> As cradle and grave,
> as unending sea,

[36] Sie [die Woge] schleicht heran, an abertausend Enden
  Unfruchtbar selbst Unfruchtbarkeit zu spenden,
  Nun schwillt's und wächst und rollt und überzieht
  Der wüsten Strecke widerlich Gebiet.
  Da herrschet Well auf Welle kraftbegeistet,
  Zieht sich zurück und es ist nichts geleistet.
  Was zur Verzweiflung mich beängstigen könnte,
  Zwecklose Kraft unbändiger Elemente!
  Da wagt mein Geist sich selbst zu überfliegen,
  Hier möcht' ich kämpfen, dies möcht ich besiegen. (10212–21)

as constant change,

as life's incandescence,

I work at the whirring loom of time

and fashion the living garment of God. (501–9)[37]

The Earth Spirit condemns Faust because he does not understand (begreifen) its essence: "Your peer is the spirit that you comprehend:/ mine you are not!" (Du gleichst dem Geist den du begreifst,/ Nicht mir! 512–13.) In Faust's attempt to control the waters, understanding no longer is an issue. Power and control are.[38]

In his final moments, Faust believes that he has triumphed over nature by reclaiming land from the ocean. Technology, whether the dams or the new tower that he plans to build to replace the destroyed trees, is a means to control nature, to order and enslave that which is chaotic and free. Yet, it is precisely at the moment that Faust believes himself to have used technology to conquer nature that nature triumphs over him: he dies. In death, Faust does not return to nature, but is assumed into heaven where the creative weaving and subsequent striving is denied to him.

Many scholars have argued that Goethe's most important texts, including the *Wilhelm Meister* novels, *Elective Affinities*, and even *Werther*, sustain multiple interpretive readings.[39] The text of *Faust*, too, contains evidence of radically alternative readings of the ending. One must re-evaluate the arguments of those who would stress the positive, utopian possibilities of Faust's reclamation project as well as those who argue

---

[37] In Lebensfluten, im Tatensturm
  Wall' ich auf und ab,
  Wehe hin und her!
  Geburt und Grab,
  Ein ewiges Meer,
  Ein wechselnd Weben,
  Ein glühend Leben,
  So schaff' ich am sausenden Webstuhl der Zeit,
  Und wirke der Gottheit lebendiges Kleid. (501–9)

[38] Rigby offers a very insightful reading of Faust's reclamation project in light of ecocritical theory. Although I agree with many of her observations, because of my interpretation of Faust's demise, I read Goethe's play as being much more critical of the modern technological project. Thus, whereas Rigby questions whether P. B. Shelley would have distanced himself from "Faust the developer," I would argue that Goethe's play questions the utopian possibilities of Shelley's Prometheism (110).

[39] See, for example, Miller, Tanner and my "New Reading" 442–65. For an argument on how *Wilhelm Meister's Apprenticeship* is able to sustain "both the liberalizing potential of this narrative and the conservative strain that many readers have detected" (161), see Schutjer (117–62).

that Faust serves as a model for human behavior and weigh those interpretations against this more negative interpretation of Faust's heavenly
future existence.[40] In many important ways, Goethe's *Faust* resembles
his *Elective Affinities*. Scholarly opinion has always been divided on
whether either of these works is moral or immoral, and Protestants and
Catholics alike have been troubled by Goethe's use of Catholic symbolism. Perhaps, most importantly, Goethe himself spoke of both works as
containing secrets that would spur the reader to read and re-read and
would engender debate. With *Faust*, however, Goethe seems to have tired
of witnessing those debates and would not allow Part II to be published
in his lifetime. He nevertheless provided hints to his close friends about
the work. He wrote to Karl Friedrich Zelter (June 1, 1831) of the whole
work's containing an "obvious puzzle or enigma" (offenbares Rätsel)
and to Johann Sulpiz Boisserée (November 24, 1831) of the regret in
not being able to enjoy discussing the "seriously meant jests" of Part II
(die ernst gemeinten Scherze), and perhaps most tantalizing, in his
last comments on Part II to Wilhelm von Humboldt (March 17, 1832)
of the "very earnest jests" (diese sehr ernsten Scherze).[41]

The last scenes of the play contain a variety of possible "seriously
meant jests": Mephisto longs for the good old days when he could be

---

[40] Goethe's works are not only known for their ability to sustain multiple interpretive
readings, but also for their ambiguous endings. *Elective Affinities* serves as perhaps the best
example. At the end of that novel, two would-be lovers are buried together: Ottilie, a woman
who starved herself to death in order to avoid the advances of her guardian's husband, and
the husband, Eduard, who may also have committed suicide to be with Ottilie. The novel ends
with the hopeful words of the narrator, who, in viewing the corpses in the chapel, speculates
about what a friendly day it will be when the two wake up together. The conclusion appears
to end on a high note: a happy reconciliation of two star-crossed lovers in the next life. Yet,
as Walter Benjamin has noted (355), this couple bears marked similarities to another couple
who wound up in a very different place: the adulterers Francesca and Paolo, whom Dante
meets in hell.

[41] There is one comment attributed to Goethe that would seem to contradict my argument
about Faust's ultimate passivity. In a conversation with Eckermann (June 6, 1831), Goethe
seemingly speaks of Faust's pure activity, reflects upon the need for divine grace (göttliche
Gnade) for salvation, and states that these sentiments correspond with his own religious views
(Es steht dieses mit unserer religiösen Vorstellung durchaus in Harmonie, FA 2, 12: 489). I
read these lines as ironic. Goethe was not a religious man, at least not in the Christian sense,
and would have been unlikely to have expressed such sentiments. Although many scholars
have viewed these comments as important for interpreting the play, others, including Schöne,
question the authenticity of the exchange between Eckermann and Goethe precisely because
of Goethe's numerous statements about religion elsewhere (782–6, 801). Schöne further
argues that the comments about Faust's activity are simply a paraphrase of the angels' speech
and not Goethe's own words, and one could sooner attribute the sentiment of the quotation
to Eckermann than to Goethe (785). See also Böhm, who likewise questions the exchange
and sees the comment as more likely stemming from Eckermann than Goethe (294).

assured of God's word and where precedent and tradition would back up the devil's rights; modern souls are hesitant, according to Mephisto, to leave bodies; and most famously, Mephisto loses Faust's soul because he is sexually distracted by the naked backsides of the half-dressed cherubs. When Mephisto's body is covered in boils, he even likens himself to Job. The final and most telling "jest" occurs, however, when part of Faust's remains are condemned — to heaven. This condemnation, moreover, is one based upon the choice of stasis over activity. Goethe's play thus embraces modernity — in its departure from a morality based upon religious strictures — while at the same time questioning the hero of this era: the scientist who seeks to control nature at any cost.

PROJECTED MODERNISMS

In the above sections, I have argued first that Goethe's *Faust* is meant to be read from several different perspectives, and second, that a very important perspective has been left out in previous interpretations of it, namely, that it is a bad thing for Faust as an individual to go to heaven. This perspective is a necessary one, because as I have been arguing throughout the entire chapter, Goethe demanded that one 1) always view problems from a variety of perspectives; and 2) analyze the advantages and disadvantages of each perspective. Only then could one begin to have a sense of the whole and be in a position to evaluate particular situations or problems more fully.

Many readers of Goethe's *Faust*, while fully recognizing the protagonist's faults, ultimately believe that Goethe's play endorses the capitalist future. They argue for the benefits that will accrue for a large number of people living on the reclaimed land. After all, Goethe in his own words (*Conversations with Eckermann* February 21, 1827) seems to support or even be excited by the capitalist-driven changes to come:

> [Goethe] spoke much and with admiration of Alexander von Humboldt, whose work in Cuba and Columbia he had begun to read, and whose views as to the project of making a passage through the Isthmus of Panama appeared to have a peculiar interest for him. "Humboldt," said Goethe, "has, with a great knowledge of his subject, given over points where, by making use of some streams which flow into the Gulf of Mexico, the end may be perhaps better attained than at Panama. All this is reserved for the future, and for an enterprising spirit. So much, however, is certain, that, if they succeed in cutting such a canal that the ships of any burden and size can be navigated through it from the Mexican Gulf

to the Pacific Ocean, innumerable benefits would result to the whole human race, civilized and uncivilized. But I should wonder if the United States would let an opportunity escape of getting such work into their own hands. It may be foreseen that this young state, with its decided predilection to the West, will in thirty or forty years, have occupied and peopled the large tract of land beyond the Rocky Mountains. It may furthermore be foreseen that along the whole coast of the Pacific Ocean, where nature has already formed the most capacious and secure harbors, important commercial towns will gradually arise, for the further-ance of a great intercourse between China and the East Indies and the United States. In such a case, it would not only be desirable, but almost necessary, that a more rapid communication should be maintained between the eastern and western shores of North America, both by merchant-ships and men-of-war, than has hitherto been possible with the tedious, disagreeable, and expensive voyage round Cape Horn. I therefore repeat that it is absolutely indispensable for the United States to effect a passage from the Mexican Gulf to the Pacific Ocean; and I am certain that they will do it. Would that I might live to see it! — but I shall not. I should like to see another thing — a junction of the Danube and the Rhine. But this undertaking is so gigantic that I have doubts of its completion, particularly when I consider our German resources. And thirdly, and lastly, I should wish to see England in possession of a canal through the Isthmus of Suez. Would I could live to see these three great works! It would well be worth the trouble to last some fifty years more for the purpose. [42]

---

[42] Bei Goethe zu Tisch. — Er sprach viel und mit Bewunderung über Alexander von Humboldt, dessen Werk über Cuba und Columbien er zu lesen angefangen und dessen Ansichten über das Projekt eines Durchstiches der Landenge von Panama für ihn ein ganz besonderes Interesse zu haben schienen. "Humboldt, sagte Goethe, hat mit großer Sachkenntnis noch andere Punkte angegeben, wo man mit Benutzung einiger in den Mexikanischen Meerbusen fließenden Ströme vielleicht noch vorteilhafter zum Ziele käme, als bei Panama. Dies ist nun Alles der Zukunft und einem großen Unternehmungsgeiste vorbehalten. So viel ist aber gewiß, gelänge ein Durchstich der Art, daß man mit Schiffen von jeder Ladung und jeder Größe durch solchen Kanal aus dem Mexikanischen Meerbusen in den stillen Ozean fahren könnte, so würden daraus für die ganze zivilisierte und nichtzivili-sierte Menschheit ganz unberechenbare Resultate hervorgehen. Wundern sollte es mich aber, wenn die vereinigten Staaten es sich sollten entgehen lassen, ein solches Werk in ihre Hände zu bekommen. Es ist vorauszusehen, daß dieser jugendliche Staat, bei seiner ent-schiedenen Tendenz nach Westen, in dreißig bis vierzig Jahren auch die großen Landstrecken jenseits der Felsengebirge in Besitz genommen und bevölkert haben wird. — Es ist ferner vorauszusehen, daß an dieser ganzen Küste des stillen Ozeans, wo die Natur bereits die geräu-migsten und sichersten Häfen gebildet hat, nach und nach sehr bedeutende Handelsstädte entstehen werden, zur Vermittelung eines großen Verkehrs zwischen China nebst Ostindien und den vereinigten Staaten. In solchem Fall wäre es aber nicht bloß wünschenswert, sondern fast notwendig, daß sowohl Handels- als Kriegsschiffe zwischen der nordamerikanischen westlichen und östlichen Küste eine raschere Verbindung unterhielten, als es bisher durch die langweilige, widerwärtige und kostspielige Fahrt um das Cap Horn möglich gewesen. Ich wiederhole also: es ist für die vereinigten Staaten durchaus unerläßlich, daß sie sich eine

Within this passage, one can see a number of statements that would support a positive reading of the ending of the play. Goethe very much seems to sanction the expansive trade and growth that characterizes the end of *Faust*. He speaks of expansion of land, of colonization and even links merchant and war ships in the same sentence. He praises capitalist, enterprising activities and speaks of the innumerable benefits to human beings from such endeavors. He envisions a world in which trade and communication flourish.

But however positively one may wish to read the quote above about the Panama Canal, Goethe also had extremely negative views about this type of progress, as the "Maxims and Reflections" that head this chapter demonstrate. The above conversation with Eckermann, thus, does not tell the whole story about Goethe's views on technological progress, but only one side of it. Goethe's principle of compensation postulates that all actions from which benefits arise also have certain costs. The readers who have endorsed the play in primarily positive terms have neglected to focus upon those. Indeed, however much Goethe may have praised the technologies and economies, he was well aware of their downsides. If we examine a letter that Goethe wrote (to Zelter, June 6, 1825), one can see that he is not so quick to embrace all of the fruits of the new society:

> Young people today are excited way too soon and then are carried away in the whirlpool of the time. Wealth and speed are what the world admires and toward which everyone strives; railways, express mail delivery, steamships and any possible ease of communication is that toward which the educated look, in order to surpass themselves, to overeducate themselves and thereby to persist in mediocrity. And this, of course, is the consequence of making everything generally available: that a culture of mediocrity becomes the general norm. This is that toward which Bible groups, the Lancaster pedagogy ["learn through teaching method" AOT], and who knows what all else strive.[43]

Durchfahrt aus dem Mexikanischen Meerbusen in den stillen Ozean bewerkstelligen, und ich bin gewiß, daß sie es erreichen."

"Dieses möchte ich erleben; aber ich werde es nicht. Zweitens möchte ich erleben, eine Verbindung der Donau mit dem Rhein hergestellt zu sehen. Aber dieses Unternehmen ist gleichfalls so riesenhaft, daß ich an der Ausführung zweifle, zumal in Erwägung unserer deutschen Mittel. Und endlich drittens möchte ich die Engländer im Besitz eines Kanals von Suez sehen. Diese drei großen Dinge möchte ich erleben, und es wäre wohl der Mühe wert, ihnen zu Liebe es noch einige funfzig Jahre auszuhalten." (FA 2, 12: 580–1)

[43] Junge Leute werden viel zu früh aufgeregt und dann im Zeitstrudel fortgerissen; Reichtum und Schnelligkeit ist was die Welt bewundert und wornach jeder strebt; Eisenbahnen, Schnellposten, Dampfschiffe und alle mögliche Fazilitäten der Kommunikation

In his comments both here and in the maxims above, Goethe anticipates certain trends: the desire for quick and easily digestible news and knowledge, a debt-driven economy, and the devaluation of high culture and knowledge. The first maxim that introduces the chapter even seems to predict the paparazzi- and reality-show driven pop-culture of today, where everyone's actions are dragged in front of the public. Goethe certainly predicted the overall push for greater ease and speed of communication as well as the displacement of high culture for low that would result. In the letter to Zelter above, Goethe foresees that once everyone has greater access to the goods of modernity, from trade to culture to education, the end result will be a leveling one. Education and culture will not be what they once were but will become something quite ordinary.

Living as we now do in the Faustian world where technology gives us a great many comforts, it is perhaps much easier to see the advantages of this world than the disadvantages, and indeed many who have written about this play in the twentieth century argue that we are to take Faust's project and his salvation at face value. The economist Hans Binswanger, writing in the economic heyday of the 1980s, talks about the joy of creating a surplus economy. Taking the example of Faust's act of land reclamation, he waxes poetic about the economic joy of large-scale projects and dismisses the more intimate realm of love between two people as being less pleasurable:

> A similar joy is experienced by all who in some form — as entrepreneur, worker, or researcher — perform an economic act. Not without reason does Faust find the greatest happiness not in love but in the achievement of such a deed [the land reclamation project]. The happiness it brings is more wide-ranging and lasting than the happiness that love — as experienced with Gretchen — can grant. The latter is merely a private happiness which exhausts itself in the individual relationship. The former is a happiness that should benefit all humanity, opening up ever more "future" with its promise of eternal progress. (39)

Binswanger weighs advantage, as many contemporary economists do, in terms of scale and power. His analysis shows how far we have come to accept the Faustian realm. Whereas Goethe's readers of the

---

sind es worauf die gebildete Welt ausgeht, sich zu überbieten, zu überbilden und dadurch in der Mittelmäßigkeit zu verharren. Und das ist ja auch das Resultat der Allgemeinheit, daß eine mittlere Kultur gemein werde, dahin streben die Bibelgesellschaften, die Lancasterische Lehrmethode, und was nicht alles. (FA 2, 10: 277)

nineteenth century primarily viewed the love story as the focus of the play, Binswanger argues that the dams and future work space for millions is the true core.[44] If we follow this kind of argument here, then Faust's abandonment of Gretchen is a good thing because it eventually allows him to move on with his life to a happiness that is greater because it makes thriving millions happy, too.

Faust certainly emphasizes to himself the merits of commerce and geopolitical expansion. He wishes to advance a whirlwind of free, capitalist activity that has been enabled through technological advances. He realizes that some obstacles still stand in the way of achieving this goal, and in his last speech speculates about what would happen once his land reclamation project is completed:

A marsh stretching along those mountains
contaminates what's been reclaimed so far;
to drain that stagnant pool as well
would be a crowning last achievement.
If I can furnish space for many millions
to live — not safe, I know, but free to work
in green and fertile fields, with man and beast
soon happy on the new-made soil
and settled in beside the mighty hill
a dauntless people's effort has erected,
creating here inside a land of Eden —
then there, without, the tide may bluster to its brim,
but where it gnaws, attempting to rush in by force,
communal effort will be quick to close the breach.
To this idea I am committed wholly,
it is the final wisdom we can reach:
he only merits freedom and existence
who wins them every day anew.
And so, beset by danger, here childhood's years,
maturity, and age will all be vigorous.
If only I might see that people's teeming life,
share their autonomy on unencumbered soil . . . (11560–80)[45]

---

[44] Binswanger also notes negative aspects of Faust's project, but in the end sees it primarily in a positive light.

[45] Ein Sumpf zieht am Gebirge hin,
    Verpestet alles schon Errungene;
    Den faulen Pfuhl auch abzuziehn
    Das Letzte wär das Höchsterrungene.

Faust here endorses the philosophy of "the end justifies the means." According to this view, despite his murder of Baucis and Philemon, use of slave labor, deployment of unconventional weapons, and so forth, Faust is in the end justified, because his plans will benefit a great many people. He has used his power to create a space in which people will be able to flourish, where they will be able to be active and productive, where they can be freer to pursue their work than in the monarchical, religious, and more feudal government that surrounds his lands.

In such a reading, the deaths of Baucis and Philemon and Gretchen may be regrettable, but necessary for progress. This type of argument is not that distant from the school of economic thought that had been so dominant in recent decades until the unraveling of the markets at the end of 2008. At the very least, most Chicago-school type economists would have a hard time understanding why Baucis and Philemon refused to leave their memory-filled home for the better spot of real estate that Faust offers them. Indeed, if Faust's and Baucis and Philemon's case were brought before a judge of this school of thought, adjudicating the case in terms of the principles of wealth maximization would undoubtedly give Faust the property. Although Baucis and Philemon are not willing to sell their property, a judge like Richard Posner would probably recommend "mimicking" the market, "which means imposing the result he believes a market would have reached."[46] Faust has more resources at his disposal, and he would have been the victor in an auction-type setting. In other words, under a Chicago-school model, Baucis and Philemon would lose their case.

Eröffn' ich Räume vielen Millionen,
Nicht sicher zwar, doch tätig-frei zu wohnen.
Grün das Gefilde, fruchtbar; Mensch und Herde
Sogleich behaglich auf der neusten Erde,
Gleich angesiedelt an des Hügels Kraft,
Den aufgewälzt kühn-emsige Völkerschaft.
Im Innern hier ein paradiesisch Land,
Da rase draußen Flut bis auf zum Rand,
Und wie sie nascht gewaltsam einzuschießen,
Gemeindrang eilt die Lücke zu verschließen.
Ja diesem Sinne bin ich ganz ergeben,
Das ist der Weisheit letzter Schluß:
Nur der verdient sich Freiheit wie das Leben,
Der täglich sie erobern muß.
Und so verbringt, umrungen von Gefahr,
Hier Kindheit, Mann und Greis sein tüchtig Jahr.
Solch ein Gewimmel möcht ich sehn,
Auf freiem Grund mit freiem Volke stehn. (11559–80)

[46] See, for example, Dworkin's explanation and critique of Posner's principles (198).

Faust would also have such a court's approval because he advocates a more productive use of the land.

Although economists generally stop short of advocating violence to achieve financial or market advantages, other propositions suggested, from selling babies to body parts on the free market (as Posner has proposed),[47] may seem to some equally abhorrent. Indeed, what happens to Baucis and Philemon is clearly related to contemporary economic models of analysis. Could they not, after all, symbolize a Third World, less developed worldview (Berman)? A private, but leaked memo written by Lawrence Summers (December 12, 1991) while he was the Chief Economist at the World Bank, serves as an illustrative example:

Just between you and me, shouldn't the World Bank be encouraging more migration of the dirty industries to the LDCs [Least Developed Countries]? I can think of three reasons:

(1) The measurement of the costs of health-impairing pollution depends on the foregone earnings from increased morbidity and mortality. From this point of view a given amount of health-impairing pollution should be done in the country with the lowest wages. I think the economic logic behind dumping a load of toxic waste in the lowest-wage country is impeccable and we should face up to that.

(2) The costs of pollution are likely to be non-linear as the initial increments of pollution probably have very low cost. I've always thought that under-populated countries in Africa are vastly under-polluted; their air quality is probably vastly inefficiently low [sic] compared to Los Angeles or Mexico City. Only the lamentable facts that so much pollution is generated by non-tradable industries (transport, electrical generation) and that the unit transport costs of solid waste are so high prevent world-welfare-enhancing trade in air pollution and waste.

(3) The demand for a clean environment for aesthetic and health reasons is likely to have very high income-elasticity. The concern over an agent that causes a one-in-a-million change in the odds of prostate cancer is obviously going to be much higher in a country where people survive to get prostate cancer than in a country where under-5 mortality is 200 per thousand. Also, much of the concern over industrial atmospheric discharge is about visibility-impairing particulates. These discharges may have very little direct

---

[47] So, too, does he advocate the use of torture when used to protect American interests: the Constitution is not "a suicide pact."

> health impact. Clearly trade in goods that embody aesthetic pollution
> concerns could be welfare-enhancing. While production is mobile the
> consumption of pretty air is a non-tradeable.

> The problem with the arguments against all of these proposals for more pollution
> in LDCs (intrinsic rights to certain goods, moral reasons, social concerns, lack of
> adequate markets, etc) could be turned around and used more or less effectively
> against every Bank proposal for liberalisation.

Although one would imagine that this memo might have resulted in a
large outcry, the *Economist*, the source that published the leaked memo,
reflected: "The language is crass, even for an internal memo. But look
at it another way: Mr Summers is asking questions that the World Bank
would rather ignore — and, on the economics, his points are hard to
answer. The Bank should make this debate public" (February 8, 1992).
Summers, of course, went on to become US Secretary of the Treasury,
president of Harvard (until other controversial opinions about women
and science and his troubled relationship to African-American professors led to his ouster there) and now is again in the White House. It is
difficult to imagine Summers' political resurrection but for the troubled
economic times and perhaps serves as yet another example of how
willing we are to trade principles for a perceived economic good.

In his book, *The Dismal Science*, the Harvard economist Stephen
Marglin reflects on Summers' 1991 memo and the possible reactions
that it elicits:

> In my experience, people who have not been exposed to a college course in
> economics are likely to be outraged by the memo . . . But what a difference a
> year makes. After a freshman course in economics, college students begin to
> think like economists . . . and will explain why and how both the low-wage and
> the high-wage countries benefit from the relocation of toxic wastes.
>
> Make a list of all the things that you feel should not be traded in markets, even
> if there are willing buyers and sellers. If you are an economist, or even if you have
> had a year of freshman economics, your list is likely to be a short one, maybe
> limited to addictive drugs and one or two other things. But if you are among the
> uninitiated you might include anything from sexual relations to votes in public
> elections, not to mention toxic wastes. It might include body parts, pornography
> (perhaps only child pornography). (37)

That Faust does not trouble himself with the source of the finances
of his land reclamation project (it is financed through theft and

colonization masked as trade), or the deaths of the couple, places him in the modern, economic camp. Looking over the fields that will employ and house so many, he believes that his name will live on, and he is blissfully happy. That he will be able to maximize wealth for so many at the price of the deaths of so few seems a reasonable trade. So, too, are many readers willing to see the merits of Faust's claim in this light and turn to Faust's economic boom town to justify his assumption into heaven — even in light of murder.

Given this conservative economic analysis of Faust-like dealings, one might expect the left to be horrified at Faust's actions. The extent to which the socialists and communists have also embraced Faust's project and seeming salvation is therefore quite surprising. One might think that in light of Faust's attempts to realize his land reclamation project at the expense of slave labor and the lives of two lower-class people, socialist thinkers would find the end, a rewarded Faust, quite troubling. The very opposite, however, is generally the case with the socialists, who see the ending of *Faust* as a necessary step toward the progress of a better state. But even here, the better state is primarily so in economic rather than in aesthetic (or ethical) terms. Arts and culture come equally under attack in the Faustian new world, no matter if read from a left- or right-wing perspective. The eminent Marxist theorist Georg Lukács, for example, takes Goethe's interest in the technology of the last pages at face value.[48] Goethe, according to Lukács, does "nothing to mitigate the diabolical character of the capitalist form of this progress" and claims that capitalist activity is indeed the fulfillment of Faust's life-long striving (192). Faust is saved because capitalism does not have the power to corrupt the nucleus of the human being (194): "despite Mephisto, despite capitalism — mankind is not condemned to fall into the diabolical and to 'eat dust'" (217).[49] Because capitalism

---

[48] "No one acquainted with the pronouncement of Goethe's last decades can be surprised at this ending. He ironically rejects the confused illusions of the wars of liberation but later thinks that good highways and railroads will necessarily bring about the unity of Germany. He takes a passionate interest in every technical and economic achievement of capitalism and even expresses the desire to be able to live long enough to witness the construction of the Danube–Rhine canal and the Suez and Panama canals. Here too belongs his envious recognition — very rare in Germany then — of the nascent ascendance of the United States." (192)

[49] For further discussion of *Faust* and twentieth-century socialism, see Bullitt (184–95). She discusses how several socialist writers adopted Goethe's theme in their own works. She also reports that both Marx and Lenin admired the play, and "it has even been suggested as a kind of artistic buttress to the *Communist Manifesto*" (195). For a more critical look at the connection between *Faust* and socialism, see Yurick (67–95).

cannot destroy that which is the best in us, society can progress to a later stage in history, even though, as Lukács argues, Goethe himself could not have had an idea of what that stage might be. Even recent commentators believe that Faust deserves to be saved "in the name of and for the sake of his sheer energy, his drive, his avidity for experience" (Swales "Drama" 91) or for his "Promethean ambitions" (Rigby 212). Details of the play, however, time and again problematize this point of view, especially since we are given not only Faust's perspective on his life goals, but also the devil's.

Faust is very much a modern man, and one who is willing to engage in Realpolitik. The world is a messy place, and one has to give up on absolute principles if one wishes to get ahead — if one is going to spread the fruits of capitalism, with the aid of science and technology, far and wide. When confronted with the war in Act IV, Faust at first is hesitant to take a lead part, but is convinced to do so by Mephisto: first because Faust will gain property and power; and second because Faust can be sure to win due to his superior weapons. Mephisto supplies the army and the magic that insures Faust's success. As we have seen above, Faust hopes to use this power for the benefit of others. In some ways, it may be unfair to call him the murderer of Baucis and Philemon because he never outrightly tells Mephisto to kill them. He just tells Mephisto to take care of it and then does not bother with the details. Even here, Faust has an excuse. He wanted to trade them in land, not rob them (11371). In fact, Faust believes that the older couple will profit by an exchange of land; he promises to give them a superior piece of it in exchange. Because he has lost his connection to nature, poetry, and beauty, he no longer fathoms that someone could be attached to an object, a house and its adjoining garden, out of love or sentiment.

Faust's trade is quite reminiscent of the account of Cyrus's education according to Xenophon (*Cyropaedia* 1:3:17), a classical story about justice and right behavior. Cyrus is told a story about a small boy with a big coat and large boy with a small coat. The large boy uses force to exchange coats, and Cyrus is asked to adjudicate the matter. When he rules that the state of affairs is just because each boy now has the coat that is most appropriate for him, Cyrus is whipped by his teacher for failing to see the injustice of using violence to achieve the desired means. Roderick Long contrasts this older means of adjudicating with a more contemporary one: "Xenophon has Cyrus describe his training in judicial arbitration; the passage is a telling anticipatory reply to the Coase-Posner approach to law, which recommends rendering verdicts in accordance with social utility rather than antecedent rights."[50] Faust, the modern man, has embraced the concept of using global utility to trump older forms of justice. Might does make right as long as a greater number of people benefit by the act of power than those who are harmed. These same principles are behind the booming world of trade in Faust's colony. As Mephisto notes:

> On the open sea your mind is open,
> and no one gives a fig for prudence;
> you have to grab things in a hurry:
> you catch a fish or catch a ship,
> and once you've three in your possession,
> you soon have caught a fourth as well;
> the fifth then hasn't got a chance,
> since it is a fact that might is right —
> not *how* but *what* will be the only question asked.
> Unless I'm all at sea about maritime matters,
> war, trade, and piracy together are
> a trinity not to be severed. (11177–88)[51]

Mephisto makes these statements after he has (at Faust's bidding) sent out two ships for trade, but 20 return — trade has flourished, but only because it was accompanied by theft. The trinity of the Christian world is replaced by that of the new: war, trade, and piracy. The new technology that enables trade and the community to thrive has a considerable downside for those not in Faust's colony. The success of this enterprise is at the cost of peace, law, and justice. Baucis and Philemon are the symbols for all of the others who are similarly robbed or murdered to enable the new society to flourish. It is noteworthy that the Three Mighty Men who were so necessary for winning the war

---

[50] <http://www.strike-the-root.com/4/long/long5.html>.
[51] Das freie Meer befreit den Geist,
  Wer weiß da was Besinnen heißt!
  Da fördert nur ein rascher Griff,
  Man fängt den Fisch, man fängt ein Schiff,
  Und ist man erst der Herr zu drei
  Dann hakelt man das vierte bei.
  Da geht es denn dem fünften schlecht,
  Man hat Gewalt, so hat man recht.
  Man fragt ums Was? und nicht ums Wie?
  Ich müßte keine Schiffahrt kennen.
  Krieg, Handel und Piraterie,
  Dreieinig sind sie, nicht zu trennen. (11177–88)

for the emperor are still around as necessary elements to the world of trade and capital.

Mephisto, in this sense, is much more old-fashioned than Faust. His ultimate assessment of the Baucis and Philemon incident is that Faust is in the wrong. As a devil, he is quite happy to accommodate Faust's wishes, but he nevertheless also supplies the moral commentary upon the whole: "Here's an old story, ever the same —/ Naboth's vineyard once again" (1 Kings 21)[52] Mephisto is referring to an Old Testament teaching about justice. King Ahab wishes to acquire Naboth's vineyard because it abuts his own property. Naboth refuses to sell or to trade properties. King Ahab's wife, Jezebel, has trumped-up charges brought against Naboth so that he is killed and his property confiscated. Elijah is sent by God to inform Ahab: "In the place where dogs licked up the blood of Naboth, dogs will also lick up your blood . . . The dogs shall eat Jezebel within the bounds of Jezreel" (1 Kings 17–23). Although Ahab repents and is granted some reprieve — the punishment will not come to him directly but to his children — he is not able to escape punishment for his act of injustice. Mephisto's stance toward this biblical injustice is not surprising. Mephisto himself trusts God to uphold contracts, precedents, and property rights. After all, these are the principles that must rule if he is to gain Faust's soul according to their blood-signed agreement.

However much Goethe's play portrays the appeal of technology and capitalism (or at least its inevitability), it also quite profoundly draws our attention to its costs — costs that are as true in today's Faustian world as they were within the confines of the play. Whereas readers in the past were more likely to see Faust's redemption in terms of God's forgiveness and the intercession of the "penitent" Gretchen, today's readers are more likely to see Faust's heavenly assumption as a reward for works well done. This trend, I believe, is a demonstration of how Faustian and economically driven we have become. Unlike Lukács, I believe that capitalism has destroyed Faust's humanity and serves as a cautionary tale of our own. A close reading of the play demonstrates not only what we have paid in order to get to where we are today, but also what additional costs may accrue unless we strive to strike a balance between the competing forces that so define Faust. In the end, as I have argued above, it turns out to be a bad thing for Faust to go to heaven, and thus his assumption does not necessarily imply a happy ending for

---

[52] Auch hier geschieht was längst geschah,
  Denn Naboths Weinberg war schon da. (Regum I, 21) (11286–7)

technology or capitalism. Rather, the play contains a profound critique of the man who gives up his love of nature and the arts to embrace the technologies of capitalism.

RELIGION IN A CAPITALIST WORLD

Mephisto, of course, does not ultimately gain Faust's soul, so it would appear as if the God of the play favors more modern principles of social utility as well. Indeed, if we compare the Archbishop's attitude toward his own building project at the end of Act IV and Faust's project in Act V, numerous parallels arise. Most striking is that the Archbishop, too, believes that the ends justify the means, even in the case of unpaid labor. In this scene, the Archbishop warns that God and the Pope are upset with the Emperor for his reliance upon Faust and black magic to win the war. In order to expiate this sin, the Emperor must cede some land to the Church. Just as he has given land to Faust for his project, so too must the Emperor give the Church its due. The Archbishop then gives an impassioned speech, with numerous elements that echo Faust's last words. He speaks of reclaiming land, of future flourishing and thronging, of a populace that will enjoy and utilize that which he plans to build. Towers will also play a major role in this vision:

> But, first, the place that sin has so defiled must be
> proclaimed at once as sacred to God's service.
> The mind already sees great walls that quickly rise,
> the shafts of morning sun that flood the choir with light,
> the edifice that grows and widens to a cross,
> the soaring, lengthening nave, a joy to all the faithful
> who in their fervor now pour through the solemn doors —
> from lofty towers that aspire heavenwards
> the bells' first summons has sung out through hill and valley,
> and penitents approach to start their lives anew.
> At this great consecration — may its day be soon! —
> your presence, Sire, will be the chief and crowning glory. (11005–16)[53]

[53] Erst! der entweihte Raum wo man sich so versündigt,
   Sei alsobald zum Dienst des Höchsten angekündigt.
   Behende steigt im Geist Gemäuer stark empor,
   Der Morgensonne Blick erleuchtet schon das Chor,
   Zum Kreuz erweitert sich das wachsende Gebäude,
   Das Schiff erlängt, erhöht sich zu der Gläubigen Freude,

At first glance, the Archbishop's goal appears quite different from Faust's. He seems to be building in order to provide spiritual inspiration and foster religious worship. The building will be a joy to those who worship there and will inspire those who visit it to reflect upon God's glory. As a result, the pilgrims will spiritually benefit from their visit and will be able to start their lives anew. The Emperor, excited that he will be part of an enterprise that will praise God, feels elevated in contemplating this project.

The very next speech by the Archbishop, however, reveals that the Church's motives are more complex. The Church, like Faust, desires power and money and will justify the use of unpaid labor in the process. The transaction between the Emperor and the Archbishop parallels the pact scene of Part I and concludes in a rather dubious and open-ended contract. Rather than concern for the pilgrims' souls, the Church seems to be using this opportunity to enrich itself and to awe its members into compliance with its rules. As the Archbishop explains to the Emperor:

> You will, besides, devote to the work's furtherance,
>
> in perpetuity, all local revenues;
>
> tithes, tributes, rents. The costs of proper maintenance
>
> are great, and so are those of careful management.
>
> To speed construction in so desolate a place
>
> you'll give us from your loot some of the gold you have won.
>
> Moreover, we shall need — a fact I won't gloss over —
>
> wood from a long way off, and lime and slate and such like;
>
> the people shall haul these, instructed by the pulpit;
>
> the Church will bless the man whose team toils in her service. (11022–31)[54]

Sie strömen brünstig schon, durchs würdige Portal,
Der erste Glockenruf erscholl durch Berg und Tal,
Von hohen Türmen tönt's, wie sie zum Himmel streben,
Der Büßer kommt heran, zu neugeschaffnem Leben.
Dem hohen Weihetag, er trete bald herein!
Wird deine Gegenwart die höchste Zierde sein. (11005–16)

[54] Dann widmest Du zugleich dem Werke, wie's entsteht,
Gesamte Landsgefälle: Zehnten, Zinsen, Beet,
Für ewig. Viel bedarfs zu würdiger Unterhaltung,
Und schwere Kosten macht die sorgliche Verwaltung.
Zum schnellen Aufbau selbst auf solchem wüsten Platz
Reichst du uns einiges Gold, aus deinem Beuteschatz.
Daneben braucht man auch, ich kann es nicht verschweigen,
Entferntes Holz und Kalk und Schiefer und dergleichen.

This subsequent speech is a worldly one in which the Archbishop attempts to enrich the Church as much as possible by obtaining money and goods from the Emperor and free labor from its parishioners. Ironically, the Church here envisions a rather modern mode of existence. On the surface, this may seem counter-intuitive. The play takes place in Reformation and pre-1789 Europe, so it would appear as if the Church reflects the older power structure of that time. The Church is powerful because the government supports it and makes sure that it continues to receive wealth and, with it, power.

The portrayal of the Church here, however, could also be seen as presciently modern. It is, after all, a Church that embraces the advantages of capitalism as long as it benefits by receiving portions of that money. It is one that has gained in power as the Emperor has lost his. The Emperor not only has divided his rule and eliminated the hereditary monarchy, but he has also asked the Church, among other powers, to oversee the election of the next monarch (10961–70). An interesting parallel could be drawn here between the power of the Evangelicals within the political structure of the USA. Although the USA has a secular government, the Evangelical movement has in recent decades been an influential political force. The Emperor is informed that he will not be able to be in power without the support of the Church, which he in turn will need to support. Similarly, it is widely held that George W. Bush never would have been elected without the support of religious groups, which other Republicans have sought to appease, with greater and lesser success, ever since. It is a commonly held opinion that John McCain selected Sarah Palin as his running mate in order to please the Evangelicals. Even Barack Obama, raised as an atheist, joined an Evangelical Church, Trinity United, when he became seriously interested in politics. (America may be ready for a black president but not an atheist one.) This Church, which he has since left, also has an unabashedly political agenda. One could even see how in our contemporary world, just like in the Faustian one, capitalism thrives alongside polities governed by religious extremists. Iran in most ways is a modern state, but one where religious extremism exists side-by-side with capitalism. One could also think of the growing power of Islam in countries such as Turkey or Pakistan, where the secular government does constant battle with the powers of religious groups. The Archbishop in Goethe's play has so much foresight that he even

Die Fuhren tut das Volk, vom Predigtstuhl belehrt,
Die Kirche segnet den der ihr zu Diensten fährt. (11023–32)

requests future taxes on the land that Faust has been given — land that at that point in the play does not even exist.[55] The Church, therefore, hopes to profit further from Faust's successes even if they are gained through the powers of the devil. The Archbishop, like Faust himself, is willing to engage in Realpolitik.

Faust and the Archbishop both believe in their projects. In the case of the Church, a beautiful building will be built that will inspire generations to come while the Church itself will gain great wealth. In the case of Faust, new land is to be forged from the ocean where millions can live and praise Faust's name in the eons to come. If we return to the quote above in which Goethe discusses the Panama Canal, many scholars believe on the strength of it that Goethe indeed endorsed this modern view, warts and all. Those scholars who wish to align Goethe with this understanding of modernity argue that he realized that the advances of capitalism had their problems, but that these were in the end outweighed by the advantages.[56]

Goethe, as I have already argued above, embedded an alternative to reading Faust's assumption into heaven as simply a reward, and this perspective provides a much-needed balance to the views that Goethe, when all is said and done, wholeheartedly supported the efforts of modernity. Other scholars, of course, have noticed conflicts inherent within the play and have turned to a variety of theories to explain them. Bennett, for example, argues that the play represents the tragedy and alienation of life itself, i.e., that the only tragedy is that there is no real tragedy and we are forever thwarted in our desire for catharsis and closure because one interpretation incessantly interrupts the other: "*Faust* is constructed to *deny the audience an adequate point of view from which to receive its meaning or accept its teaching* (100). Any way we look at the world is thus a false one (101)." Bennett's reading of the play, however, does not take into account Goethe's notion of wholeness and balance within his natural scientific texts. In Goethe's worldview, opposites do not negate but complete each other. It is not therefore tragic that the play has multiple interpretations, nor is it without meaning because it does so. Rather, Goethe asks us to view the play from a variety of perspectives in order to gain a better understanding of the modernisms

---

[55] As Bennett has pointed out, Faust's people will not be living as freely as Faust imagines. They will be subject to the "tithes, rents, and tributes" of the Church.

[56] See, for example, Berman who writes that while Goethe understood the tragedy that accompanied such development, he nevertheless embraced its utopic potential (73). See also Swales ("Drama" esp. 91) and Lamport, who provide an overview of those scholars who view Faust in a positive light.

that confront us and to try to find balance among competing desires. Goethe's play does not deny us a point of view, but provides us with many and then asks us to decide the pros and cons of each.[57] In this way, scholars such as Noyes come closer to a Goethean understanding of the purpose of this multiplicity. Noyes eloquently summarizes the dual pulls of modernity within *Faust*: "[Cosmopolitanism and colonialism] hold great promise and great danger; their challenge is the challenge of modernity. In cosmopolitanism and colonialism Goethe sees the European dream of a mobile, self-fulfilled subjectivity, but he also sees the nightmare of self-aggrandizement, destruction of the environment, and violation of human rights" (458). Although Noyes does not use the principle of compensation, one can readily see how it could be applicable to his conclusions. There is a heavy cost to Faust's colony, and the play encourages us to see this.

While approaches such as that of Noyes are clearly important in analyzing Goethe's critique of modernity, one important aspect is still missing from such analyses — an aspect that I believe comes to light through reading Faust's assumption in a negative light. Goethe is not only critical of modern capitalism rooted in technology because of what it needs to do in order to succeed and function, but he also has serious reservations about the very philosophical underpinnings of such endeavors. What gives him concern is not only the fact that people must suffer in order for many more to thrive. The circumstances of Faust's death and afterlife open the door to a different brand of criticism entirely: one that questions the desirability of a scientist who is more interested in controlling nature than in understanding it or a captain of industry who is more interested in creating a capitalist economy than in pursuing or supporting the liberal arts. In other words, Goethe worried about what would happen to the soul of the individual who found happiness in business and technological endeavors. In our struggle to find an image of the whole by balancing the pros and cons of each perspective, we have to take into account these other, negative aspects of Faust's endeavor.

---

[57] Although Blessin, in his book on Goethe's novels, also argues that Goethe's works contain multiple strands, he believes that Goethe meant to provide a unified structure for his works. That we see a variety of perspectives today, according to Blessin, is due to the growth in the social sciences and the perspectives that such fields as psychology, economics, and sociology bring to interpreting literary works (39).

BEAUTY AND THE NEW ECONOMY

One way to begin to address these negative aspects is to turn once again to Goethe's cautionary words about trade and communication, cited at the beginning of this chapter. If we compare Goethe's statements with Faust's speeches, it is important to note that Faust does not conceive of his grand development project until after absolute beauty (Helen) and poetry (Euphorion) have died in Act III. Before Faust embraces his land reclamation project, he is heavily involved in the arts, including classical values and high culture. Much of his journey until this point has been about finding beauty: from his love of Gretchen in her quiet simplicity to his grand love affair with Helen of Troy. Throughout the whole journey through Act III, Faust has voiced a strong appreciation for nature, and it is to nature that he turns when the devil's presence becomes oppressive. The last time that Faust expresses a sublime appreciation for nature is right after Helen has disappeared, but before he has lost his final concrete remembrance of her. Faust has ridden to the peaks of high mountains by grasping an article of her clothing that has turned into a cloud. In this scene, Faust then watches this garment/cloth and other clouds go by. Within the images of the clouds, he sees not only Helen's image, but Gretchen's as well. I will quote the passage in its entire length, because it is an important moment of transition for Faust into the less intellectually and spiritually rich world of modernity:

> As my eyes see the utter solitude below
> I step with care onto the margin of these peaks
> and send away the cloud that during sunlit days
> softly transported me across the land and sea.
> It slowly separates from me without dispersing.
> The greater part, a massive sphere, is pressing eastward,
> followed by my admiring and astonished gaze:
> although its changing billows, as they move, divide,
> it seems to shape a figure. — Yes, my eyes are right! —
> I see, stretched out in sun-gilt splendor on a couch,
> a gigantic, yet still godlike, woman's form.
> In its majestic loveliness, it hovers there
> Within my sight, resembling Juno, Leda, Helen!
> Already it moves on! Like distant icy masses
> piled high upon each other, there in the east it stays,
> a dazzling symbol of these fleeting days' vast import.

Yet one bright tenuous streak of mist still hovers near
and cheers me with its cool caress on heart and brow.
Lightly it rises, hesitates, goes higher still,
and draws together, — Am I entranced by a mirage
of what, when young, I valued most, but lost long since?
Deep in my heart youth's first rich springs well up; I see
the image of love's dawn, its carefree happiness —
that swiftly felt, first, scarcely comprehended vision
which, had it lasted, would surpass all other treasures.
Like inward beauty of the soul the lovely form
grows clearer, rises, not dissolving, to the ether,
and draws with it my best and inmost self. (10039–66)[58]

In the first half of Faust's monolog, he describes his final parting from
Helen. He releases her image (*entlassen*) and then watches wistfully
as it departs to the east — back to the land of Greece and ancient
Classicism. This cloud is a cumulus one, and Faust enjoys watching it
take on various shapes until it culminates in majestic, godlike beauty.

---

[58] Der Einsamkeiten tiefste schauend unter meinem Fuß,
 Betret' ich wohlbedächtig dieser Gipfel Saum,
 Entlassend meiner Wolke Tragewerk, die mich sanft
 An klaren Tagen über Land und Meer geführt.
 Sie löst sich langsam, nicht zerstiebend, von mir ab.
 Nach Osten strebt die Masse mit geballtem Zug,
 Ihr strebt das Auge staunend in Bewundrung nach.
 Sie teilt sich wandelnd, wogenhaft, veränderlich.
 Doch will sich's modeln. Ja! das Auge trügt mich nicht! —
 Auf sonnbeglänzten Pfühlen herrlich hingestreckt,
 Zwar riesenhaft, ein göttergleiches Fraungebild,
 Ich seh's! Junonen ähnlich, Leda'n, Helenen,
 Wie majestätisch lieblich mir's im Auge schwankt.
 Ach! schon verrückt sich's! Formlos breit und aufgetürmt,
 Ruht es in Osten, fernen Eisgebirgen gleich
 Und spiegelt blendend flüchtger Tage großen Sinn.
 Doch mir umschwebt ein zarter lichter Nebelstreif
 Noch Brust und Stirn, erheiternd, kühl und schmeichelhaft.
 Nun steigt es leicht und zaudernd hoch und höher auf,
 Fügt sich zusammen. — Täuscht mich ein entzückend Bild,
 Als jugenderstes, längstentbehrtes höchstes Gut?
 Des tiefsten Herzens frühste Schätze quollen auf,
 Aurorens Liebe, leichten Schwung bezeichnet's mir,
 Den schnellempfundnen, ersten, kaum verstandnen Blick,
 Der, festgehalten, überglänzte jeden Schatz.
 Wie Seelenschönheit steigert sich die holde Form,
 Löst sich nicht auf, erhebt sich in den Äther hin
 Und zieht das Beste meines Innern mit sich fort. (10039–66)

In the second half, another cloud, a more ethereal cirrus one, reminds him of his earlier love, Gretchen. As with the first cloud form, this one changes shapes but never loses its overall essence. It, too, disappears from Faust's sight, and notably, he states that as it moves away from him, it "draws away with it my best and inmost self." Faust recognizes that with the loss of both Helen and Gretchen, and the love of beauty and nature that they represent, the better part of him is lost as well. As discussed above, with them dies Faust's desire to understand nature. He now wants to rule and possess nature rather than understand it (10185–8). The Faust, then, who speaks of possessing, conquering, and ruling over nature, is one who emerges only after he has lost his ability to love and with it his imaginative side. This explains how he can so little regret the murder of Baucis and Philemon, and why the bells no longer touch his heart as they did quite early in the play. The appreciation for pastoral beauty and religious remembrances are destroyed within Faust on top of the mountain after Helen's death. Although he is able to accomplish a great deal in the practical realm once he gives up these ethereal aspects of his life, he becomes much the loser in his spiritual side.

It would hence appear that Faust's divided soul has already been endangered by his participation in the realm of commerce. When both the earthly and the spiritual souls fought within him, although he made mistakes, he continued to strive and be active. Once capitalism has taken root, the power of one of his two souls seems to have atrophied to such an extent that Faust is capable of being satisfied. By adopting his plan to harness the powers of the ocean, he loses that which most characterized him, and that which the God of the Prolog characterizes as the best part of humanity: his ability to strive. Faust, the businessman and developer, loses his imagination for grand things, for beautiful things, and once he has lost this part of himself, he can easily find self-satisfaction. Baucis and Philemon represent not only resistance to his plan of complete control over the land, but they also represent part of his own lost past. His possession of the land is not "pure" (rein) because it still contains a remnant, as the older couple symbolizes, of his more liberal past. Even the irritation he feels at their presence is stated in terms of "stunted profits" (verkümmern herrlichsten Gewinn).

Faust the technolog can imagine a moment of satisfaction that Faust the lover of nature and the beautiful never could have. The Faust of Part I made a pact with the devil that he thought he could never lose. He never believed that he could find satisfaction because his internal dynamic tension would keep that from happening. The Faust at the end of Part II, however, does give up striving, and with it, as I have argued above, loses his ability to act: a fate if not worse than death, then certainly equivalent to it. Mephisto thus fittingly characterizes the moment (Augenblick) that has done Faust in as "this final, mediocre, empty moment" (den letzten, schlechten, leeren Augenblick, 11588). His dreams have become mediocre. Aristotle remarks that the art of money-making is not interesting because it is a low endeavor not befitting of a gentleman. It is a coerced activity that is always done for some other purpose — it is not a good in itself (*Nicomachean Ethics*). Similarly, the art of land reclamation does not seem to be befitting of the poet and nature lover that Faust once was. The level of discomfort that he experiences in seeing a beautiful old cottage, grove, and church within his modern fields, the ease with which he erects a tower where beautiful old trees stood, and his lack of conscience in employing slave labor where he was once horrified at the death of Gretchen's brother, all illustrate how the dual soul that sought complementary experiences has lost out.

The dark side, thus, of Faust's project is not simply that human sacrifices become necessary. It is also the deadened state of the soul of the person who is the driving force behind it. The person who believes that the highest human calling is to build a new subdivision has already demonstrated his impoverished soul by the very expression of this desire. While Faust sees this subdivision as enabling new freedoms, these revolve around the freedom to work:

> If I can furnish space for many millions
> to live — not safe, I know but free to work
> in green and fertile fields, with man and beast
> soon happy on the new-made soil. (11563–6)[59]

The happiness that he envisions for his people is a commonplace one, and one that certainly would never have satisfied the ever-striving Faust of the beginning of the play. That someone who could teach poetry to Helen of Troy finds satisfaction in building a subdivision and is willing to die for it is quite telling.

---

[59] Eröffn' ich Räume vielen Millionen,
    Nicht sicher zwar, doch tätig-frei zu wohnen.
    Grün das Gefilde, fruchtbar; Mensch und Herde
    Sogleich behaglich auf der neusten Erde (11563–6)

If we apply Goethe's comments to Zelter to the society that Faust has created (June 6, 1825), then we can draw further connections to contemporary society. High culture, liberal education, and anything that smacks of elitism are often attacked in today's world. In Chapter 3, I will discuss issues of elitism, business, and the liberal arts in more detail. It is of note here, however, that the drive toward business principles that eventually dominates Faust is evident in higher education. Many books and articles have recently been written about the trend in higher education to run universities more like businesses. A recent *New York Times* piece analyzes how the more practical fields in universities have gained ground at the expense of the more liberal ones as a result: "Health sciences, computer science, engineering, and business . . . have grown in importance and size compared with the more liberal social sciences and humanities . . . At the same time, shrinking public resources overall and fewer tenure-track jobs have pushed younger professors in those fields to concentrate more single-mindedly on their careers. Academia, once somewhat insulated from market pressures, is today treated like a business" (Cohen A18). In other words, the humanities are being attacked from two sides. On the one side, there are fewer jobs since a liberal education is no longer valued as a good in itself, and on the other, those who are in these fields have to act more according to business models (e.g., be measured more in terms of productivity — articles published, grants received, invited lectures given, etc.) than according to older models of teaching and enriching the lives of students.

The pressures to run universities like businesses seem to be everywhere, and often at the cost of liberal education. A couple of quick examples from my own university may shed some light on how this capitalist drive manifests itself. For the last several years, our provost has run a one-day leadership workshop for deans and department heads before the beginning of the school year. A recent topic was: "Collaboration and Community: Bridging Organizational and Social Boundaries in Pursuit of Entrepreneurship, Innovation and the Academic Mission." While I believe that this topic speaks for itself, it came upon the heels of the University of Illinois system's endeavor, at the urging of our former president, Joseph White, to found an online university, completely for profit, like Phoenix University (to which our president overtly referred as a kind of model at an earlier workshop). In its initial conception, the online program was to be divorced from faculty input and quality control, although the online degree would bear the University of Illinois imprimatur. (The faculty senate intervened and refused to support this extreme model.)[60] Nevertheless, that one of the premiere public university systems in America would even consider such a profit scheme shows how Faustian we have become. So, too, have the foreign languages come under attack across the USA. Too often, the languages that are taught at a university are based not upon any standard but upon popularity. Increasingly, the ancient languages or even German are being cut from instructional budgets simply because of tuition dollar calculations. Languages are deemed unworthy of support unless large numbers of students flock to them.

Where once the university was seen as a complement to (if not a check on) the business world, it now turns more and more towards business's practices and seeks to justify itself according to the market. Like Faust, the justification is that the new model will open the world of the university to many more than is now possible. The question remains here, as in the case of Faust, whether at least half of the soul has been sacrificed in order to do so. Does the selling of the academic soul lead to the mediocrity that Goethe predicts in his letter to Zelter? Everyone can now access culture (and even a university degree of sorts) from one's computer, but it is an extraordinarily common one. The bacchanalia that Mephisto offers Faust on Walpurgis Night (a witches' sabbath) is but a faint shadow to what one can experience daily on the reality shows of television. The Faust of Part I is bored by such frolics; the Faust of Part II would undoubtedly invest in their production.

One of Goethe's contemporaries, Alexis de Tocqueville, also weighed the pros and cons of the modern world. His *Democracy in America* (1840, based upon an 1831 trip to America) raises similar concerns about the leveling of culture as Goethe feared. Tocqueville notes of the Americans:

> Few pleasures are either refined or very coarse, and highly polished manners are as uncommon as great brutality of tastes. Neither men of great learning nor extremely ignorant communities are to be met with; genius is rare, information more diffused . . . Almost all extremes are softened or blunted: all that was most prominent is superseded by some middle term, at once less lofty and less low, less brilliant and less obscure, than what before existed in the world.
>
> When I survey this countless multitude of beings, shaped in each other's

---

[60] For a discussion of White's plans, see Foster's report in the *Chronicle of Higher Education.* April 27, 2007.

likeness, amid whom nothing rises and nothing falls, the sight of such universal uniformity saddens and chills me and I am tempted to regret that state of society which has ceased to be. (350)

According to Tocqueville's analysis, the advantages of the American way of life in the new age of technological advances and greater ease of communication are that one eliminates the horrors of the extremes: extremes of poverty, vice, cruelty, and brutality. The subsequent costs, however, are high as well: a mediocrity of cultural achievement, the elimination of heroes and other high characters of virtue, and the loss of great learning. Like Goethe, Tocqueville concentrates on how modernity tends toward a mediocrity from which he believed it would be difficult to emerge, and one that threatened the very benefits of freedom that the Americans cherished. Using language akin to Goethe's theory of compensation,[61] Tocqueville warns:

Providence has not created mankind entirely independent or entirely free. It is true that around every man a fatal circle is traced beyond which he cannot pass; but within the wide verge of that circle he is powerful and free; as it is with man, so with communities. The nations of our time cannot prevent the conditions of men from becoming equal, but it depends upon themselves whether the principle of equality is to lead them to servitude or freedom, to knowledge or barbarism, to prosperity or wretchedness. (352)

Goethe's *Faust* similarly speculates about the direction that society will take. Although Faust himself believes that his colony is a secure one in which generations to come will extol his name, the devil predicts a very different outcome. Mephisto prophesies a kind of apocalypse for the human race. In the end, it will be destroyed because of the very technology that it has embraced in the hope of grand, capitalist endeavors:

And yet with all your dams and levees
Your striving serves no one but us;
In fact, you're now preparing a grand feast
For the water-daemon, Neptune.

---

[61] Goethe corresponded with the great French scientist Geoffroy Saint-Hilaire (1772–1844) on compensation, and Geoffroy, who praises Goethe's works, developed a related theory to explain changes in animal formation. It is therefore quite possible that Tocqueville, given Geoffroy's fame, was familiar with the workings of this theory.

All of your kind are doomed already; —
The elements have sworn to help us;
The end will be annihilation. (11544–50)[62]

---

[62] Du bist doch nur für uns bemüht
   Mit deinen Dämmen deinen Buhnen;
   Denn du bereitest schon Neptunen,
   Dem Wasserteufel, großen Schmaus.
   In jeder Art seid ihr verloren,
   Die Elemente sind mit uns verschworen,
   Und auf Vernichtung läufts hinaus.

Chapter 2

WERTHER THE EVANGELICAL

Goethe's novel, *The Sorrows of Young Werther* (1774), quickly became a European sensation, and it was the work for which he was known for the rest of his life. The story of the novel is rather simple. A very sensitive, nature-loving young man falls in love with a sympathetic young woman, Lotte (Charlotte). At the time of their meeting, she is engaged to a worthy and serious man, Albert. Although Werther is encouraged by his friend, Wilhelm, to make an offer to Lotte, he runs away, and she marries Albert. He tries to occupy himself with a position at court, but his free-spiritedness causes him trouble, and he feels forced to leave. He finds himself unable to stay away from Lotte. His love for her continues to grow, and in a passionate scene, he kisses her, and she, torn between Werther and the respectable life that her husband offers, locks herself in a room away from his reach. Werther decides to spare her and to save her marriage by killing himself. He shoots himself at midnight using a pistol borrowed from Albert that has passed through Lotte's hands. (She dusts off the weapon before handing it to Werther's servant.) He is discovered in the morning, barely alive, and dies about 12 hours after shooting himself. The news of his suicide so shocks Lotte that the last we hear of her, she is near death, and we do not know if she will survive. ·

Many readers have viewed the novel as a valorization of democracy, emotions, and a heightened sense of individualism. During the course of its pages, the protagonist wishes to live in a society that we have largely realized: the aristocracy is dismantled, individuals are allowed to follow their own hearts in matters of religious values, aesthetic objects are valued only in the eye of the beholder, and marriage ties have loosened. The novel thus correctly predicted many of the directions that contemporary society would take, and the main character,

Werther, serves as the spokesman *par excellence* for these changes. Why should one class of people tell another what to think, where to work, how to write and with whom to associate? At the same time, however, the protagonist suffers a great deal for such newly-won perspectives. With his rejection of Christianity and societal strictures, he feels alienated and alone and has no outlet for his feelings of guilt. His sense of belonging to a community is destroyed. Nor is there any formal structure left to check his passions and avert his suicide. And while many readers may be sympathetic to Werther's rejection of rules of grammar, not many would be so amenable to his willingness to allow a murderer to go free.

The portrayal of the growing power of individualism within the novel's pages serves as an excellent background to explore the American ideological and cultural divide. We commonly think of America as a polarized place: we have red states and blue states. The values of each are further considered to be different: blue states are liberal while red are conservative; religion is more likely to be a factor in the red rather than in the blue. The divide between the two seems large. Europeans are often puzzled about Americans and their connection to religion. That Barack Obama's church or pastor played a role in whether people would vote for him (and indeed that candidates need professed religious affiliations at all), that evolution is a political issue on which even presidential candidates (such as Sen. Sam Brownback) take stands, that George W. Bush is generally thought to have won the 2004 election because of Karl Rove's (an atheist's) strategy to mobilize the Evangelicals — all these are things that are hard to understand for the much more secularized Europe. Universities, too, have seen the polarizing events of the culture wars. Has the left-wing of academe so taken over that we need an affirmative action policy, as David Horowitz suggests, for conservative professors? Does the right — with its concern for standards, assessment, and job employment skills — or the left — with its demand for diverse voices and self-esteem — have the best interest of the students at heart?

Are these divides, however, as large as they seem? What if both sides share cultural and historical influences to the extent that they both are heading toward the same end result albeit by different paths? Conservatives, for example, often claim the 1960s as the source of the decline of American educational values. What if the "watering down" of the canon, of values, of standards, and so forth, is not to be found within the cult of the pot-smoking, free-loving, self-indulgent hippie, but within the foundational tenets of Evangelicalism, historically understood? Similarly, what if the call for diversity at no matter the cost stems not from a rejection of traditional values, as conservatives at times claim, but from a natural extension of them?

The debates surrounding the novel's interpretation mirror in many ways the polarizing debates of our own time. Should we endorse a society with even more freedoms or should we struggle against these forces to maintain some more traditional and ordering aspects of society? In other words, do those aspects of society that Werther wishes to change — fewer rules, a leveling of the classes, freedom of expression — completely outweigh whatever negative consequences that such changes would bring, including fewer societal support mechanisms for those in need of them, a lack of external controls on the passions, and a questioning of the rules of justice that are perhaps the most basic for any society? By once again turning to Goethe's principle of compensation, one can analyze these issues in terms of gains and losses. To the extent that the novel represents the growing power of individualism, what, then, are the costs associated with those gains?

Most readers of the novel have been in agreement that it deftly portrays the spirit of the times: a period in literature that is known as Storm and Stress because of its emphasis on individual passions and youthful rebellion. Those of the novel's contemporaries who valorized the novel saw it as a manifesto for rebellion. Within the course of the novel, the young protagonist questions and challenges nearly every aspect of contemporary society, from strict class distinctions to religious conventions to sexual mores. The outfit of the novel's protagonist, "a blue jacket, a yellow vest, and breeches made of tanned leather, a tall hat with a wide rounded brim, a pair of high leather boots suitable for wandering in the countryside" became a fashion trend that, as Daniel Purdy has argued, became the "*de rigueur* masculine uniform of rebellion" (147). This costume made not only an aesthetic statement that identified its wearers with the literary movement of sensibility, but also a social protest that rejected the finery of the aristocracy and the tendency of the middle class to imitate it. Instead, the middle class felt empowered to create its own, more democratic uniform that echoed the democratic tendencies it saw within the novel.

Conservative elements of society viewed the novel's liberal side with horror, especially since they attributed a spate of suicides to it, and fought against its influence. The city council of Leipzig, for example, "in response to a petition from the theological faculty, made it an offence (punishable by fine) to sell copies of the novel — and also to wear the 'Werther costume.' The ban was imposed in January 1775 and

.remained in force until 1825" (Swales, *Werther* 97). The obituary section in the November 1784 *Gentleman's Magazine* tells the warning tale of a young woman: "*The Sorrows of Young Werter* [sic] were found under her pillow: a circumstance which deserves to be known, in order, if possible to defeat the evil tendency of that pernicious work." When the novel appeared in Italian translation, the bishop of Milan ordered his priests to buy up all of the copies to prevent the spread of its influence.

Some of the novel's early readers, however, were skeptical that Goethe wholeheartedly embraced his protagonist and his actions.[1] For them, the graphically gruesome way in which Werther dies signals a distancing of the author from his character. After shooting himself, he lies for hours with his brains hanging out, is discovered, his brains are pushed back in, and he lingers for hours more and dies on Christmas Eve.

Part of the reason that the history of the novel's interpretation is so complex is that it was so widely read and imitated. Many who read the novel (just as the conservative authorities feared) used it as a source of inspiration.[2] The novel, however, not only set a variety of fashion

---

[1] These debates on how to interpret the novel have continued through the last two hundred years. Many scholars read the novel in a positive light. Although those who view the novel positively generally admit to some level of pathology in the protagonist's actions, they admire his attempts to challenge societal strictures and blame society for causing his death. Viëtor, for example, argues that the book illustrates an admirable idealism as well as the limited opportunities that were available to the middle class: "Goethe's expressions leave no doubt as to what he considers the cause of Werther's ruin in the outer world. The cause lies in the fatal conditions under which the intellectual young men of the age had to live" (32). In such readings, that Werther fails in his efforts to combat society is, accordingly, a testimony to the strength of society and its norms, but not at all about any salutary aspects of rules, traditions, or hierarchies. Other scholars see that the novel contains criticism of Werther but argue that these criticisms are absent in the 1774 version of the novel and only appear in the 1786 version. According to this interpretation, Goethe only later outgrew this Storm and Stress period to go on to write more classical and restrained texts. For Marxist readers like Lukács, Werther's challenge of authority is a step in the right direction toward individual freedom and the struggle for equality (45). Thus, although Lukács does not focus on the Pietist influences as I do, he argues forcefully that those critics of the novel who focus on its challenge of traditional, bourgeois, religious mores understood its revolutionary qualities.

[2] Purdy's book gives a wonderful background to the novel's effect. Pedagogues complained that young people all wanted to be Werther, a 1781 Viennese pamphlet decried the influence of the novel on the servant class, and a Werther cult that Purdy compares to the Freemasons staged midnight processions in the geographical settings of the novel. Such processions continued well into the nineteenth century, even after the authorities had banned them and sought to hide the grave of Jerusalem, a man whose suicide was one of the inspirations for the novel (Purdy 148–51). *Werther* scenes appeared on porcelain cups and pots, and there was even a perfume named after its protagonist. The novel was hugely popular throughout Europe, especially in Britain where many assumed that Werther himself was English. William Godwin went so far as to proclaim his late wife, Mary Wollstonecraft,

trends, whether in dress or speech. It also reflected cultural and social phenomena that had already established themselves. This chapter focuses upon the Pietist mood of the novel, both to unlock Goethe's criticism of the growing power of the individual and to show how this Pietist-inspired individualism manifests itself today. Pietism has proven to influence two vastly different, and opposing, camps: the conservative, American, Evangelicals (via the path of Pietism itself) and the more liberal brand of secular spiritualism that has since revealed itself in movements as disparate as Transcendental Meditation to self-help to Yoga to the People (via influential readers of *Werther* like Ralph Waldo Emerson). By following both strands of influence, one can see how the novel foreshadows such modern phenomena, which are related to its Protestant roots, as the movement against grammar and Standard English in schools to the popularity of blogs. The "philosophy" of the organic farm from which I buy my vegetables in Hyde Park (Chicago) even takes its source, via an albeit circuitous route, from the *Sorrows of Young Werther*.[3]

However influential Goethe's novel was in promoting certain aspects of modernity, it also contains criticisms of it. Although the novel has been read from a variety of perspectives, this chapter will primarily examine those aspects that view Werther's quest for individualism unfavorably. I have decided not to look at the pro-Werther side for two reasons. First, it is much more evident, as the novel's early reception demonstrates, and, as it is written from primarily Werther's perspective, it is not necessary to outline the aspects in his favor. He does so himself in language both eloquent and persuasive. If the principle of compensation requires us to see the benefits and the disadvantages, most of

---

a "female Werter"[sic] (Burwick). Mary Shelley herself gave the novel special prominence in her *Frankenstein or the Modern Prometheus* (1818). It is one of the three books (together with Plutarch's *Lives* and Milton's *Paradise Lost*) that her monster reads and that form his understanding of the world.

[3] The cookbook which accompanied my order from the farm is laced throughout with quotes from Rudolf Steiner, who began his career as a Goethe scholar but eventually founded his own school of thought, anthroposophy. Anthroposophy takes the following as its main manifesto: "Anthroposophy is a path of knowledge, to guide the spiritual in the human being to the spiritual in the universe. It arises in people as a need of the heart and feeling life. Anthroposophy can be justified only to the degree that it satisfies this inner need. It may be acknowledged only by those who find within it what they themselves feel the need to seek. Therefore, anthroposophists are those who experience, as an essential need of life, certain questions on the nature of the human being and the universe, just as one experiences hunger and thirst" (Steiner 1904. <http://www.steinerbooks.org/aboutrudolf.html> accessed July 1, 2008). The organic cookbook by Farmer John Peterson begins with a quotation from Steiner that emphasizes individual freedom in what one eats or drinks.

its readers already see the attraction of Werther's position. Second, Goethe's critical stance is much more central to our investigation of his analysis of contemporary aspects of society. In many ways, our society has become more "Wertherized" in its focus on individuals and their emotions, personal quests toward spiritual discovery, intense appreciation for nature, and environmental advocacy. We therefore no longer need to make the case for his mode of being; we are largely living it. In short, the advantages are clear; it is from studying the disadvantages that we can most stand to gain in understanding the shortcomings of our own society and how we got where we are. A close examination of key passages in the novel demonstrates not only the distance that Goethe already had toward his protagonist in the first version of the novel (Goethe published a revised and slightly expanded version in 1786),[4] but most importantly, that he was critical of the growing sense of individuality within modern society of which Pietism was but one outgrowth.

Much ink has been spilled, especially since Karl Rove's engineering of Bush's 2004 re-election campaign, in investigating the political power of Evangelical groups in America. Goethe's *Werther* certainly does not provide answers for politicos searching for clues to sway this group. What it does illustrate, however, are tendencies that Goethe identified as central to modernity: what happens when the irrational side of individualism flourishes? To what extent are modernity's successes (capitalism, democracy, acute sense of self) related to its darker side (self-absorption, disconnectedness, anti-intellectualism, lack of appreciation for things greater than self)? In short, how can analyzing Goethe's literary treatment of a religious movement and its cultural and psychic influences help us to understand a key influence today?

THE SORROWS OF YOUNG WERTHER

Pietism

It is well known that the novel contains many Pietist influences.[5] Pietism was a seventeenth- and eighteenth-century religious movement

---

[4] Goethe added several new letters and rewrote and reordered sections primarily at the end of the novel. Many scholars have argued that Goethe's criticisms of his protagonist arise only in this version. See my "A New Reading."

[5] Many scholars have written upon aspects of Pietism. Atkins ("Lavater") analyzes it in terms of Lavater's sermons on "üble Laune," whereas Flitner examines Werther as a Pietist mystic, heretic, and pious man. See also Kemper who links Pietist forms in the novel with Goethe's concept of genius and Kowalik who examines the novel as being critical of Pietist

that broke away from the Lutheran Church in Germany. Pietists found mainstream Protestant Churches to be too orthodox. To Pietist taste, the Lutheran Church was too hierarchical in structure, too much influenced by scholarly and religious traditions and rules, and gave too much credence to reason and learning at the expense of the emotions. Like modern Evangelicals, Pietists believed that one had to be born again, one should speak about such personal experiences to others, and that individuals could interpret biblical texts for themselves. Pietism therefore was a continuation of the break with tradition, learning, and hierarchy that began with the Reformation. Pinson, who in his book examines the close connection between Pietism and the rise of German nationalism, provides an overview of its tenets:

> Pietism represented a turning towards a more inward, emotional, and enthusi-
> astic form of Christianity. Under the emotional stress of the havoc and misery
> caused by the Thirty Years War, a mystical wave spread over Germany. A reaction
> took place against the emphasis on dogma and on scholastic argumentation
> concerning the tenets of creed and purity of doctrine. People turned to a simpler
> and more heartfelt form of religion which would be an expression of immediate
> feeling rather than an outcome of prolonged study and discussion. The second
> characteristic, closely related to the first, was the emphasis on a more practical
> Christianity. Learning was not sufficient. Purity of life, saintliness of behavior,
> active Christianity came to be regarded as the most essential mark of Christian
> life. The third mark of Pietism was the greater emphasis placed on the doctrine
> of general priesthood. Pietism in all its forms and aspects sought to remove
> that wide gulf between the official clergy and the lay classes which had hitherto
> prevailed . . . The encouragement of Biblical reading and study, which in Luther's
> day was largely limited to the clergy, was extended by Pietism to include all classes
> of population. (14–15)

Because Pietists believe that the path to God lies within the emotions of the individual and his or her own powers of understanding apart from any authority, whether academic, scholastic, or orthodox, they have no pressing need to be educated in a book sense nor do they need to turn to an authority figure or more educated person for guidance.

---

stances toward grief. As Kemper reports, Goethe had contact with a variety of Pietist sources, whether in his reading of Gottfried Arnold's work, his familiarity with Pietist hymns and poems from a variety of schools, his knowledge of the various movements, or his close friendship with several important Pietists, including the physiognomist Lavater (175–6). For a discussion in the secondary literature about Pietist elements in *Werther*, see Kemper, Soboth, Schöffler, and Anstett.

This movement was democratic, in that everyone was equally capable of interpreting the Bible and everyone was equally suitable to preach to others. As is discussed in more detail below, this approach serves as the opposite to that of the Catholic Church, whose scholasticism is rooted in the tradition of Aristotelianism and has among its fundamental beliefs that one can approach God through the use of one's intellect but that we need guidance from a complex hierarchy and traditions in order to do so. This hierarchical understanding of religion is further connected to the Catholic Church's emphasis on the liturgy. As Shea notes, there is a huge gap in the role of the liturgy between Catholic and Evangelical Churches (of which Pietism is an original feeder group): "Conservative Christians practice Biblical Christianity — a religion centered on the Bible as the sole (sola) source of authority without any need for a Church or liturgy. Catholics on the other hand practice Liturgical Christianity — the Bible as understood within a worshipping Church" (quoted in Greeley and Hout 13). In other words, Catholicism requires a liturgy, structure, and authority. Evangelicals are largely free of these restrictions.

The eighteenth-century German establishment — whether religious or political — felt threatened by Pietism's subversive and democratizing tendencies and sought ways to suppress its popularity. Rulers and the clergy believed that Pietism would have profound political and social consequences. Adherents would gather together without regard to gender or class and without the need for ordained clergy. These gatherings were radical indeed when one remembers that at this time the rules for the classes were regulated down to the smallest detail of who was and was not allowed to wear silk stockings or gold and silver ornamentation (Chiarloni 134–9). Women, moreover, were not only allowed to preach by some sects, but they were believed by many to be closer to God because they were considered less reasonable and less well educated than the men: their emotions brought them closer to God. Susanne von Klettenberg, the Pietist who perhaps had the most influence on Goethe, rejoices in the fact that she is a woman and thus more readily able to communicate directly with Christ (Dohm 114, Chiarloni 148).

The pages that follow examine Goethe's treatment of religion and emotions in *Werther* and argue that he linked Pietism and its influences to the modern obsession with the individual. While today one often links this obsession to the counter-culture age of the 1960s and its descendants, it has as its antecedent a much earlier tradition and one that today is more often than not considered politically and socially conservative.

What is perhaps most striking in this novel is Goethe's favorable treatment of Catholic traditions. In *Werther*, he uses Catholic symbols to provide a balance against which to measure the democratizing and individualizing elements of Evangelicalism and secular spiritualism. In short, by drawing our attention to the past benefits of a more structured and ordered society, Goethe hints at the costs of a liberalizing and secularizing society. While by no means endorsing Catholicism *per se*, the decline of Catholicism becomes a means — much in the same way as the decline of the aristocracy does in the *Elective Affinities* — by which to measure the radical nature of the changes as well as identifying part of what has been lost in the wake of those changes.

Werther's *Pietism*

Before analyzing Goethe's critical stance, it is important to review those elements of the novel that are considered to be Pietist inspired or influenced. Goethe was well versed in Pietism. Not only was his mother involved in these religious circles, but he himself had close Pietist friendships that were formed while he was recovering from an illness as a young man. He read many of the key texts, poems, and hymns and was involved in Pietistic, hermetic science — even setting up a small lab in his house to conduct alchemical experiments. The very first letter of *Werther* contains many features of Pietism that are characteristic throughout, and hence although somewhat lengthy, the portion provided below gives a flavor of the whole:

> How glad I am to have got away! My dear friend, what a thing is the heart of man! To leave you, from whom I was inseparable, whom I love so much, and yet be happy! I know you will forgive me. Were not all my other attachments especially designed by fate to torment a heart like mine? Poor Leonore! And yet I was not to blame. Was it my fault, that, while the capricious charms of her sister afforded me agreeable entertainment, a passion for me developed in her poor heart? And yet — am I wholly blameless? Did I not encourage her emotions? Did I not find pleasure in those genuine expressions of Nature, which, though but little amusing in reality, so often made us laugh? Did I not — but oh! What is man, that he dares so to accuse himself? My dear friend, I promise you, I will change; I will not longer, as has always been my habit, continue to ruminate on every petty annoyance which fate may have in store for me; I will enjoy the present, and the past shall be for me the past. No doubt you are right, my best of friends, there would be far less suffering among mankind, if men — and God knows why they are so constituted — did not use their imaginations so assiduously in recalling the memory of past sorrow, instead of bearing an indifferent present . . .

For the rest, I am very well off here. Solitude in this terrestrial paradise is a wonderful balm to my emotions, and the early spring warms with all its fullness my often-shivering heart. Every tree, every bush is a bouquet of flowers; and one might wish himself transformed into a cockchafer, to float about in this ocean of fragrance, and find in it all the food one needs.

The town itself is disagreeable; but then, all around it, nature is inexpressibly beautiful. This induced the late Count M. to lay out a garden on one of the sloping hills which intersect here and form the most lovely valleys. The garden is simple and you feel upon entering that the plan was not designed by a scientific gardener, but by a man who wished to give himself up here to the enjoyment of his own sensitive heart. I have already shed many a tear to the memory of its departed master, in a summer house which is now reduced to ruins, but was his favorite retreat, and now is mine. I shall soon be master of the garden. The gardener has become attached to me within the few days I have spent here, and, I'm sure, it will not be to his disadvantage. (11: 5–6)[6]

Werther's epistolary form follows Pietist models. Pietists privileged

---

[6] Wie froh bin ich, daß ich weg bin! Bester Freund, was ist das Herz des Menschen! Dich zu verlassen den ich so liebe, von dem ich unzertrennlich war und froh zu seyn! Ich weiß du verzeihst mir's. Waren nicht meine übrigen Verbindungen recht ausgesucht vom Schicksal, um ein Herz wie das meinige zu ängstigen? Die arme Leonore! Und doch war ich unschuldig! Konnt ich dafür, daß, während die eigensinnigen Reize ihrer Schwester mir eine angenehme Unterhaltung verschafften, daß eine Leidenschaft in dem armen Herzen sich bildete? Und doch — bin ich ganz unschuldig? Hab' ich nicht ihre Empfindungen genährt? hab' ich mich nicht an den ganz wahren Ausdrücken der Natur, die uns so oft zu lachen machten, so wenig lächerlich sie waren, selbst ergetzt, hab ich nicht — O was ist der Mensch, daß er über sich klagen darf! — Ich will, lieber Freund, ich verspreche dir's, ich will mich bessern, will nicht mehr ein bißchen Übel, das uns das Schicksal vorlegt, wiederkäuen, wie ich's immer gethan habe; ich will das Gegenwärtige genießen, und das Vergangene soll mir vergangen seyn. Gewiß du hast recht Bester, der Schmerzen wären minder unter den Menschen, wenn sie nicht — Gott weiß warum sie so gemacht sind! — mit so viel Emsigkeit der Einbildungskraft sich beschäftigten, die Erinnerungen des vergangenen Übels zurück zu rufen, eher als eine gleichgültige Gegenwart zu ertragen . . .

Übrigens befinde ich mich hier gar wohl. Die Einsamkeit ist meinem Herzen köstlicher Balsam in dieser paradiesischen Gegend, und diese Jahrzeit der Jugend wärmt mit aller Fülle mein oft schauderndes Herz. Jeder Baum, jede Hecke ist ein Strauß von Blüthen, und man möchte zum Maykäfer werden, um in dem Meer von Wohlgerüchen herumschweben und alle seine Nahrung darin finden zu können.

Die Stadt selbst ist unangenehm, dagegen rings umher eine unaussprechliche Schönheit der Natur. Das bewog den verstorbenen Grafen von M . . . seinen Garten auf einem der Hügel anzulegen, die mit der schönsten Mannichfaltigkeit sich kreuzen, und die lieblichsten Thäler bilden. Der Garten ist einfach und man fühlt gleich bey dem Eintritte, daß nicht ein wissenschaftlicher Gärtner, sondern ein fühlendes Herz den Plan gezeichnet, das seiner selbst hier genießen wollte. Schon manche Thräne hab' ich dem Abgeschiedenen in dem verfallenen Cabinetchen geweint, das sein Lieblingsplätzchen war und auch meines ist. Bald werde ich Herr vom Garten seyn; der Gärtner ist mir zugethan, nur seit den paar Tagen, und er wird sich nicht übel dabey befinden. (FA 1, 8: 11–15)

confessional accounts of their experiences. Like so many who write blogs today, they favored public forums to portray to others the personal, emotional discoveries they had made. Letters written at that time were often meant to be shared and hence served as a semi-public sphere that enabled people to share their emotions with others. The whole of *Werther* conforms both from its epistolary form to its confessional contents to this practice. Other aspects of the novel are also closely related to Pietism. Specifically, as Pietists turned toward their emotions and imaginations and away from reason, so too does Werther take pride in his intense emotional sense and his rejection of anything that smacks of calm rationality. The quote above shows Werther's stance toward his heart and emotions that is characteristic throughout.[7] He praises the garden not because it is beautiful, but because it avoids a rational plan and seems rather to follow a passionate one. Later in the novel, he will so valorize his imagination that he will believe himself to be a great artist on the strength of it, even though at that very moment he is incapable of drawing anything. He also does not want his books to be sent to him, "for the love of God, keep them away from me! I no longer want to be guided . . ." (May 13, 1771).[8] Most importantly, his language throughout is impassioned and is studded with many exclamation points and dashes for unfinished or interrupted thoughts. Emotions and not rational evaluations are what determine the state of affairs. The world is seen and evaluated according to his frame of mind, and because he is happy, the unhappiness of others can be brushed away. So, too, does he expect his friend to forgive him simply because he is happy at heart. Werther's character often demonstrates Pietist qualities taken to their extremes, but this, I would argue, is the point. Goethe is exhibiting with this charming but self-absorbed individual the directions that such personalized philosophies could take.

This emotional propensity, of course, is that which leads to Werther's suicide. Within the novel, he hopes through the strength of his own individualism to change several aspects of society, from class distinctions to writing practices. He commits suicide when he senses his failure to change the greater world around him. In the second version of the novel,[9] Goethe illustrates the societal consequences that extreme

---

[7] One scholar has noted that Werther uses the term "heart" (Herz) 111 and "soul" (Seele) 75 times (Michéa 213).

[8] Ich bitte dich um Gotteswillen, laß mir sie vom Halse. Ich will nicht mehr geleitet . . . seyn. (FA 1, 8: 17)

[9] Even within the first version of the novel, we see reason denigrated in favor of passion. When Werther meets an insane, but happy man, he is somewhat envious of his position and

individualism could bring about. In this version, Goethe introduces a laborer who murders out of jealousy. If liberal justice is about exploring the background and emotional state of mind to search for mitigating or extenuating circumstances and the conservative form of justice is about the letter of the law and punishment, then Werther's position represents the extreme liberal case. He feels empathy for the man and seeks not only to justify his behavior, but to help him escape the law. Even Werther himself knows that such behavior is not representative of "sound judgment," but his passions hold sway: "He felt for the man, thought his crime quite excusable, and identified so completely with the fellow that he was convinced he could make everyone view the matter in the light in which he saw it himself" (11: 68). When confronted by the fact that the case must go through "regular channels," Werther suggests that "the judge should look away if someone tried to help the prisoner escape" (68).[10]

Another important aspect of Pietism that is prevalent within the pages of the novel is introspection. Pietists believed that the best way to evaluate the world and their place in it was through meditation, especially in solitude. In this, as is discussed in more detail below, they foreshadowed the later Transcendentalists who then morphed into many different New Age groups. Of further note is the number of sentences that contain first-person pronouns. For the Pietists, even the Bible was to be interpreted not with the help of any commentaries, but through one's own experiences. Werther has the propensity to evaluate art, music, society, relationships, and so on, primarily through his own perspective. He appropriates texts, for example, to the extent that he speaks of texts as "his," as in "his" Homer — implying that he has made Homer his own property through his interpretation of him. His notion of the self, ego, "I" is front and center, and it is through this self-absorbed perspective that everything is digested. He liberally quotes from the Bible and uses particular passages to reinforce his own way of life. For instance, he enjoys playing with children and acting in a childlike way. He finds support for this behavior through the biblical

---

notes: "God in heaven! Is this the destiny of man? To be happy only before he has acquired reason and again after he has lost it?" (11: 63) "Gott im Himmel! hast du das zum Schicksale der Menschen gemacht, daß sie nicht glücklich sind als ehe sie zu ihrem Verstande kommen und wenn sie ihn wieder verlieren!" (November 30, 1772, FA 1, 8: 189)

[10] Er fühlte ihn so unglücklich, er fand ihn als Verbrecher selbst so schuldlos, er setzte sich so tief in seine Lage, daß er gewiß glaubte auch andere davon zu überzeugen. And further: . . . der Amtmann möchte durch die Finger sehn, wenn man dem Menschen zur Flucht behülflich wäre! (FA 1, 8: 205, 207)

passages in which Christ praises children (June 29, 1771). His reading of texts is in general so idiosyncratic that he reads a passage that prefaces one of the bloodiest parts of the *Odyssey* and sees it as relevant to his solitary, pastoral supper of self-picked, buttered peas.

Werther sees within the texts that he reads what fits into his own interpretation of the world. Much like the prostitute Ilya (Melina Mercouri) in the film, *Never on Sunday* (1960), who believes that Greek tragedies have happy endings, Werther as a reader creates his own reality. The film, in the end, endorses the prostitute's approach. Homer (Jules Dassin), the man who tries to educate her through books and music, is portrayed as a buffoon, who ultimately must admit the superior ways of the prostitute's heart. Goethe's stance on such individualized reading is more complex and can be found by looking at the ironies of the text. First, there is a profound irony in the fact that Werther, who is so opposed to books in the beginning of the novel, tries consciously at several points to re-enact literary works, including those by Goldsmith, Homer, "Ossian," and Lessing. Second, the editor's footnotes provide a further bit of irony by which to gain a critical distance to Werther's views. The editor provides two sets of commentaries on Werther's literary tastes in footnotes. In one, the editor leaves out the titles of the works that Lotte and Werther criticize, because he deems neither a young woman nor an unsteady man a proper judge of literature. The very next footnote, however, leaves out the titles of the works Werther and Lotte praise for an entirely different reason: one should be able to know in one's heart which works are being addressed.[11] While literary interpretations certainly are subject to a variety of perspectives, Werther's at times have little or no basis in the text he is reading. The irony of the fact that many of the readers of *Werther* began dressing and acting like the protagonist was not lost on Goethe, who in his autobiography comments: "my friends were misled into thinking that poetry must be transformed into reality, that they must reenact the novel, and possibly shoot themselves" (4: 432).[12] That Goethe a few short years later (1777–8) wrote a parody of his own novel

---

[11] As I have argued elsewhere: "On the one hand, Goethe appeals to the rational critics and tells them to disregard the untaught opinions of two young people, while on the other hand, he appeals to the sentimental reader by acknowledging the importance of one's heart. While Goethe here presents two conflicting opinions, the first is generally disregarded when interpreting the book" ("A New Reading" 457).

[12] [. . .] so verwirrten sich meine Freunde daran, indem sie glaubten, man müsse die Poesie in Wirklichkeit verwandeln, einen solchen Roman nachspielen und sich allenfalls selbst erschießen [. . .]. (FA 1, 14: 639–40)

in which the Werther-imitating "hero" chooses a doll over a living, breathing woman is perhaps the best commentary that Goethe could provide about interpreting texts through one's emotions.

One of the most telling aspects of Werther's heightened introspection is his eventual inability to communicate. At first, this is manifested in his rejection of rules of grammar — a rejection, as we shall see, that has been taken up in America since the early part of the twentieth century. When employed as an attaché, he is angry when his superior wishes him to write in a grammatically correct way and expects him not to leave out words in the documents (December 24, 1771). Werther strongly believes in the authenticity of the moment and hence disregards the need ever to rewrite his prose — even in the business setting. Like many English teachers of the twentieth century, Werther dismisses correctness of form as an evil against the individual right of idiosyncratic expression.

Whatever similarities Goethe may have given his alter ego of himself, this criticism of form was certainly not one of them. Goethe was notorious for writing and rewriting his works in order to find that "right word" that Werther's superior challenges him to find so much to Werther's disdain. One does not, however, need to search outside of the novel for an indication of how the reader is to interpret Werther's relationship to his own introspective language. By the end, Werther is no longer able to communicate effectively. His sentences are so unfinished and incoherent that the novel requires an editor to finish the story that was begun from Werther's perspective alone. Of course, Werther could not describe his own suicide, but the editor takes over the story days before this event. Where once his letters were enough to tell his story, by the end, an editor must try to piece together scraps and fragments of sentences and to interview others to tell the hero's story.

Werther's relationship to formal language is associated to his largely democratic spirit that one can again trace back to the Pietist religion. Pietists worshipped democratically; they did not believe that it was necessary to have an ordained intermediary between themselves and God and felt that all classes and genders could find their way to God equally. As is discussed in greater detail in the next section, Werther, too, believes that he can directly appeal to God without the need for intercession. His politics to the extent that they are evident are mixed, but tend toward the democratic. He is highly critical of those who keep a distance from the lower classes, calling this a cowardly act to ensure that levels of respect are maintained. He himself befriends several people of the lower classes throughout the novel. He is at his most aristocratic when he notes that "we are not all equal, nor can we be" (Ich weiß wohl daß wir nicht gleich sind, noch seyn können, May 15, 1771, FA 1, 8: 19), yet he finds it hard to accept this principle when applied to himself. When members of the aristocracy treat him as an inferior, and he is asked to leave a party, he becomes unhinged. While he can admit difference in equality between himself and those below him, he cannot acknowledge class principles when he is in the inferior position. As Wilson has pointed out, "Werther's failure of the attempt to overcome class-based attitudes is responsible for the scandal of Werther's ejection and ultimately for his suicide" (205). In the episode as Werther tells it, his enemies are glad to see him punished for his democratic notions and rejoice in the expulsion as a punishment for Werther's flouting of conventions, "for his want of esteem for others" ("meiner Geringschätzung anderer," March 15 and 16, 1772, FA 1, 8: 147). His reaction to this event is extreme (for all that has happened is that he has been asked to leave a social event), and he contemplates suicide: "A hundred times have I seized a knife to give ease to this oppressed heart. I have heard of a noble race of horses that instinctively bite open a vein when they are hot and exhausted by a long run, in order breathe more freely. I am often tempted to open a vein, to gain everlasting liberty for myself" (March 16, 1772).[13]

It is well worth noting that Werther is not a Pietist in one very important respect: he does not make Christ the center of his life. In fact, in the end, he overtly rejects a personal relationship to Christ. Rather than symbolizing Werther's break with the Pietist tradition, this tendency shows its natural evolution. Once one believes that one does not need an intermediary to commune with God, and once one believes, as some Pietists did, that one could become one (and hence equal) with Christ through one's own suffering and imaginative re-creation of his wounds on one's own body (Dohm 116, 120), what need does one have for Christ at all? In other words, if our imagination allows us to feel as Christ did and hence allows us to be at one with him, it is not that far a step from the one that Werther takes, i.e., declaring a direct relationship to God. In this way, as is discussed below, Werther's form of spirituality is related to contemporary, secular forms of it. As far apart as the Evangelicals and the secularists who practise modern

---

[13] Ach, ich habe hundertmal ein Messer ergriffen um diesem gedrängten Herzen Luft zu machen. Man erzählt von einer edlen Art Pferde, die wenn sie schrecklich erhitzt und aufgejagt sind, sich selbst aus Instinct eine Ader aufbeissen um sich zum Athem zu helfen. So ist mir's oft, ich möchte mir eine Ader öffnen, dir mir die ewige Freyheit schaffte. (FA 1, 8: 147)

forms of spirituality may seem to be, *Werther* may illustrate that their differences could very well be in degree and not in kind. Both begin in the emphasis upon the individual and his or her emotional state and both emphasize fulfillment through individual quests. After we have examined Goethe's treatment within *Werther* of such religious and spiritual tendencies in some detail, especially through the counter lens of Catholic symbolism, we can gain a better idea of what Goethe believed the anthropological downsides were to Pietist-influenced social changes and how they are manifested today.

Werther's *Catholic vestiges*
Scholars have long noted the strong Pietist overtones of Goethe's novel as well as other religious sources and influences.[14] What has not — to the best of my knowledge — ever been discussed, are its Catholic elements.[15] Catholic references, however, provide the necessary historical context to the novel's complicated portrayals of Pietism and religion and provide a contrary cultural force by which to evaluate certain Pietist trends. By examining the novel in the light of Catholicism, we gain insight into Goethe's anthropological understanding of religion, i.e., his understanding of how religious customs, in this case Catholic ones, positively influence society and culture and how the growth away from such a tradition has had certain consequences. In particular, in Goethe's discussions of Catholicism, he focuses on its ability to create community and its efficacy in creating interior wholeness. According

---

[14] Strikingly, it was not until Schöffler's 1938 piece that anyone noticed the clear references to the Gospel of John throughout the text. Within his path-breaking work, Schöffler compares the passions of Werther to those of Christ (71). While Kahn sees important parallels between *Werther* and a "Passionsgeschichte," he discounts the possibility of evaluating the work according to Christian principles (124). However, whereas Kahn reads the secularization of society in positive terms (16), I argue that the religious references point to the opposite conclusion. See also Anstett, who, like Kahn, reads the novel within the framework of changing religious sensibilities and also excludes Catholicism from the discussion (172–3). For an analysis of how Schöffler's work was received for the decades that follow, see Zabel. Graefe, in her study, carefully documents the biblical sources within the novel to analyze Werther's religious propensities. Throughout her article, she focuses upon its Protestant elements, although at the very end she provocatively suggests in passing that parts of the novel allude to the Catholic philosophy of *analogia entis* (98).

[15] Scholars have, of course, commented upon the two sacraments that most clearly appear (and the only two that are shared by both Protestants and Catholics) in the novel: communion and baptism. These sacraments, however, have been examined through the Protestant and Pietist perspective and not the Catholic one (Saul 109–10). Some scholars have investigated other religious aspects of the novel. See, for example, Sauder, who canvasses the religious influences upon the young Goethe. Within the course of the overview, he discusses Lutheran orthodoxy, Pietism, the Hermetic tradition, and Spinoza, but not Catholicism.

to Goethe's analysis, Catholicism's emphasis on a priestly intermediary enables inner peace and unity that is lost with Protestantism in general. Moreover, whereas the Pietists (and subsequent Evangelicals and secular spiritualists) believe that knowledge of a divine force is gained through an individual, emotional process, Catholicism has a rational approach to the divine as one of its core tenets. By examining the Catholic elements in the novel, we therefore gain a necessary counterbalance to earlier interpretations that valorize Pietist trends. While many commentators have studied the positive side to breaking free of tradition, I will argue that Werther's pathological side also represents the negative side of having abandoned aspects of the type of society and cultural values that Catholicism once offered. In effect, the Catholic symbols of the novel serve as a reminder of what has been abandoned in the modern world, or to put it in terms of Goethe's principle of compensation, they illuminate some of the costs associated with the modern individualism that Werther so embodies.

What becomes of central issue in the novel is the question of Werther's sense of guilt and the divided nature of his soul. Some scholars, for example, have argued that *Werther* is a tragedy of a new era because there is no guilt (Schöffler). I would argue in stark contrast that it is a tragedy because guilt has no formal outlet. Werther shoots himself because he has no recourse to traditions or hierarchies that would provide an outlet for his guilt. He is left with himself, and this is not enough to prevent his suicide. He represents a modern man who is living in a society that is growing ever more secular and ever more self-absorbed. He tries to find divinity first through nature and then through his bourgeois love of Lotte, and when that fails, through himself. Although he deeply desires forgiveness, he can find no outlet to ease the guilt of his self-perceived sins. Thus, whereas Reiss finds society to be healthy and Werther to be sick, I argue that Goethe's novel also points to the shortcomings of a secularizing, Evangelical society. As a consequence, it is not only Werther's "neurotic personality" that is particularly modern (Reiss 45), but also the society that brings it about.[16]

To avoid any misunderstanding, I would like to emphasize that I am not arguing that Goethe was in some way a closet supporter of Catholicism. Indeed, he is very well known for his harsh criticism of converts to Catholicism and for pointed anti-Catholic statements. At

---

[16] Schöffler, too, sees the text as demarcating the end of a religious tradition. He, however, views the whole according to Goethe's Lutheran background (85).

the same time, however, he heavily used Catholic symbols in many of his important works (*Faust, Elective Affinities*) and praised certain aspects of the Catholic Church — praise that has gone largely unnoticed in scholarship. In other words, as in many other spheres, Goethe in his works, letters, and conversations discusses both the advantages and disadvantages to this tradition. I contend that as an astute observer of society, Goethe recognized long-lasting influences of Catholic traditions and wrote about the consequences of the philosophical shift from the patriarchal hierarchy of the Church to the individualism of Protestantism and its various sects.[17] Such a reading illuminates a striking critique of a Werther-character type.

Goethe himself provides the framework for this discussion in his autobiography, *Poetry and Truth* (*Dichtung und Wahrheit*). Recalling his youth, he examines some of the social and emotional consequences of the rise of Protestantism and contrasts them with Catholicism. Notably, he comments upon how individualized the Protestants have become because they lack ritual to hold them together:

> The Protestant service is not rich or consequential enough to hold the congregations together, and so it can easily happen that members detach themselves, either to form smaller congregations or to conduct their daily affairs quite peacefully without church affiliations. (4: 219)[18]

Goethe's close friend, the Pietist von Klettenberg, for example, despite her affinities with certain Pietist groups, refused to join any of them formally, seeing herself as a free spirit (Frey-Geist, Chiarloni 146). The more individualized a person's religious preferences are, the less need he or she has of others and the more likely he or she is to reject the types of traditions that once united people. In this context, Goethe especially focuses upon the paucity of Protestant sacraments. He views sacraments as essential features in holding people together. Whereas Catholics have seven, Protestants have only two:

[17] In several important passages throughout his corpus, Goethe comments upon the way in which religious doctrines have been used for social or political aims. For example, in his "Metamorphose der Pflanzen: Zweiter Versuch," he discusses the political usefulness of the doctrine of teleology but warns of its dangers to the progress of science (FA 1, 24: 154–5). Below, I will consider the most central one to my argument: his discussion of the Catholic sacraments in *Poetry and Truth*.

[18] Der protestantische Gottesdienst hat zu wenig Fülle und Konsequenz, als daß er die Gemeine zusammenhalten könnte; daher geschieht es leicht, daß Glieder sich von ihr absondern und entweder kleine Gemeinen bilden, oder, ohne kirchlichen Zusammenhang, neben einander geruhig ihr bürgerliches Wesen treiben. (FA 1, 14: 315)

It can be said that the Protestant service in general lacks a rich content, but when this is closely investigated it will be found that Protestants have too few sacraments . . . The sacraments are the most sublime part of religion, the physical symbol of extraordinary divine grace and favor. (4: 218)[19]

Goethe here values those aspects of religion that provide cultural meaning ("rich content") and metaphysical experiences. The sacraments allow individuals an opportunity to transcend themselves. In the discussion that follows, he canvasses all seven of the Catholic sacraments: communion, baptism, confirmation, marriage, priestly orders, confession, and the last rites. In particular, however, he focuses upon the Eucharist and confession. Although he writes that for both Protestants and Catholics communion will always remain "great and sacred," if it stands as the only sacrament (and here Goethe dismisses the sacrament of baptism, since it is not consciously selected by the individual), then the entire religion loses its nourishing elements:

But such a sacrament [communion] should not stand alone; no Christian can receive it with the true joy it is meant to give unless a sense of the symbolical and sacramental has been nourished in him. He must be accustomed to view the inner religion of the heart as completely one with that of the visible church, as the great universal sacrament, which is divided again into a multitude of others, but communicates to each of these parts its holiness, indestructibility, and eternity. (4: 219)[20]

Although Goethe makes his pronouncements from an anthropological rather than a theological perspective, he correctly characterizes the central importance for Catholics of the sacraments, especially that of the Eucharist.[21] He here describes a pre-Wertherian state. The Church

---

[19] Fehlt es dem protestantischen Kultus im Ganzen an Fülle, so untersuche man das Einzelne, und man wird finden, der Protestant hat zu wenig Sakramente . . . Die Sakramente sind das Höchste der Religion, das sinnliche Symbol einer außerordentlichen göttlichen Gunst und Gnade. (FA 1, 14: 316)

[20] Ein solches Sakrament dürfte aber nicht allein stehen; kein Christ kann es mit wahrer Freude, wozu es gegeben ist, genießen, wenn nicht der symbolische oder sakramentliche Sinn in ihm genährt ist. Er muß gewohnt sein, die innere Religion des Herzens und die der äußeren Kirche als vollkommen Eins anzusehen, als das große allgemeine Sakrament, das sich wieder in soviel andere zergliedert und diesen Teilen seine Heiligkeit, Unzerstörlichkeit und Ewigkeit mitteilt. (FA 1, 14: 316)

[21] *The Catechism of the Council of Trent* states: "But if we consider the dignity of the Sacraments, the Eucharist, for holiness and for the number and greatness of its mysteries, is far superior to all the rest" (Borromeo 154). *The Catechism* also emphasizes that one of the effects of the sacraments is to indelibly stamp an impression upon our souls. This impression, moreover,

provides a structure which allows people to go beyond their own concerns to think about ideas greater than themselves. Such an approach allows individuals to find unity within themselves as well as with the larger community of the Church. Their inner lives need not be in conflict with their external, social ones. This unity exists, according to Goethe, in large part because of the sacrament of confession, a sacrament that soothes one's mind and allows one fully to participate in communion (FA 1, 14: 317). Without confession, Goethe argues, the conflicting demands of nature and religion would result in confusion and turmoil for the individual. Confession remedies this condition. The priest is able to help the individual and "calm, warn and strengthen him" (4: 219, zu beruhigen, zu warnen, zu stärken, FA 1, 14: 317). Confession, moreover, becomes a "remedy (Heilmittel) for one's whole life" where the priest is able to "set erring persons back on the right path and to relieve those who are tormented" (4: 220).[22]

It is important to note that although Goethe did not consider himself a Christian, and even less a Catholic, he nevertheless believes that for many people sacraments are necessary for psychic health. Two things are especially important here. First, that confession serves to unify the split in an individual's soul (a split that Goethe characterizes as torturous); and second, that this is accomplished through an intermediary. Individuals cannot find solace and forgiveness from within themselves, but require the priest, who in the sacraments of confession and communion stands in Christ's place and through whom God acts. Whereas a Protestant can speak directly to God, a Catholic priest becomes God's agent through whom one can receive God's graces. Goethe discourses at some length on the source of priestly authority: we do not revere the priest, but his office; his blessing, moreover, is not seen as earthly but heavenly and is hence not invalidated by the sinful nature of the priest.[23] In his sacramental functions, the priest brings unity between the inner and outer realms, the individual and the community, and the ordinary and the sacred. The advantages that such wholeness brings to the individual are, according to Goethe, destroyed with Protestantism (FA 1, 14: 319). Throughout these passages, the words and phrases that describe Catholicism emphasize unity whereas those that describe Protestantism emphasize its power to separate. Goethe tells us that

becomes a unifying mark of one's internal and external existence (Borromeo 159).

[22] Irrende zurecht zu weisen und Gequälte zu erledigen. (FA 1, 14: 317–18)

[23] In these observations, Goethe is very closely following Catholic doctrine. See, for example, Aquinas, "That the Sacraments Can Be Dispensed by Evil Ministers" (*Summa*, Book 4, ch. 77).

he was so captivated with the Catholic tradition of confessing one's individual sins that he as a young man attempted to fashion such a confession within the form of a Protestant one — a type of confession that forbade the listing of individual sins.

Several of Goethe's acquaintances were shocked when they read the passages above that seemed so favorable to the Catholic Church and its traditions. Voss (1804), Böttiger and Rochlitz (June? 1812) found the statements to be out of character for Goethe (Goethe, *Anhang* #1793, 1659). These comments, however, were not as unusual as these men may have believed. Goethe, as is well known, had many critical things to say about the Catholic Church and the ways in which its doctrines impeded the progress of philosophy and the development of bourgeois culture. At the same time, he also recognized that certain cultural aspects were lost with the Reformation. In particular, the difference between Protestant and Catholic notions of confession was an issue upon which he commented throughout his life. For Goethe, the main advantage to the practice of Catholic confession was its notion of immediate absolution. Thus, whereas Pietists were well known for making public "confessionals," i.e., personal statements about their own faults and shortcomings, the purpose was not to gain immediate forgiveness of sins. For example, Voss, in a letter dated later than his comments expressing surprise above (February 24, 1805), writes to Karl Wilhelm Ferdinand Solger (1780–1819) about how Goethe in a conversation compared the strengths and weaknesses of both religious traditions. He reports that Goethe blamed Luther for the changes that gave the individual too much to bear: "In former times one could have the burden of one's conscience taken away by another." Now, Goethe observes, one has to deal with the burden oneself and thereby lose the ability to regain a sense of harmony.[24] One never, Goethe adds, should have taken away the Catholic forms of confession. Similarly, in a diary entry a couple of years later (September 7, 1807), Goethe notes that the priest through confession unifies the divided soul and makes one whole again so that individuals do not have to grapple with such problems on their own (FA 2, 6: 233–4). Late in life Goethe even muses to Karl Wilhelm Göttling (1793–1869) that Protestants are more likely than Catholics to write autobiographies because Catholics are able to rid

---

[24] Ehemals konnte eine Gewissenslast durch andere vom Gewissen genommen werden, jetzt muß sie ein belastetes Gewissen selbst tragen, u verliert darüber die Kraft mit sich selber wieder in Harmonie zu kommen. (FA 2, 5: 551)

themselves of their sins through their confessors (March 4, 1826).[25]

The sentiments expressed in these personal comments certainly coincide with Goethe's more extensive analysis in *Poetry and Truth* cited above. Although they are written well after the composition of *Werther*, Goethe provides information within his autobiography that places his mood within a Catholic mindset at the time of the novel's composition. He was spending a great deal of time within the Catholic circle of the LaRoche family, and letters written by Goethe as well as his acquaintances at the time substantiate his close connection to the Catholic priest, Father Damian Friedrich Dumeix (1729–1802). Within his autobiography, Goethe emphasizes his close ties to him: "he was a very perspicacious man, who beautifully and adequately explained to me the beliefs and usages, and the external and internal condition of the oldest church" (4: 430).[26] At this point, Goethe reports that he even participated in Catholic "religious practices" (Religionsübungen, FA 1, 14: 637).[27]

Given this background, when Goethe then speaks of a "general confession" (Generalbeichte) in his autobiography in respect to the process of writing *Werther*, it should be read as more than one of the several confessional metaphors within the autobiography (Müller

---

[25] Diese haben immer einen Beichtvater zur Seite und können ihre Gebrechen hübsch einzeln los werden.

[26] Er war der erste katholische Geistliche, mit dem ich in nähere Berührung trat, und der, weil er ein sehr hellsehender Mann war, mir über den Glauben, die Gebräuche, die äußern und innern Verhältnisse der ältesten Kirche schöne und hinreichende Aufschlüsse gab. (FA 1, 14: 637)

[27] It is important to note that during Goethe's own infatuation with the real life Charlotte Buff (later Kestner 1753–1828), he viewed his emotional attachment to her in terms of religious symbolism. In a letter to her fiancé Johann Christian Kestner (1741–1800), he references a catechism and declares that the receipt of any object from Buff's hands would be viewed as receiving an object of grace: "ein sinnliches Zeichen wodurch die geistlichunsicht-baare Gnadengüter pp wies im Cathechismus klingt" (December 15, 1772, FA 2, 1: 276). Buff is hence viewed as a priest (for we receive sacraments through the hands of priests) and objects that pass through her hands are considered to be blessed. In another letter to Kestner (April 6, 1773), he compares Charlotte Buff to Christ when he relates how on Good Friday he "would like to make a holy grave and bury Lotte's silhouette" (wollt ich heilig Grab machen und Lottens Silhouette begraben, FA 2, 1: 298). While working on *Werther*, he excuses his long silence to the now married Charlotte Buff Kestner (March 1774) by telling her that she has actually been more present to him than ever before: she has been with him "in, cum et sub" (FA 2, 1: 354). Although this formula characterizes the Lutheran understanding of the change that happens to the communion wafer during consecration (Lutheran consubstantia-tion versus Catholic transubstantiation of the bread), it is nevertheless noteworthy that she is linked to this sacrament in his mind. Finally, in a letter to her (August 26, 1774), he compares the effects of spending time with a woman who knew her from her youth to the effects of the relics of saints. In this same letter, when announcing that he will be soon be sending her a copy of the novel, he characterizes it as a "prayer book" (Gebetbuch, FA 2, 1: 393).

1232). The term "Generalbeichte" is a Catholic one and has a very specific meaning. A general confession covers a larger time span and may include as much as the whole of one's life. It "is necessary and obligatory for all who have made one or more sacrilegious Confessions" or is "useful for . . . a desire to begin a new life" (Benedictine 36, 38). The Doctor of the Church St Francis de Sales writes of general confession: "it gives us a more complete knowledge of ourselves; . . . it relieves our mind of much anxiety and gives peace to our conscience; it excites in us good resolutions . . ." (quoted from Benedictine 38). Indeed, within the context of *Poetry and Truth* Goethe speaks of this confession using similar terms as Catholic theologians. Goethe the artist has found a way to wholeness outside of the Catholic tradition of confession that mirrors its results:

> For through this composition, more than any other, I had saved myself from a stormy element on which I had been tossed back and forth most violently, by my own and others' doing, by chance and chosen mode of life, by resolve and rashness, by obstinancy and pliancy. I felt as glad and free again as after a general confession, and entitled to a new life. (4: 432)[28]

Goethe speaks of guilt and how he was driven emotionally from pillar to post because of his actions and experiences. He, of course, does not gain new life and wholeness by going to confess his sins to a priest. His art serves that function for him. He recognizes, however, within the autobiography as well as in his comments on confession elsewhere, that individuals suffer certain psychic consequences in no longer having recourse to religious confession. Goethe's notions on this score are hierarchical. He does not need religion, but sees that others — because they have no recourse to art or other avenues — do. In this very important sense, Werther is unlike Goethe. Werther's art notoriously fails him throughout: when most enthused by nature, he cannot portray the image on paper; when most in love with Lotte, he cannot draw her portrait; when driven mad by his feelings, he has difficulty in writing complete sentences.[29] The hero of Goethe's novel

---

[28] Denn ich hatte mich durch diese Komposition, mehr als durch jede andere, aus einem stürmischen Elemente gerettet, auf dem ich durch eigne und fremde Schuld, durch zufällige und gewählte Lebensweise, durch Vorsatz und Übereilung, durch Hartnäckigkeit und Nachgeben, auf die gewaltsamste Art hin und wider getrieben worden. Ich fühlte mich, wie nach einer Generalbeichte, wieder froh und frei, und zu einem neuen Leben berechtigt. (FA 1, 14: 639)

[29] Werther himself reports: "Ich leide viel, denn ich habe verlohren was meines Lebens

is representative of an individual who cannot find release through art and can no longer seek it through confession. His isolation grows in part because he has a need for some form of spiritual communion that he can neither find in his Pietist forms of worship or within himself. In the end, Werther shoots himself, as I argue below, because the new religious beliefs are inadequate to deal with the new emphasis upon the individual apart from a larger community. Werther himself realizes this aspect of modernity when he notes that he has not been called to be one of Jesus's chosen ones (November 15, 1772).

At important junctures within the novel, the reader is presented with references to Catholic sacraments. They have, however, been so changed and subverted that they act as fossils: their existence demonstrates how far society has evolved away from these traditions. Throughout the story, Lotte takes on a priestly function. She distributes communion, confirms allegiance with a slap, baptizes, provides unction to the dying, and most importantly, hears Werther's confession but denies him absolution. She therefore serves as an intermediary between the old religion and the new. She mimics in some form the rites of Catholicism, but in doing so as a woman, represents the new spirit of religious reform. Goethe's portrayal of the consequences of these changes, however, suggests that new forms of sentimentalized religion lack the strength of former traditions and ultimately fail to bring comfort to Werther's divided self.

Communion is the first sacrament that makes an appearance. Although commentators have noted that Werther's last meal is a sacrilegious version of the Lord's supper, it is not the only reference to this sacrament. In fact, we learn a great deal about Werther's decline by comparing his final communion with the earlier instances of it: initially he partakes of communion with others, but by the end he partakes of it alone. Significantly, when Werther first meets Lotte, she is distributing bread (the Catholic version of the sacrament, i.e., without wine) to children who would refuse to take it from anyone else.[30] Whereas in

---

einzige Wonne war, die heilige belebende Kraft, mit der ich Welten um mich schuf; sie ist dahin!" (November 3, 1772)

[30] Although it may seem a stretch to read the first encounter with Lotte in terms of the Eucharist, there is evidence to support this interpretation. Many scholars have already argued that the scene has significance for interpreting the whole work. Most, however, focus upon its maternal connotations. I believe that the religious symbolism goes well beyond seeing Lotte as a maternal or even Marian symbol. Both Kowalik (101) and Dye (90–1) provide overviews of the connection between Werther and his relationship to mothers and mother figures. Kowalik focuses upon the psychoanalytic perspective, whereas Dye focuses upon the mother/whore dichotomy.

the Catholic Church, priests are virginal father figures, in this subverted form of the sacrament, Lotte, a virginal mother figure, serves as a priest. Werther's later characterization of her echoes such an image when he views her as so holy a figure that his desire dissipates in her presence (July 16, 1771). Second, it is clear that Werther is deeply affected by witnessing this scene and undergoes a kind of spiritual transformation so that his "whole soul" (ganze Seele) changes (June 16, 1771). His encounters with Lotte, moreover, have made his days as happy as those God gives to his saints (June 19, 1771). Third, there is a direct reference to Catholic ritual once Werther has taken over distributing bread from Lotte. Significantly, this activity is accompanied by its own canon. A Catholic Mass is characterized by parts that are changeable (e.g., the particular scriptural readings for the day, the introit, Gospel, etc.) and the part that is always — word for word — the same, the canon. The canon is the part of the Mass where the bread and wine are consecrated and communion takes place. In the "communion" in the novel, Werther, when giving out the bread, always tells the same story to the children, "unchanged in a singsong tone like reciting away the beads on a rosary" (my translation, August 15, 1771).[31] In other words, Werther's secular fairy tale is recited like the canon part of the Mass: in a singsong way without altering a syllable. Notably, his own analogy of this event is to the Catholic recitation of prayers on the beads of a rosary.[32]

The next vestige of a sacrament occurs at the ball during the counting game. In the Catholic Church, the sacrament of confirmation is similar to baptism, but whereas baptism is generally performed upon an infant, people are confirmed when they have achieved the age of reason. Traditionally, confirmation is given during the time of Pentecost because this day is its source.[33] According to this tradition, after Christ's resurrection, when the disciples were gathered together, "suddenly there came a sound from heaven, as of a mighty wind coming, and it

---

[31] . . . unveränderlich in einem singenden Sylbenfall an einem Schnürchen weg zu recitiren. (FA 1, 8: 105)

[32] The origin of the phrase, "an einem Schnürchen" is the rosary. See the entry for "Schnürchen" in Grimms' *Das Deutsche Wörterbuch.*

[33] Pentecost is a moveable feast and, depending upon the day for Easter, occurs any time between May 10 and June 13. Goethe wrote about Pentecost in his 1773 "Zwo wichtige bisher unerörtete biblische Fragen, zum erstenmal gründlich beantwortet." The purported author of this piece, a Swabian pastor, argues that the disciples did not actually speak in tongues on this day, but were inspired to speak the language of emotions, the language of the heart. Strikingly, even this "pastor" who advocates sentiment warns that it can go too far: "Auf der Höhe der Empfindung erhält sich kein Sterblicher." For a discussion of this work, see Boyle 140–2.

filled the whole house, where they were sitting. Divided tongues, as of fire, appeared among them . . . And they were filled with the Holy Ghost" (Acts 2.2–4). Notably, the phenomenon has certain similarities to a storm, with strong winds and the sudden appearance of light. This sacrament is meant to strengthen the courage of those who receive it. Whereas even Jesus's disciples were afraid at the time of the Passion, after Pentecost, they became brave in the face of death (Borromeo 210). As the *Catechism* explains: "In baptism man is enlisted into the service; in confirmation he is equipped for battle" (Borromeo 201). Within this ceremony, the confirmant becomes a "soldier for Christ": "The person when anointed and confirmed . . . receives a gentle slap on the cheek from the hand of the Bishop to make him recollect that, as a valiant combatant, he should be prepared to endure with unconquered spirit all adversities for the name of Christ" (Borromeo 211–12).

The ballroom scene supports a reading of the sacrament of confirmation in several different ways. First, it is during this scene that Werther pledges himself as a kind of "soldier" to Lotte. He writes Wilhelm that he would willingly risk his life to insure that a girl that he loved would never waltz with another (June 16, 1771). When the strong storm arises, people are frightened and gain their courage through a game that Lotte organizes and in which she slaps people when they make a mistake. Werther's attraction to Lotte is strengthened as a result of this game. The conclusion of the ball is a religious experience, though not one oriented toward God, but rather to the Pietist poet, Klopstock. Notably, it is through Lotte's powers that Klopstock is elevated to divinity: "It was more than I could bear. I bent over her hand, kissed it in a stream of ecstatic tears, and again looked into her eyes. Divine Klopstock! If only you could have seen the apotheosis in those eyes! And your name, so often profaned, may I never hear it uttered again" (June 16, 1772).[34] Werther's ecstatic description of this scene demonstrates how quickly he has begun to transpose his sentiments from the divinity of nature of the first pages of the novel to the divinity of Lotte. Later, we will see that Werther's rejection of Christ occurs at the same time that he realizes that he must renounce Lotte. During his happier times, however, Lotte serves as a priest, as an intermediary for Werther to a form of spirituality outside of himself.

---

[34] Ich ertrug's nicht, neigte mich auf ihre Hand und küßte sie unter den wonnevollesten Thränen. Und sah nach ihrem Auge wieder — Edler! hättest du deine Vergötterung in diesem Blicke gesehen, und möcht ich nun deinen so oft entweihten Nahmen nie wieder nennen hören. (June 16, 1771, FA 1, 8: 55)

Lotte's actions next take on a priestly manner when Werther describes her relationship to the sick: "What Lotte can be to an invalid I feel in my own heart," and describes her in terms of a priest giving divine unction (July 1, 1771).[35] When an ill woman is told by her doctors that she is about to die, she wishes to have Lotte "in these last moments" (in diesen letzten Augenblicken) by her side (July 1, 1771). Later, Frau M. even confesses (bekennen) in the presence of Lotte that she has stolen from the family till in order to keep the household running. Without such a confession, Frau M. feels incapable of facing eternity with any confidence (July 11, 1771). Lotte's presence, in Werther's mind, allows the woman to die in comfort and peace, just as the last rites for a Catholic assure that one can enter eternity with peace of mind.

Baptism is the next sacrament to appear in the novel. In this case, the analogy is directly made in the text itself and has indeed been analyzed by other commentators.[36] The "baptism" takes place because Werther has kissed one of Lotte's sisters, making her upset. Lotte takes the child to the well, where the young girl rubs her cheeks with water "in the fervent belief that all the impurities would be washed off by the miraculous water and that she would surely be spared the disgrace of an ugly beard" (July 6, 1772). As Werther tells his friend: "I have never attended a baptism with greater reverence" (July 6, 1771).[37] Whereas the sacrament of baptism, according to Catholic doctrine, takes away the stain of original sin from the one being baptized, Lotte's baptismal act in Werther's eyes is even more powerful: "and when Lotte came up, I could have fallen on my knees as before a prophet who has washed away the sins of the people" (July 6, 1772).[38]

---

[35] Was Lotte einem Kranken seyn muß, fühl' ich an meinem eigenen armen Herzen. (July 1, 1771, FA 1, 8: 61)

[36] Saul, for example, believes that the baptism scene is a turning point for Werther in which he leaves all religious traditions behind (119). (He also sees Werther's last meal as a substitute for Protestant rather than Catholic communion.) Although I, too, see Werther as ultimately abandoning religious tradition, this decision occurs much later and only after Lotte has refused Werther absolution. Saul believes that Werther's relationship with Christ is primarily at stake. I argue that Werther's view of Lotte as a priest, as a mediator to the divinity, is just as central to the text. Graefe similarly sees only the two Protestant sacraments as being present in the novel (88).

[37] . . . mit welchem Glauben, daß durch die Wunderquelle alle Verunreinigung abgespühlt, und die Schmach abgethan würde, einen häßlichen Bart zu kriegen (July 6, 1771, FA 1, 8: 71) . . . ich habe mit mehr Respect nie einer Taufhandlung beygewohnt (July 6, 1771, FA 1, 8: 73). Some scholars (Saul) wish to argue that the scene is not a baptism to Werther at all. After all, Werther does not initially equate it with a baptism, but compares it to one. The surrounding text, however, closely links Lotte's ritual with that of a baptism.

[38] . . . und als Lotte herauf kam, hätte ich mich gern vor ihr niedergeworfen wie vor einem Propheten der die Schulden einer Nation weggeweiht hat (July 6, 1771, FA 1, 8: 73).

Of course, this language in the examples above illustrates the exaggerated heights of Werther's emotions. Yet, that he closely connects Lotte with the forgiveness of sins also demonstrates the religious functions that she has for him. The point here is not that Werther is a Catholic searching for a priest, but rather that the vestiges of Catholicism exercise a strong influence upon his worldview (however subconsciously). These vestiges, moreover, embody a human need that was once, according to Goethe, fulfilled by the Catholic sacraments. Werther seeks to find a way to spiritual wholeness and community through the sacraments, if only by analogy, through his relationship with Lotte. In this way, his views of her strongly echo the Catholic, Thomistic doctrine of *analogia entis*, i.e., that one can gain approximate knowledge of God through one's earthly experiences.[39] Whereas Lutherans argue that one gains knowledge of God through grace or scriptural revelation, Thomists assert that since God created the world (and it was good) and he created human beings (in his image), we can approach and learn about the divinity by studying the world around us. In this way, the Catholic religion is more intellectual in a strict understanding of the term than either the mainstream Lutheran one (where knowledge is acquired through God's gift of grace) or Evangelical ones (whose members believe that one approaches God primarily through one's emotions).

For Catholics, reason can assist one in finding God and is not seen as an impediment. While it is denied us in this world to know God in his entirety, one can nevertheless begin to approach such knowledge in this one.[40] In a conversation with Johannes Daniel Falk (1768–1826),

---

[39] As mentioned above in note 14, Graefe makes this observation in passing (98). It is interesting to observe that Pope Benedict XVI was discoursing on this very aspect of Catholicism in his Regensburg speech that has since become notorious for other reasons.

[40] The prayer by Thomas Aquinas that priests traditionally said before Mass succinctly describes this phenomenon: "Oh, most loving Father, grant that I may one day forever contemplate Him (Jesus) unveiled and face to face, whom, on my pilgrimage, I receive under a veil" (Hoever 80). Although Goethe was clearly not a Catholic, he was heavily influenced by Spinoza, who also advocated studying nature in order to understand God. For Spinoza, to study nature was to study God as he ultimately saw the two as being the same. Goethe, too, believed that in studying nature one could learn about the divine, but in a slightly different context. In my earlier book on Goethe's philosophy of nature, I have argued at some length how Goethe's conception of God was that of a creative principle. Nature or human beings participate in the divine to the extent that they are creative: nature through its acts of procreation or in its formation of new organisms and human beings through their productive activities. (It is for this reason, then, that the God of the Prolog in *Faust* praises Faust, as well as any human being, so long as they remain productive.) *Analogia entis* fits into this general approach, but, of course, for a Catholic the image of God is a very different one than for Goethe or Spinoza.

Goethe echoes the sentiment that one learns about God by studying nature, and indeed stresses the interconnectedness between faith and scientific inquiry:

> Strictly speaking I cannot have any knowledge of God beyond what is warranted by the rather limited scope of my sense-perceptions . . . But it by no means follows that these limitations of our study of nature also set limits to faith. On the contrary, the immediacy of divine intuitions within us is such that it may very well come to appear that our knowledge is but . . . imperfect, requiring for this very reason that faith should supplement and complete it . . . Where knowledge suffices we of course do not need faith, but where the power of knowledge fails or seems insufficient, we should also give faith its due. Provided only we start from the principle that knowledge and faith are not meant to cancel each other out but to complete each other, we shall surely be on the right road to truth in all things. (January 25, 1813, Trans. from *Conversations and Encounters* 89–90)[41]

Werther seeks to find God, absolution, and a new life through Lotte. He begins to worship himself because she loves him (July 13, 1771) to the extent that he becomes a pilgrim when he returns to his hometown (May 9, 1772), his physical desires depart in her holy (heilig) presence

---

[41] Streng genommen kann ich von Gott doch weiter nichts wissen, als wozu mich der ziemlich beschränkte Gesichtskreis von sinnlichen Wahrnehmungen auf diesem Planeten berechtigt . . . Damit ist aber keineswegs gesagt, daß durch diese Beschränkung unserer Naturbetrachtungen auch dem Glauben Schranken gesetzt wären. Im Gegenteil kann, bei der Unmittelbarkeit göttlicher Gefühle in uns, der Fall gar leicht eintreten, daß das Wissen als Stückwerk besonders auf einem Planeten erscheinen muß, der, aus seinem ganzen Zusammenhange mit der Sonne herausgerissen, alle und jede Betrachtung unvollkommen läßt, die eben darum erst durch den Glauben ihre vollständige Ergänzung erhält . . . Wo das Wissen genügt, bedürfen wir freilich des Glaubens nicht; wo aber das Wissen seine Kraft nicht bewährt oder ungenügend erscheint, sollen wir auch dem Glauben seine Rechte nicht streitig machen. Sobald man nur von dem Grundsatz ausgeht, daß Wissen und Glauben nicht dazu da sind, um einander aufzuheben, sondern um einander zu ergänzen, so wird schon überall das Rechte ausgemittelt werden. (FA 2, 6: 177–8)

See also Goethe's 1824 essay, "Ernst Stiedenroth," where he turns to the notion of balance and compensation in order to discuss overtly human personalities, especially in terms of reason and faith. Each person must analyze his or her own self, discover which characteristic is missing or imbalanced, and then strive to cultivate that aspect. In order to illustrate this point, he turns to analyze the general characteristics of scientists and followers of religion: "Thus a man born and bred to the so-called exact sciences, and at the height of his ability to reason empirically, finds it hard to accept that an exact sensory imagination might also exist, although art is unthinkable without it. This is also a point of contention between followers of emotional religion and those of rational religion: while the latter refuse to acknowledge that religion begins with feeling, the former will not admit the necessity for religion to develop rationally" (12: 46). Goethe does not privilege one mode of being — emotional or rational — above the other. Both ought to coexist, and adherents of either approach stunt their own development to the extent that they exclude the other.

(July 16, 1771), he worships those that have been in her company
(July 18, 1771) and most significantly: "I cannot pray except to her.
My imagination sees nothing but her; nothing matters except what
has to do with her" (August 30, 1771).[42] In the end, he even believes
that his clothes have been made sacred (geheiligt) through her touch
(FA 1, 8: 263). Although the religious language certainly is indicative
of an intense emotional state, the contexts of the various sacraments
point to further meaning. In each of the above instances, Werther is
seeking something more than a relationship with a woman. He seeks
a transcendence that will combine the earthly with the heavenly and
one that will include the forgiveness of his sins.

Werther, however, is thwarted in this quest. At issue is the question
of intercession. He comes to reject the intermediacy of Christ (i.e.,
that human beings are saved through his sacrifice) and believes that he
can make a direct appeal to God. Notably, even Werther realizes that
religion is useful to some and claims to respect it:

> I respect religion — you know I do. I feel that it can give strength to the feeble
> and comfort to the afflicted. But does it affect all men alike? . . . Does not the Son
> of God himself say that they are His whom the Father has given to Him? Have I
> been given to Him? What if our Father should want to keep me for himself, as
> my heart sometimes tells me? (November 15, 1772)[43]

According to Christian beliefs, Christ died so that human beings could
be saved. The Catholic religion teaches that through the sacraments,
"as through a channel, must flow into the soul the efficacy of the
Passion of Christ, that is, the grace which He merited for us on the
altar of the cross, and without which we cannot hope for salvation"
(Borromeo 149). Within the sacraments, the priest stands in for Christ.
He becomes his representative during the Mass, and he has the ability
to confirm and to forgive sins because Christ gave the disciples the
power to act in his stead. In the novel, Werther rejects the intermediacy
of Christ because he believes he has direct access to God. His rejection

---

[42] Ich habe kein Gebeth mehr, als an sie; meiner Einbildungskraft erscheint keine andere
Gestalt, als die ihrige, und alles in der Welt um mich her sehe ich nur im Verhältnisse mit
ihr. (August 30, 1771, FA 1, 8: 113)

[43] Ich ehre die Religion, das weißt du, ich fühle daß sie manchem Ermatteten Stab,
manchem Verschmachtenden Erquickung ist; Nur — kann sie dann, muß sie dann das einem
jeden seyn? . . . Sagt nicht selbst der Sohn Gottes, daß die um ihn seyn würden die ihm der
Vater gegeben hat? wenn ich ihm nun nicht gegeben bin? wenn mich nun der Vater für sich
behalten will, wie mir mein Herz sagt! (November 15, 1772, FA 1, 8: 181)

occurs at the same time that his relationship with Lotte is at a turning point. He can no longer find the same religious connection through her, through her intermediacy, that he did earlier in the novel. On November 24, 1772, he still sees her in a divine and sacred light: "Never will I dare kiss you, beautiful lips which the spirits of Heaven guard."[44] Werther does dare to kiss those lips, and this kiss leads to the crisis that is his demise. Notably, he afterwards seeks a kind of absolution, and with its denial, commits suicide.

After Werther has kissed Lotte, the climax of a heightened emotional scene, she runs into the next room and shuts the door. This scene contains several gestures that point toward confession. He is in a kneeling position (er lag auf der Erde, den Kopf auf dem Kanapee) and appeals for forgiveness in a whispered voice (mit leiser Stimme) through a partition. He begs for one word from Lotte, a phrase that echoes the part in the traditional Mass when one asks God for forgiveness before taking communion. God needs to say one word (*sed tantum dic verbo*) and our sins will be forgiven. Lotte does not answer Werther — she does not give him the one word — and he goes away in the depths of despair (FA 1, 8: 247). In the pages that follow, he repeatedly asks for her forgiveness in the notes that he leaves behind. Because he cannot receive forgiveness either from Lotte (because she would not speak to him and has sworn never to see him again) or from Christ (because Werther does not acknowledge his status as an intermediary), he decides to punish himself (ich strafe mich dafür) for "a sin in the eyes of the world" (diese Welt Sünde, FA 1, 8: 251).

If we return to Goethe's description of confession in *Poetry and Truth*, we can see how important he thought confession was in making an individual feel whole and in re-establishing a sense of community:

> Just when the conflict between natural and religious demands has, of necessity, involved him in endless confusion, he is given the admirable expedient of confiding his good and bad deeds, his frailties and his doubts, to a worthy man who can calm, warn, and strengthen him, chastise him with punishments that are again symbolic, and lastly gladden him by completely absolving him of his guilt and returning the slate of his humanity washed clean. (4: 219)[45]

---

[44] Nie will ich's wagen einen Kuß euch aufzudrücken, Lippen! auf denen die Geister des Himmels schweben. (November 24, 1772, FA 1, 8: 185)

[45] Hier ist ihm nun in der unendlichen Verworrenheit, in die er sich, bei dem Widerstreit natürlicher und religioser Forderungen, verwickeln muß, ein herrliches Auskunftsmittel gegeben, seine Taten und Untaten, seine Gebrechen und seine Zweifel einem würdigen, eigens dazu bestellten Manne zu vertrauen, der ihn zu beruhigen, zu warnen, zu stärken,

Goethe praises the sacrament of confession and sees his art (as discussed above) as salutary in the same way — it allows one to release one's guilt through an intermediary/medium and regain peace. For Werther, however, that is not possible. His art has long failed him. Lotte, who has served as a type of priestly intermediary, has not only refused him absolution, but he even sees her handing over the pistols as a sign from heaven that he should shoot himself (FA 1, 8: 259). Moreover, whereas Christ asks God his father whether he must drink of the bitter cup, Werther sees Lotte as handing it to him: "You see, Lotte, I do not shudder to take the cold and fatal cup from which I shall drink the frenzy of death. Your hand gave it to me, and I do not tremble" (11: 86).[46] Werther fears that Lotte has closed her heart against him (FA 1, 8: 259), and he believes the way to expiate his sin is to die.

A close examination of Werther's reaction to the knowledge that Lotte has dusted off the pistols demonstrates how her refusal to forgive accelerates his despair and leaves him alone without recourse to any sort of community. His first act after receiving the pistols is to order bread and wine. This communion, however, is the very opposite of the one that Goethe describes in his autobiography. Whereas the Eucharist emphasizes community, whether Jesus shares the Passover meal with his disciples or members of a congregation share in a communal ritual, Werther takes his last supper alone. The sacrament is done by himself and for himself. And whereas the Catholic sacrament fosters, according to Goethe's cultural observations, a unity of the inner and outer worlds, Werther's last supper illustrates the exact opposite: the complete disjunction between his inner hopes and outer reality.

Werther believes that he is dying on behalf of Lotte (FA 1, 8: 262), and many have noted that he sees himself as a Christ figure because he claims to die for the good of others. This desire is an empty wish, and one must wonder whether he does not really wish to destroy whatever is left of Lotte and Albert's happiness. Although he repeatedly comments that he hopes to restore the happiness of both (FA 1, 8: 260), the evidence that he leaves behind will accomplish the exact opposite. His notes serve to accuse Lotte and insinuate worse things than one shared kiss: "I have ill rewarded you, Albert, but you will forgive me. I have disturbed the peace of your house. I have sowed distrust between

---

durch gleichfalls symbolische Strafen zu züchtigen und ihn zuletzt, durch ein völliges Auslöschen seiner Schuld, zu beseligen und ihm rein und abgewaschen die Tafel seiner Menschheit wieder zu übergeben weiß. (FA 1, 14: 317)

[46] Hier Lotte! Ich schaudre nicht, den kalten schrecklichen Kelch zu fassen, aus dem ich den Taumel des Todes trinken soll! Du reichtest mir ihn und ich zage nicht. (FA 1, 8: 263)

you" (11: 85).[47] He has not only failed in dying for the good of others, but at the end of the novel, we are not even sure that Lotte will survive. Werther himself fails as an intermediary just as he failed to find an intermediary for himself.

Scholars have long argued to what extent Goethe distanced himself from the sentimentality of his protagonist in the first version of the novel. Many have read it at face value, i.e., as an autobiographical account in which the young Goethe seriously writes about the passions that he had himself recently experienced.[48] The Catholic symbols embedded within the novel, however, argue for a more complex understanding of the sentimentality within the pages. The references to Catholic sacraments and theology (*analogia entis*) paint a negative portrait of a new society that has enabled a Werther to emerge and to be admired. While the individual has gained a great deal of freedom in the wake of the growth of Protestantism — we witness Werther's relative ease in moving among the social classes, his questioning of societal mores, his freedom to interpret the Bible and religion quite loosely, and his leisure to obsess about his emotions and self — at the same time there are costs and consequences to those freedoms.[49] The freedom that an individual gains by breaking away from Catholic hierarchy has certain psychic consequences, and Werther embodies those: exaggerated and conflicting emotions that find no release, and isolation from a larger community. The last words of the novel emphasize his complete break with a religious community: "No clergyman attended him" (Kein Geistlicher hat ihn begleitet). In the end, Werther still seeks aid through the sacraments, but only through the vestiges of their forms. These vestiges do not have the same anthropological power that the sacraments of the Catholic Church once contained and hence are not sufficient to supply what Werther so desperately seeks. Werther, unlike the artist Goethe, cannot bear the conflicts of a modern individual, who without a venue for release tortures himself in isolation without recourse to community. Werther's self-absorption, his rejection of reason, his embracement of passions lead to his self-destruction.

---

[47] Ich habe dir übel gelohnt, Albert, und du vergibst mir. Ich habe den Frieden deines Hauses gestört, ich habe Mißtrauen zwischen euch gebracht. (FA 1, 8: 261)

[48] For an overview of such readings, see my "New Reading."

[49] Noyes, in the context of explaining Goethe's relationship to notions of cosmopolitanism and colonialism, similarly sees the tension in Werther as being between "free movement (desire) and its institutionalized restriction (the law). This tension characterizes Werther's open flaunting of convention, causing him to believe himself immune from the rules that restrict social and spatial mobility, and eventually resulting in his downfall" (446). Whereas Noyes focuses upon mores generally, I make the case here for Goethe's interest in Catholic ones.

Goethe does not privilege one mode of being — emotional or rational — above the other. Both ought to coexist and adherents of either approach stunt their own development to the extent that they exclude the other. Werther failed not only to achieve the balance of reason and passion in his own life, but he rejected the attempt even to try to do this. By now turning to contemporary religious issues in America, we can begin to trace the legacy of valorizing the emotions over the intellect in the USA. This legacy is an interesting one because it has its antecedents on both the right, American Evangelicalism, and the left, secular spiritualism.

THE LEGACY OF THE NOVEL

Werther*'s shared history with American Evangelicalism*
Many recent books have explored the influence of Evangelicalism upon the formation of contemporary American politics and culture. If we now revisit some of the characteristics of Pietism within the American sphere, we can begin to see how the same elements that Goethe questioned within *Werther* are important factors in the American religious and cultural scene. Thus, although it would be difficult to trace any direct influence of the novel upon contemporary Evangelicals, their shared values and heritage with eighteenth-century Pietists draw our attention to those elements that Goethe criticized in his novel. Pietism and American Evangelicalism are, of course, related. German Pietism represents one of the several strands that have formed American Evangelicalism (Sweeney 33–6; Collins 91). In his work on the connection between modernity and Evangelicalism, Hunter defines the latter according to several key tenets:

> At the doctrinal core, contemporary Evangelicals can be identified by their adherence to 1) the belief that the Bible is the inerrant Word of God, 2) the belief in the divinity of Christ, and 3) the belief in the efficacy of Christ's life, death, and physical resurrection for the salvation of the human soul. Behaviorally, Evangelicals are typically characterized by an individuated and experiential orientation toward spiritual salvation and religiosity in general and by the conviction of the necessity of actively attempting to proselytize all nonbelievers to the tenets of the Evangelical belief system. (7)

Pietists and Evangelicals both believe that individuals have a personal and emotional connection to God, and both believe in the necessity of converting nonbelievers to their way of worshipping. Most importantly both are anti-intellectual and anti-hierarchical, and book learning is de-emphasized by both groups. Both seek God not through the structures of a religious authority, but through personal relationships with God. While their emphasis upon the Bible may seem to belie such an assertion, it is one's personal connection to the Bible that is most at stake in being "born again." In other words, education or traditional rules do not bring one closer to God, but may indeed, according to its adherents, have a negative influence. As the scholar Collins, a self-identified member of an Evangelical Church, observes, if one places too much emphasis upon the intellect in religion, "then some of the richest wisdom of the gospel will be left unappreciated" (90).

Evangelical movements in respect to their rejection of authority are squarely in the liberal side in that they do not believe in turning to standards of knowledge or tradition to establish a relationship with the divine. For example, Sweeney, a self-professed Evangelical, describes a central tenet of Puritanism as being anti-intellectual in this sense: "[Puritans] taught that a sermon is not an occasion for the display of human learning . . . Puritans promoted what they called experimental religion or experiential Christianity, arguing that authentic, saving faith is first and foremost an affair of the heart. It cannot be inherited from one's parents or imposed on people from above. It requires an inward transformation, a real relationship with Christ" (31).[50] Thus, while Evangelicals believe in some universal principles, their outward stance toward book learning and hierarchy is very much akin to a liberal, value-based system. They have historically rejected the imposition of laws or knowledge from the outside as well as an elevated understanding of the clergy.

The link between American Evangelicalism and democracy is a strong one. What began as a rejection of Church hierarchy and customs soon expanded, as the eighteenth-century German authorities had feared, to more secular concerns of politics and social mores. As Tocqueville, that astute observer of nineteenth-century America, noted:

[50] Strikingly, these sentiments echo those of Emerson, who wrote in his journal on September 21, 1838: "Do not believe the past. You think in your idle hours that there is literature, history, science behind you so accumulated as to exhaust thought and prescribe your own future. In your sane hour, you shall see that not a line has yet been written; that for all the poetry that is in the world your first sensation on entering a wood or standing on the shore of a lake has not been chanted yet. It remains for you; so does all thought, all object, all life remain unwritten still."

> The greatest part of British America was peopled by men who, after having
> shaken off the authority of the Pope acknowledged no other religious supremacy:
> they brought with them into the New World a form of Christianity which I
> cannot better describe than by styling it a democratic and republican religion.
> This contributed powerfully to the establishment of a republic and democracy
> in public affairs; and from the beginning, politics and religion contracted an
> alliance which has never been dissolved. (1: 311)

Tocqueville goes on to remark how the individualized form of religion
contributes to the overall freedom of the country. Democracy and the
freedom to worship according to individualized preferences go hand
in hand (1: 314).

Tocqueville, while having many things to say in praise of American
democracy, also warns against certain propensities, including a destruction of community, a devaluation of the arts and letters, and valuing
equality more than liberty. Goethe's novel, too, warns of such dangers.
Like Tocqueville, *Werther* extols many aspects of the new democratizing
society, but at the same time portrays some of its negative consequences.
Here again, Goethe's principle of compensation serves to illustrate
that gains always have costs and consequences. While Tocqueville
himself admired much of the American spirit and democracy, he did
worry about what would happen to those aspects of society that were
traditionally supported by more aristocratically based societies: the arts,
literature, and speculative philosophy. He predicts that one day "faith
in public opinion will become for [Americans] a species of religion,
and the majority its ministering prophet" (1: 12). His greatest concern,
however, was that Americans were more enamored with equality than
liberty: "for equality their passion is ardent, insatiable, incessant, invin-
cible; they call for equality in freedom; and if they cannot obtain that,
they still call for equality in slavery. They will endure poverty, servitude,
barbarism, but they will not endure aristocracy" (1: 102–3).

For Tocqueville, the term "aristocracy" is not limited to the political sphere, but is to be broadly understood as a society that values
the merits (including education) and accomplishments of some
people over others. If we turn to Nathan Hatch's excellent book,
The Democratization of American Christianity, he outlines in detail what
some of these democratic tendencies might mean. Like Tocqueville,
Hatch argues that American democratic forms and Evangelicalism
are inextricable. Evangelicalism flourished in America at the time of
its founding precisely because of the Americans' democratic spirit.
He argues that fiercely democratic, populist, and anti-intellectual

forces have always been dominant in American Protestant religions: "Religious populism, reflecting the passions of ordinary people and the charisma of democratic movement-builders, remains among the oldest and deepest impulses in American life" (5). Similarly, "respect for authority, tradition, station and education eroded" (6).[51] Nor was this movement's anti-authoritarian and anti-intellectual thrust limited to the sphere of religion. We can see how far the group went in its distrust of authority by its treatment of the learned professions. The professions of law and medicine were fiercely attacked. The newly liberated American assumed that people with the most common abilities could judge right and wrong on their own and that they would fare better by turning to folk remedies than to more scientific ones (Hatch 27–30). It was therefore not only the non-useful arts that were discounted, but educated professions in general.

Of course, Hatch here is discussing trends in early America, but are such stances, after all, so distant from today? In the 2008 Democratic primary, a major focus was the supposed elitism of the two candidates. Barack Obama's education, elevated discourse, and accomplishments were often seen as negative qualities. His main appeal, moreover, has been in his success in portraying himself as an agent of change against the establishment. Hillary Clinton, in turn, went out of her way to portray herself as whiskey-guzzling bowling queen to counter any perceptions of her that were elitist. When Obama was caught on tape during the campaign stating that poor, small town people "cling to guns and religion," Clinton fiercely attacked him for being "elitist and divisive" and, for a time, no one knew how much the charges of elitism would hurt him. In the end, perhaps Obama's ease with the Pietist mode of confessionals, of public autobiographical statements, helped him to win the election. Zeleny and Knowlton of *The New York Times* (July 1, 2008) suggest that Obama gained Evangelical adherents, in part because he embraces their propensity to give personal witness: "He is also drawing on his own characteristics and story, including his embrace of Christianity as an adult, a facility with biblical language and imagery and comfort in talking about how his religious beliefs animate his approach to public life" (A16). John McCain, in contrast, who was raised in the more hierarchical and authority-based Episcopalian Church (although he attends the Baptist Church of his wife), has had a more difficult time relating to Evangelicals — a striking fact given that

---

[51] Hatch goes on to argue that scholars who have focused on early religious movements as conservative "have obscured the egalitarianism powerfully at work in the new nation" (5).

overall, his politics are more in tune with those that have characterized Evangelicals. He, as the *Times* notes, "does not talk much in public about religion, and Christian conservatives have been slow to embrace him" (A16).

Goethe, Emerson, and American spiritualism

The line of influence from Goethe and his *Werther* is a more direct one to trace within the sphere of American spirituality. There are many ways in which one could see today's modernisms in terms of Werther's propensities. The qualities that he values, qualities based upon a heightened sense of self, are reflected in many aspects of contemporary society. His diary bears similarities to blogs, his spirituality to American Evangelicalism as well as to New Age mysticism, and the tone of his anti-intellectualism can be found in many aspects of the American educational system. In the context of discussions of Goethe's modernity, it is interesting to take the case of Ralph Waldo Emerson.

Many recent scholars in disparate fields, from those writing about blogs to American forms of mysticism, have pointed to Emerson as a leading influence on many contemporary trends (Schmidt, Serfaty, Kripal). Kripal, for example, endorses the view that Emerson's reach extends to "that immense swath of mystical, Gnostic, and esoteric traditions that encompasses everything from the early Swedenborgians, the Mesmerists, Spiritualists, Christian Scientists, and Theosophists to the contemporary human-potential and New Age movements," including Esalen (B6). And interestingly, as scholars such as Van Cromphout have argued, Emerson considered Goethe to be one of the quintessential moderns and sources of influence for himself. He is one of the most discussed and quoted figures within Emerson's writings and was "a major factor in Emerson's long experiment with self-definition" (9). In his own journals, Emerson has several notable comments about the importance of Goethe as a modern and Goethe's influence on his own thinking: "It is to me very plain that no recent genius can work with equal effect upon mankind as Goethe, for no intelligent young man can read him without finding that his own compositions are immediately modified by his new knowledge" (Emerson Journals V: 314). Similarly, he comments upon his own views of Goethe's modernity: "Goethe is the pivotal man of the old and new times with us. He shuts up the old, he opens the new. No matter that you . . . were born since Goethe died, — if you have not read Goethe, or the Goetheans, you are an old fogy, and belong with the antediluvians" (Emerson

Journals XI: 430).[52] Emerson himself thus claims that one cannot read Goethe without being influenced by him nor can one read him without becoming a modern.

Of course, the effort to truly trace the influence of Goethe upon Emerson (as Van Cromphout has done) or Emerson's influence upon aspects of contemporary society (as Serfaty and Schmidt have done) is a long and complicated task and outside the confines of this present work. It proves quite fruitful, however, to examine some of the ways in which Emerson scholars argue for his influence on many of today's modernisms and to compare this influence against the issues that surface in *Werther*. Serfaty, for example, in her overview of online diaries and blogs, compares the popularity of such instruments globally and discovers that Americans are much more likely to write this kind of confessional literature. She credits this American propensity to Emerson's influence: "Emerson's philosophy of the individual has been shown to be essential to the development and articulation of the American construct of national identity, turning Transcendentalism into the most far-reaching intellectual movement of the nineteenth-century" (44). She further sees within Emerson's recommendation to write journals a close connection to his philosophy of self-reliance: "When contrasting conformity with self-reliance, Emerson insists on the persistence of conflict within the subject between authority, conformity and self-creation, even while affirming the need for self-creation" (45). Like Werther, Emerson charts a course of independence for the individual during which he or she challenges the most basic aspects of hierarchy and community. The individual becomes the sole measuring stick. Indeed, Emerson's prose within his "Self-Reliance," with its frequent mention of heart and sentiment, could very easily have flowed from Werther's pen. More importantly, however, Emerson's reflections on the shortcomings of society are very much in the same vein as Werther's:

> Society everywhere is in conspiracy against the manhood of every one of its members . . . Whoso would be a man must be a nonconformist . . . Nothing is at last sacred but the integrity of your own mind. Absolve you to yourself, and you shall have the suffrage of the world. I remember an answer which when quite young I was prompted to make to a valued adviser, who was wont to importune

---

[52] Scholars in the past have been prone to contend that Emerson's comments about Goethe could be harsh, but Van Cromphout has convincingly argued that the context of these comments has not been correctly taken into account.

me with the dear old doctrines of the church. On my saying, What have I to do
with the sacredness of traditions, if I live wholly from within? my friend suggested
— "But these impulses may be from below, not from above." I replied, "They do
not seem to be such; but if I am the Devil's child, I will live then from the Devil."
No law can be sacred to me but that of my nature . . . I am ashamed to think how
easily we capitulate to badges and names, to large societies and dead institutions.
(*Collected Works* 2: 29–30)

Emerson, like Werther, is proud to be a nonconformist and to follow
the sentiments of his own heart. Emerson, too, believes that society
would be a better place were it to abandon all traditions and allow individuals to foster their own beliefs. Notably, he believes that individuals
could therefore absolve themselves, just as Werther, in the end, believes
the only source of absolution resides in his own sacrifice. Serfaty, in
her analysis of the contents of blogs with their quotidian, banal topics,
claims the intellectual source in Emerson. Emerson in his American
Scholar lecture (August 31, 1837) rejoices in the fact that his age has
rediscovered the "common, the familiar, the low" and abandoned the
"sublime and the beautiful" (93).

Indeed, one could very well argue that Emerson himself has the
Sorrows of Young Werther in mind when he expresses these sentiments.
He cites Goethe as well as Goldsmith as sources for the tendency of his
own age. Not only is Goldsmith's *Vicar of Wakefield* overtly cited within
Werther (June 16, 1771), but many scholars have noted numerous
similarities between the style and content of the two works. Within his
lecture, Emerson's stance toward hierarchy and high art is clear. He
asks "not for the great, the remote, the romantic; what is doing in Italy
or Arabia; what is Greek art, or Provençal minstrelsy; I embrace the
common, I explore and sit at the feet of the familiar, the low" (93).
The leap from exalting the common and the low to the promulgation
of blogs is not a far one. Nor is it a far leap from Werther's elevation of
simple folk to Emerson's anti-intellectual sentiments. There is, however,
a great divide between Werther's wholehearted endorsement of these
sentiments and Goethe's. As I have argued above, Goethe clearly saw
the consequences of Werther's anti-intellectual views and embedded
criticisms of them within his text. Moreover, Goethe's admiration and
emulation of Classical literature and the arts are well known. He very
well included the common and low within his literary works, but would
not be one to sit at their feet alongside of Emerson.

The elevation of the individual and the common is, as argued
through much of this chapter, a characteristic of both Pietism and

Evangelical thought. Emerson's position on mysticism and spirituality, however, further sheds light on the close connection between the more "conservative" Evangelicalism and the more "liberal," mystical strains in American thought. Meditation, self-help, gurus, and yoga are all part of the more liberal, value-driven side of religious exploration. (And it is, I would argue, no coincidence that Goethe finds himself on this turf today through Emersonian channels. Yoga to the People's webpage, for example, uses a quote from Goethe for promotional purposes, as do many other secularized spiritual groups.)[53] Although scholars such as Schmidt have wished to argue that the manifestations of contemporary American spiritualism are a phenomenon quite separate from the more conservative based one of American Evangelicalism, Pietism and its influences may actually serve as a bridge between the two. Schmidt, for example, places Emerson smack in the middle of the birth of American mysticism or spirituality (29). In his *Restless Souls*, he is careful to distinguish this movement from Evangelical ones. He sees the Evangelicals as conservative in their orthodoxy while characterizing those following various mystical and spiritual schools as being freer. His descriptions of American mystics and spiritual movements, however, closely coincide with those of the Evangelicals in their stance toward hierarchy, formal learning, and traditions as a whole. Schmidt is at pains to show that the spirituality movement is at heart different from the Evangelical one because of its emphasis upon the democratic values of individualism. The irony here, however, is that both the more conservative strand (Evangelicalism) and its more liberal cousin (Spirituality)

[53] <http://www.yogatothepeople.com/stories/decisive-element.html>. Global Yoga Journeys promotes one of its hikes as a favorite of Goethe's <http://www.globalyogajourneys. com/hiking.html>. "Awakening Arts" even offers a class, "The Sacred Cycle of the Plant through Color" on the theme of Goethe's "Metamorphosis of Plants" <http://www.awakearts. com/schedule.html>. A personal revelation found on the Kripalu website, "Seekers, Then and Now," outlines the writer's journey of discovery. The author muses that where some might find their path to Yoga from "Nietzsche, Schleiermacher, and Goethe," the writer's "own awakening to the views of the strivers came first through the bold stream of *sramanism* in American spiritual life — particularly through the incandescent spiritual explorations of Emerson, Thoreau, and the Transcendentalists . . . All wisdom traditions insist upon a healthy mistrust of other people's answers — or even upon the revealed experience of others . . . The tradition of the strivers points us not backward toward ancient answers, but toward the immediacy and urgency of our own inquiry. To be heirs of the tradition of the strivers, we must each finally write our own scriptures" <http://www.kripalu.org/pdfs/kavi_book_ prologue.pdf>.

Goethe quotes appear on many yoga sites. See, for example, <http://www.edeneastyoga studio.com/yoga-info.htm>, <http://www.spiritmatters.ca/Retreats/teachers/index.html>, <http://www.stretchways.com/FifthStab5/Poems.html>, <http://pages.prodigy.net/steven malkus1/currentevents.htm>. All above sites accessed July 4, 2008.

both come to represent the true modern characteristic of valuing the individual and his or her emotions and inner life above all else, whether book learning, governmental structures, or religions based upon traditional interpretations, hierarchy, or scholarship. There are certainly important differences between the two groups. The spirituality movement, for example, is open to non-Christian influences. Yet, strikingly, Schmidt's descriptions of this movement's attempts to break away from traditions and authority mirror the sentiments of the Evangelical groups. The various strains of American spirituality "charted a path . . . away from the old 'religions of authority' into the new 'religion of the spirit'" (7).[54] Following Emerson's philosophy of self-reliance, tenets of this spiritual philosophy included "individual aspiration after mystical experience or religious feeling," "the valuing of silence, solitude, and serene meditations," and "an emphasis on creative self-expression and adventuresome seeking" (12). In this sense, Werther's background could be said to be Evangelical because of his clear Pietist inclination toward individualism, sentiment, and self-expression. By the time he comes to reject Christ as his savior, however, he veers into the territory of the spirituality movement.[55]

The close connection between modernity, Emerson, and Werther becomes more apparent if we turn again to Emerson's own words. In his 1842 speech "The Transcendentalist," he explains the core beliefs of Transcendentalism and its accompanying spirituality. Like Werther, Emerson focuses on the spiritual, subjective experiences of the individual:

> The Transcendentalist adopts the whole connection of spiritual doctrine. He believes in miracle, in the perpetual openness of the human mind to new influx of light and power; he believes in inspiration, and in ecstasy. He wishes that the spiritual principle should be suffered to demonstrate itself to the end, in all possible applications to the state of man, without the admission of anything unspiritual; that is, anything positive, dogmatic, personal. Thus, the spiritual measure of inspiration is the depth of the thought, and never, who said it? And

---

[54] Schmidt goes to great pains to distinguish the two groups, but I wonder whether they are not in the end more related than he presents. He bases much of his claim on the fact that spirituality traces its roots back to the Transcendentalists. Key members of this group (Emerson, Thoreau, Margaret Fuller), however, were extremely influenced by the German Romantic tradition which sprang in large part from the Pietist one.

[55] Kripal, for example, reads Emerson's famous July 15, 1838 Harvard Divinity School Address as an invitation "to move beyond 'historical Christianity,' an institution whose perverse mythologization of Jesus as the only divine human being and whose slavish reliance on the Bible as somehow final and complete he found particularly odious" (B6).

so he resists all attempts to palm other rules and measures on the spirit than its own. In action, he easily incurs the charge of antinomianism by his avowal that he, who has the Lawgiver, may with safety not only neglect, but even contravene every written commandment. (270)

In other words, the Transcendentalist, like the Evangelical, does not need book learning, but discovers only inner truths through his or her spiritual connection. Of course, there is marked difference between the Evangelical and Transcendental relationship to the Bible, and this certainly separates the two groups. Yet, the core beliefs — the anti-intellectualism and the focus on the individual — certainly are shared. Even the Wikipedia definition underscores these aspects of Transcendentalism: "Transcendentalism began as a protest against the general state of culture and society at the time, and in particular, the state of intellectualism at Harvard and the doctrine of the Unitarian Church which was taught at Harvard Divinity School. Among their core beliefs was an ideal spiritual state that 'transcends' the physical and empirical and is only realized through the individual's intuition, rather than through the doctrines of established religion."[56] Although American Transcendentalism fosters a greater freedom for the individual to break free of all religious traditions, the core beliefs between Transcendentalists and Evangelicals could be viewed as differing in degree rather than in quality. Emerson's quest to establish a new spiritualism was anti-hierarchical and anti-book learning. According to Schmidt, Emerson wanted to declare for religion, the "freedom from dogmatic and canonical constrictions, and the awakening of spiritual intuition and individuality" (33). Emerson in a speech to the Harvard Divinity School in 1838 even used the born-again image. One was to "throw off 'secondary knowledge'" and consider oneself "a newborn bard of the Holy Ghost" (Schmidt 33).

Hierarchy and Werther's *case against grammar*
Of course, it is noteworthy that a movement associated with conservatives has as its heart values that are traditionally liberal, but this is a sign of how much the individualism that is both touted and criticized within Werther has become ingrained in the modern psyche. The party that once prided itself on its educated gentlemen has become a party that values the strength of personal and emotional convictions — characteristics once ascribed more to the democrats and characteristics that

---

[56] Accessed June 2, 2008.

certainly are central in defining American spirituality.[57] Both conservative and liberal quests coincide with their rejection of authority as well
as ideas based upon scholarly leanings. This gradual uniting of these
once polar groups has been noticed in other contexts. David Brooks,
in his amusing analysis of Bobos (a term he uses to explain the mix
of bohemian and bourgeois values in today's society), focuses upon
precisely this aspect of modernity. The two opposing sides of liberal
thinking, former hippies and the more conservative traditionalists have
melded precisely over issues of individualism:

> The bohemian sixties and the bourgeois eighties were polar opposites in many
> ways. But they did share two fundamental values: individualism and freedom . . .
> The bohemian revolt in the sixties was about cultural freedom. It was about free
> expression, freedom of thought, sexual freedom. It was an effort to throw off
> social strictures and conformist attitudes, to escape from the stultifying effects of
> large bureaucracies and overbearing authority figures. The bourgeois resurgence
> of the 1980s, on the other hand expanded economic and political freedom. The
> economy was deregulated and privatized in order to unleash entrepreneurial
> energies . . . Even as late as 1994, the congressional Republicans swept into power
> calling themselves the Leave Us Alone Coalition. They wanted to get government
> off people's backs in order to maximize individual freedom. (260–1)[58]

Brooks finds the growing similarities of the two groups to be a positive
development. I would argue, however, that despite the economic and
social benefits that such a confluence may bring, it also has significant
drawbacks, especially in respect to education. Although I analyze
educational issues in more detail in the next chapter, the case study

---

[57] Greeley and Hout note that "Conservative Protestants are less educated than most
Americans. Seventeen percent of them have graduated from college (5 percent going on to
earn advanced degrees) compared to 64 percent of Jews (30 percent with advanced degrees),
31 percent of adults with no religion, 30 percent of Mainline Protestants, and 26 percent of
Catholics" (98).

[58] Brooks also notes that the corporate world has adopted the rules of radical individuals
(128 ff.). Ironically, he notes that for all of the anti-hierarchical lip service, "today's CEOs
tend to dominate their companies even more than those at the old corporations" (133). So
too, the more people began to be convinced that their jobs required their creativity and
appreciated their self-expression, the longer hours they were willing to work: "Companies
learn that Bobos will knock themselves out if they think they are doing it for their spiritual
selves, for their intellectual development" (136). See also Kripalu Center for Yoga's webpage
for an interesting melding of East and West. In their online bookstore, books include those
that aim at spiritual development as well as at monetary gain, including *Easy Tips for Marketing
Your Yoga Business and Business Mastery* (3rd edition) and *A Guide for Creating a Fulfilling,
Thriving Business and Keeping it Successful* <http://www.kripalu.org/shop/shop/Book/>
accessed July 4, 2008.

of grammar — especially since Werther is so outspoken against grammatical rules — provides an interesting example in the abandonment of hierarchy within education today.

It has long been the fashion in English Departments that students' opinions are more important than their ability to express them correctly. Many English teachers agree with Werther that grammar is a bore and that those who teach it perpetuate a morally corrupt hierarchy. One should care about students' ability to emote and their self-esteem rather than teach them accepted writing styles and elegant ways to express their ideas. I realize that such language on my part may seem as if I am caricaturing their position, but if one looks at the literature put out by the principal professional organization of English teachers, the National Council of Teachers of English (NCTE),[59] one will find this terminology. In 1974, this group adopted a resolution entitled, "Students' Right to Their Own Language." The title gives a fairly accurate summary of the whole. The main point of the piece is that it is "immoral" both to claim the superiority of one English dialect over another and to insist on American Standard English (or Edited American English) in coursework. Further, the piece argues that if we want to encourage our students to write interesting prose, we should convince them "that spelling, punctuation, and usage are less important than content" (9). To enforce rules of grammar and style is "destructive of the students' self-confidence" and self-esteem (15) and displays a lack of respect for diversity. Although the resolution was passed in 1974, the NCTE reaffirmed it in 2003 and still lists it on their website as one of its stances on issues of education. (It also proclaimed an edict against grammar in 1985.) Before examining this resolution in detail, it is helpful to look at the background of this council and its historical push against tradition and standards.

What is striking about the NCTE is its historical opposition to grammar and canonical texts. In many ways, the 1974 resolution cannot simply be read as a by-product or an outgrowth of 1960s anti-establishment thinking, although the movement against hierarchies in the classroom picked up steam and adherents at this time. Rather,

---

[59] The NCTE considers itself to be the "principal professional organization supporting research and teaching in the field of writing and advocating writing as a central tool for learning, thinking, and communication" <http://www.ncte.org>. It boasts 60,000 members and has been in existence for almost one hundred years. Its mission is to "promote the development of literacy, the use of language to construct personal and public worlds and to achieve full participation in society, through the learning and teaching of English and the related arts and sciences of language" (NCTE Strategic Plan 8/90).

I would suggest that such stances toward rules, grammar, and the canon arose out of the eighteenth-century views that have been discussed above: valorization of the individual above the community as well as the passions above reason. A brief overview of some of the resolutions and addresses of this organization demonstrates how standards of all kinds have been under attack for a long time. In 1913, for example, the organization "expressed the conviction that the classics were not of much value for educational purposes" and that colleges ought "to teach modern authors" (*New York Times* (*NYT*), November 30, 1913).[60] By 1928, Dr Kemp Malone of Johns Hopkins University announced to the NCTE delegates "that the teaching of English grammar has done students more harm than good" (*NYT*, December 2, 1928). Even then, the reasons were politicized and emphasized a democracy of language. Because "America is not dominated by any cultural center or standards of speech," variations in language ought to be accepted. In her 1932 presidential address, Dr Stella Center admonished teachers "to have done with the old theory that teachers should live remote in academic seclusion, preoccupied with traditions only" (*NYT*, November 24, 1932). As Ruth Mary Meeks, the former president of NCTE, summarized at that time: "To make your meaning clear — that is the secret of good punctuation, good usage, good speech and good writing. Freed by such studies . . . from the crushing load of outworn formalities, we shall perhaps have time to stimulate in our students the clarified thought from which alone a composition worth punctuating can result" (*NYT*, December 4, 1932). Content was to be weighed over the formalities. Grammar and certain types of form were seen as an oppressing force from which students needed to be liberated.

In 1938, some members of the organization were campaigning for even more radical reforms. They argued that adults were imposing too much of themselves upon children, whereas in a truly democratic spirit, the children ought to make choices about their education themselves. A Brooklyn principal contended that "adult rules and standards have been imposed on the younger generation, resulting in a resentful attitude toward the subject . . . Why should you have to drill into children that this or that is really good, in literature? If they don't recognize that it's good when they read it, they won't like it ever" (*NYT*, June 30, 1938). Children, moreover, should only write essays based upon their own lives and not upon topics selected and imposed upon them by

---

[60] Authors on the "approved" list included Alexandre Dumas, Jack London, and Rudyard Kipling. What is modern one day becomes classic the next.

their adult teachers. Like Werther, who emphasizes his own childlike tastes, children according to the precepts of the NCTE do not need to be educated to achieve judgment, but are simply encouraged to follow their "natural" tastes.

These anti-rational, anti-hierarchical stances echo very much Werther's values, whether his criticisms of hierarchy, valorization of the poorly educated, or beliefs that one's opinions are more important than how one expresses them. Two hundred years after *Werther* was published, the NCTE's 1974 proclamation argued that one should not teach students Standard English or formal grammar because this is to impose a false hierarchy upon them: "The claim that any one dialect is unacceptable amounts to an attempt of one social group to exert its dominance over another. Such a claim leads to false advice for speakers and writers, and immoral advice for humans."[61] Whether to teach Standard English becomes a moral question for this influential group. They reject teaching the grammar of Standard English because to do so endorses a form of hierarchy established by the educated (and largely white) elite. To perpetuate the teaching of proper English is to perpetuate a form of hierarchical and hence "oppressive" culture.

If we now look closely at this resolution, we will see that it contains many echoes of Werther's stance toward language (de-emphasizing grammar and correct forms), emotions (valuing passions more than rationally based forms of study), and valorizing the less educated. Two main problems exist with these sentiments as expressed in the resolution. The first and main problem is that this manifesto subverts its main principle of equality. Rather than guaranteeing equal opportunity to all students regardless of their background, it ultimately limits the opportunities of poorer students. The end effect is the worst kind of pejorative and patriarchal agenda imaginable. An educated class of people (the teachers of English) has as an overt agenda to keep those students most likely not to speak Standard English — poor, minority, or immigrant students — in their current economic class by denying them the same education that they themselves have received. And rather than really valuing all dialects as equal, the very resolution admits to hierarchies of form — at least when it comes to the class to which the teachers themselves belong. Such teachers of English embrace the Wertherian rejection of rules, but as a consequence subject their students to remaining in a class beneath their own.

[61] <http://www.ncte.org/about/over/positions/category/div/114918.htm>

The second problem, and one which is related to the first, is that education by its very definition ought to be an edifying enterprise. Students should emerge from school better than they were before. They should have more skills, be more thoughtful, and be socially and intellectually enriched. Elitism in education is problematic when these elitist benefits are denied to one group because of its social, ethnic, or racial status. The authors of the document imply that we ought to reject an elitist educational system of any sort, and in the process, I would argue, they insure an elitism of the worst kind, where the already privileged have access to an education that allows them to flourish. In this way, they are also like Werther in that forms of democracy should apply to stations above their own rather than stations beneath them. A plumber, as the NCTE document's authors — condescendingly, I believe — point out, "who can sweat a joint can be forgiven confusion between 'set' and 'sat'" (14), but if we do not teach all of our students the difference, does that mean that poor and minority students should be plumbers and not lawyers, technical writers, and teachers? Should we also assume that plumbers are not well educated?

At the root of the entire document is the modern liberal stance that rejects standards, whether those of natural law or grammatical rules, as well as the liberal distrust of any hierarchy. Rules do not exist by nature, so the argument goes, but they arise because some dominant power has established them and then expects others to follow suit or be punished. The attitude of the resolution is that English professors of the world should unite and overthrow these hierarchically imposed rules that not only serve to inhibit our self-expression and discovery, but worst of all, support elite, political hierarchies: "By appealing to what is labeled 'proper,' they [handbooks on grammar and style] encourage an elitist attitude. The main values they transmit are stasis, restriction, manners, status, and imitation" (11). Grammar leads to anti-democratic, exclusionary sentiments. The teachers of English hope that their form of education will lead to equality and respect for diversity. If we allow students to speak and write the way in which they would like, everyone will be considered equal, and we will all be happy in our individual diversities. The problem here is that we are raising children to have Werther-like expectations and should therefore expect Werther-like consequences. Werther wanted to be considered equal with the higher classes, but when he was thwarted in this aim he became suicidal. These teachers of English imbibe their students with anti-hierarchical philosophies but then do not equip them to fight those hierarchies or to cope with the likely rejection that some of them will experience.

Conservatives like to point the finger at liberals when it comes to the watering down of education, and the example above about grammar coincides with their arguments against political correctness. However, as I have tried to illustrate, many of the qualities of the "me" generation come not solely from the counter-culture of the 1960s, but also from mainstream Evangelicalism whose doctrines privilege one's personal and emotive connection to God at the expense of intellectualism and education. The leap therefore is not too large from Goethe's portrayal of the modern individual to both liberal and conservative aspects of contemporary American society.

If we once again return to Werther, we recall that he, too, criticized formal education, discounted the court bureaucracy as a waste of time, and praised the more simple, uneducated people whom he encountered. He represents the type of individual who does not see the need for reason in his spiritual life. He is a stunted character because he rejects the possibility of balance. The rejection of reason in his spiritual life is reflected in several other important aspects as well. Grammatical rules thus can be dismissed because they stifle his creative juices, books can be interpreted as he pleases and used to justify whatever actions he feels like taking, and religious spirituality becomes so individualized that all possibility for community is cut off. Werther himself, upon re-reading his diary, is cognizant of the fact that he "deliberately . . . entangled" himself "step by step. To have recognized my situation so clearly, and yet to have acted like a child! Even now I see it all plainly, and yet seem to have no thought of acting more wisely" (August 8, 1771).[62] Werther is not lacking in the ability to reason or to evaluate his own situation. He prefers to remain as a child and to valorize his heart as sick (May 13, 1771). If we return to the budget metaphor from the Introduction, Werther has placed all of his resources into one side of his personality at the expense of the other. If Faust represents the cold and calculating side of human capacities and what can go wrong if that side overrides one's passionate, creative side, then in Werther we have the opposite pathology.

So, too, when we consider Werther's relationship to art and letters, can we see how his exaggerated sense of self leads to the deterioration of both. His emotions leave him in such a state that he can no longer

---

[62] Ich bin erstaunt wie ich so wissentlich in das alles Schritt vor Schritt hinein gegangen bin! Wie ich über meinen Zustand immer so klar gesehen und doch gehandelt habe wie ein Kind, jetzt noch so klar sehe, und es noch keinen Anschein zur Besserung hat. (FA 1, 8: 89)

draw, paint, or ultimately even speak for himself. Indeed, while the body of the work, with its beautiful writing and intense emotions, makes the case for what a passionate individual could accomplish, the structure of the whole framework — that of an editor — makes clear the shortcomings of the same. We would never have had the *Sorrows of Young Werther* but for the contributions of a more traditional-minded editor who provides what Werther's passion and self-absorption have lacked: a perspective outside of one's self, an appreciation for the damage that a self-absorbed individual can do to himself and others, and most importantly, a work of art that ultimately transcends that individual. And while Werther's condemnation of grammar begins to point to the dangers of educational systems based upon individualistic values, Goethe's *Wilhelm Meister* novels paint a more complete, if complex picture, of the issues surrounding modern, progressive education.

Chapter 3

WILHELM MEISTER AND PROGRESSIVE EDUCATION

The central topics of Goethe's novels, *Wilhelm Meister's Apprenticeship* and *Wilhelm Meister's Journeyman Years*, revolve around education. The titles of both also play with the notion of a particular type of education, that of a medieval guildsman. Even the last name of the hero refers back to this extremely hierarchical tradition: his name means "master," as in "master craftsman." Wilhelm's "apprenticeship" and his "journeyman years" refer to the efforts and progress that he makes navigating through a slew of conflicts, especially that between commerce and the arts. He begins the novels desiring to be an actor and ends them as a trained surgeon. The term *Bildungsroman*, meaning a novel of formation, self-education, or personal development, is generally considered to have been coined as a means of characterizing the *Apprenticeship*.[1]

In broad terms, the novels deal with the educational experiences of the protagonist as he matures, learns to care for his son, Felix, and sets out to select and be trained in an appropriate career. I say broad terms because, as in many of Goethe's works, there is a great deal of scholarly disagreement about the main themes and topics as well as about Goethe's position toward the issues presented.[2] Should educa-

---

[1] Ammerlahn notes, however, in the last 50 years "a scholarly debate has revolved around the previously canonical claim that *Wilhelm Meisters Lehrjahre* is a 'Bildungsroman'" (26). Ammerlahn argues, in contrast to these critics, that the novel is a "Bildungsromans eines Dichters."

[2] As in the other works that have been discussed, critics are once again divided about the main interpretive threads of the novels. Are they written to support conservative notions of family, political structures, religious values, and capitalism or the very opposite? For an overview of the history of *Wilhelm Meister's Apprenticeship*, see Curran and also Ammerlahn (25–7); for that of the *Journeyman Years*, see Bahr. In his interpretation,

tion be an elitist enterprise or a democratic one? Are the educational policies, for example, espoused by the "Pedagogical Province," the school where Wilhelm sends Felix, upheld or criticized? What makes the novels, especially the latter one, quite challenging to study is their unusual structure: letters, diaries, and aphorisms are inserted some- times seemingly at whim.[3] Mysteries are presented and never solved. Characters have strange, mystical relationships with the solar system as well as with minerals in the ground. Fairy tales are presented as reality, and religious tales are re-enacted faithfully but are done so in a completely secular light. How are readers to balance the advantages and disadvantages of the educational options presented to them when even a narrative structure is hard, at times, to discern?

While it is admittedly difficult to sort through the levels of irony and complexity,[4] I would argue that as in the case of the other works

---

Lukács, for example, sees the *Apprenticeship* as an indictment against both capitalism and the bourgeoisie: "the criticism of the bourgeoisie in this work is not only a criticism of a specifically German pettiness and narrowness but also a criticism of the capitalist division of labor, the all too intensive specialization of man and the fragmentation of man through the division of labor . . . the humanist social criticism is aimed not only at the capitalistic division of labor, but also at the constriction and deformation of human nature due to all constraints resulting from the existence and consciousness of social rank" (52–3). Blessin, in contrast, does not see the *Wilhelm Meister* novels as being critical of machine production (308–10).

[3] Many critics of both novels, from the time of their publication to today, have touted them as modern texts *par excellence*, primarily because they have a very loose narrative structure, they provide conflicting perspectives on a variety of topics, and because of their use of irony. For many postmodern critics, the style of Goethe's novels endorses a view of nihilism, where ultimately no message or meaning is to be gathered. Blessin, for example, argues that Goethe himself was not aware of the multiple strands of this work and that they only emerged in the wake of twentieth-century literary theory. It was thus not Goethe's plan to write such a complex text (124). Schutjer turns to the example of the Beautiful Soul to argue that Wilhelm learns "to sustain multiple perspectives on a person at once" (153). While arguing for a tension between conservative and liberalizing impulses in the novel, Schutjer, in the end, gives a nod to a more conservative reading of the whole in which democratic principles are questioned and the strength of the family reaffirmed (160–2). Such interpretations are in stark contrast to that of Staiger, who argues that Wilhelm constantly fluctuates between the realms of experience and idea — a sense of flux that gives the entire novel an organic structure (135).

[4] The leading German Romantic of the time, Friedrich Schlegel (1772–1829), for instance, proclaimed the first of the two novels, *Wilhelm Meister's Apprenticeship*, along with the French Revolution as one of the "greatest tendencies of the age" (*Athenaeum Fragments*). According to Schlegel, instead of having a narrative structure, the novel contains many "conversations" about the characters, but these conversations prevent the reader from "one-sidedness" because the perspective is constantly changing as the speaker changes ("On Goethe's Meister" 283). Similarly, critics today focus on the loose ends of its structure. As Curran notes: "*Wilhelm Meister's Apprenticeship* does not offer solutions, it presents life in the raw, with all its loose threads, all its unfinished business, all its changing facets, and Goethe found it easier to show these through the strivings of an indecisive and sometimes irresponsible dreamer, than by

examined so far, the principle of compensation helps us to see how ideas and perspectives compete for dominance. As one educational philosophy is pitted against another in the *Wilhelm Meister* novels, we quite literally see the dynamics of compensation in action. What should an individual do if his or her career inclinations run counter to family expectations or even against his or her own talents and abilities? What effect does a bad education have on modern endeavors, whether capitalist or aesthetic? What role should a liberal education play in a person's life? How should one weigh a hierarchical form of education against the desires of the individual?

This chapter has four main parts. The first provides a context and overview of contemporary educational debates. The second examines *Wilhelm Meister's Apprenticeship* and the educational examples it presents. The third critically compares these literary models with contemporary ones. The fourth explores a hybrid solution within the context of the *Journeyman Years*. By analyzing both novels against the backdrop of current educational disputes, I argue that while they anticipate many of our pedagogical approaches, we have also adopted those that they most warn against and have rejected those they present as the most central to human and national flourishing. By applying the examples of the novels to current educational patterns, we will see how contemporary approaches — advocated from either the left or the right — encourage ever-narrowing educational possibilities to the detriment of both individuals and society.

choosing to create a stable, mature, exemplary young man" (312). As an interesting point of comparison, Carlyle makes the very opposite point in his reading of the novel: "Here the ardent high-aspiring youth has grown into the calmest man, yet with increase and not loss of ardour, and with aspirations higher as well as clearer. For he has conquered his unbelief; the Ideal has been built on the Actual; no longer floats vaguely in darkness and regions of dreams, but rests in light, on the firm ground of human interest and business, as in its true scene, on its true basis" (Goethe 1: 231). While the sequel to *Wilhelm Meister's Apprenticeship*, *Wilhelm Meister's Journeyman Years*, was not valued as highly by the critics when it was first published, it, too, has largely been read as a prototypical modern text, i.e., one that does not have a center, closure, a real narrative structure or even a main character. Critics today read the novel as a "seminal text for the 'disappearance — or death — of the author,'" (Bahr xv). Bahr, for instance, claims the book prefigures Joyce's *Ulysses* as the first truly modern text because of its multiple perspectives and authorial voices (diary, letter, fairy tales, aphorisms, etc.), its "instability of discourse and the avoidance of closure" (97). See also Muenzer and Bennett.

Goethe's novels explore several different pedagogical models. Extreme student-centered versions of education (where student desires are considered paramount) are defended alongside extraordinarily hierarchical forms of education (where those in a position of authority seek to control what is taught and how). Simultaneously, the reader is exposed time and again to the weaknesses of each of these approaches. Goethe is very much aware in his engagement with the two main conflicting pedagogical models that each is based upon very different views of human nature. In his day, many of his contemporaries were abandoning teacher-centered models and instead were embracing more Rousseauian ones where the students and their desires were placed in the center. A brief overview of the history of these views helps to clarify why the lines between the two camps are so sharply drawn.

Pedagogy and human nature: Aristotle and Rousseau
The followers of a teacher-centered methodology implicitly believe on some level in classical notions of education and childhood. According to these principles, education does not come easy, but is the result of practice, hard work, correction, challenges, and properly ingrained habits. The Greeks believed that one had to train both the mind and the body through vigorous exercises to achieve an ideal. Nature alone was not sufficient but had to be carefully guided, trained, and controlled. The image of pruning comes up frequently in Classical works that address education. Nature, if allowed to run its own course, often runs too wild for its own good. As Aristotle explains in his *Nicomachean Ethics* when he compares the vice of profligacy to the inclinations of children:

> The words profligacy or wantonness we also apply to the naughtiness of children, which has some resemblance to the licentiousness of adults . . . The metaphor appears apt enough, since it is that which desires what is disgraceful and whose appetites grow apace that needs chastisement or pruning, and this description applies in the fullest degree to desire, as it does in the child. For children, like profligates, live at the prompting of desire; and the appetite for pleasure is strongest in childhood, so that if it be not disciplined and made obedient to authority, it will make great headway. In an irrational being the appetite for pleasure is insatiable and undiscriminating, and the innate tendency is fostered by active gratification; indeed if such gratification be great and intense it actually overpowers the reason. Hence our indulgences should be moderate and few, and never opposed to principle — this is what we mean by 'well-disciplined' and

'chastened' —; and the appetitive part of us should be ruled by principle, just as
a boy should live in obedience to his tutor. (1119b, 1–15)

Aristotle is seeking to establish several different principles in this passage. Children, if unguided, are (to adapt a phrase from Hobbes) nasty,
brutish, and short. For Aristotle, the problem lies not with desire, as
one needs to have desires if one wants to learn, be a good citizen, or be
happy. Problems arise when desires are allowed to run unchecked by
reason. Desire alone, according to Aristotle, will not necessarily lead us
to make the right choices about our happiness or well-being. The desires
of children need to be carefully pruned so that they can learn what
is appropriate and what is not. In essence, we need to be able to have
reason rule over the passions just as a tutor should rule over his pupil.
The goal is to instruct, control, and discipline nature so that it better
serves our ultimate needs. Children are not assumed to be born perfect,
but rather they must be cultivated to achieve their highest potential.

In student-centered classrooms, the opposite philosophy rules.
Society is that which is corrupt, not the natural state of one's desires.
Rather than seeking to diminish student desire, teachers are to be
ruled by it and should try to use it to keep students interested. In this
model, teachers are dethroned from their position of authority and
the power is given to the students. Students are not considered passive
receptacles of knowledge, but rather as their own teachers. Rousseau
is the philosopher *par excellence* of such methods as the very first lines
of his educational tome, *Emile or On Education* (1762), demonstrate.
Here he directly argues against the Classical imagery of pruning and
declares it monstrous and deforming:

> Everything is good as it leaves the hands of the Author of things; everything
> degenerates in the hands of man. He forces one soil to nourish the products
> of another, one tree to bear the fruit of another. He mixes and confuses the
> climates, the elements, the seasons. He mutilates his dog, his horse, his slave.
> He turns everything upside down; he disfigures everything; he loves deformity,
> monsters. He wants nothing as nature made it, not even man; for him, man must
> be trained like a school horse; man must be fashioned in keeping with his fancy
> like a tree in his garden. (37)

Much of Rousseau's work on education is taken as a handbook on
how to raise children so that they are denatured as little as possible.[5]

---

[5] Rousseau's philosophy is quite complicated, and a close reading of his texts often serves

His book was enormously influential throughout Europe, where it was touted by such educational reformers as Johann Heinrich Pestalozzi (1746–1827) and Johann Bernhard Basedow (1724–1790). Even today's Montessori and Waldorf schools take much of their underlying pedagogical philosophy from Rousseau.

The relevance of these two differing philosophies of education goes well beyond certain specialized schools. Our entire educational system could be characterized today as swinging between these two philosophies, i.e., between progressive, non-hierarchically-based notions of education and ones that emphasize the role of the teacher and the measurable end product. A brief overview of how both are manifested in today's school systems will set the stage for Goethe's prescient criticisms of each as well as his portrayal for a possible hybrid solution.

Teacher-centered versus student-centered models today

We already saw in the last chapter one extreme form of student-centered education. The push to allow students the right to their own language is part of a much broader trend in contemporary educational methodologies, a trend that is rooted in extreme notions of democracy and one that is highly prevalent today, although it has been recently under attack through initiatives like NCLB. Student-centered models in the USA — which are also called progressive, collaborative, communicative, anti-intellectualist, transformative, informal, or democratic — were heavily influenced by the philosophy of Rousseau, the educational reforms of John Dewey, and the progressive ideals of the 1960s.[6] In student-centered models, students are placed in the driver seat. They work in groups to try to teach one another collaboratively, their interests are much more likely to determine the subject matter, and they are often even encouraged to grade their own work. Imagination, innovation, and creativity are highly prized in such classrooms. The subject matter itself generally mirrors the democratic approach. High culture is de-emphasized, and everyday aspects and life experiences take precedence. Thus, in composition courses, students are more likely to be asked to write opinion papers about local topics of interest rather than to analyze literary texts. Similarly, in foreign language classes, instruction focuses more upon oral communication (and hence

---

to provide alternative interpretations to his work. My use of him here, therefore, refers more to the general way in which his works have been traditionally read. See, for example, Bloom's introduction to his translation of *Emile.*

[6] For an excellent discussion of the historical background of the development of student-centered education, see Chall and also Rivers (esp. 65 ff.).

upon the vocabulary of the everyday) than upon reading literature. In student-centered classes, effort often matters more than learning facts or principles. The process is more valued than the product. Students may earn credit for trying even if they do not learn the material; sometimes it is nearly impossible for them to fail a course "if they have tried." The last chapter examined some of the consequences of this type of instruction.

The student-centered method contrasts sharply with that of a teacher-centered one. This method is also called traditional, old-fashioned, classic, aristocratic, standard, intellectualist, mimetic, or autocratic. As one can imagine, how one labels each of these methodologies depends upon one's stance toward them. In teacher-centered models, the emphasis is upon the end product of education. It does not matter so much whether students have made a good-hearted effort; what matters instead is whether they have learned specific things. If students do not know the material, they fail. Teacher-centered education is what most of us think of when we think of the traditional classroom dynamic. The teacher is in charge, whether he or she is lecturing, instructing, grading, or disciplining the students. It is a hierarchical model in that the underlying assumption is that the teacher knows more than the student, and it is the teacher's job to teach the student discrete subject matters. The subject matter in such classrooms is more conducive toward "high culture" because these topics require more directed teaching. Knowledge of forms and structures in literature, music, or art, for example, are quite difficult to learn collaboratively. Thus, in a teacher-centered foreign language classroom, students would be more likely to practise language lessons on literary texts rather than everyday items (called realia) like magazine advertisements or soap operas. The NCLB Act is also very much in the spirit of teacher-centered models, in that what matters is the material that students know rather than their emotional or social development.

However much teacher-centered approaches have been labeled "aristocratic," we can begin to see how NCLB is fast becoming an attack on aristocratic education, traditionally understood as an educational philosophy that values both the individual and knowledge as goods in themselves, and one that values high culture as part of its mission. The philosophical underpinnings of NCLB have become so business-related that students are considered instrumentally: the end goal of education is to insure that students contribute to the nation's productivity. This emphasis is in stark contrast to earlier pedagogical goals that were concerned with the formation of well-rounded, ethical, civic-minded, critical-thinking, free-thinking, or simply happy individuals. Not only do the particular subjects that are currently tested (mathematics and the reading arts) focus upon fields most closely related to business, but the focus on the standardized tests has begun to erode the valuing of truly exceptional abilities, creativity, and imagination as well as the subjects of history, music, and the liberal arts in general. For example, computer-graded essay tests give high marks to essays written according to formulas: exceptionally creative works fail because they do not fit the formulaic models that computer programs look for. Teachers therefore have to teach students to pass tests (in other words, to write according to restrictive formulas) rather than to be excellent writers. The aim is to make everyone write competently but no one to write brilliantly. Moreover, with a growing emphasis on reading and mathematics, subjects that relate to success in the business world — and ones that can more readily be tested — there is a decided move against courses in the liberal arts, particularly music and art. This trend is especially prevalent because, as schools have to focus more of their efforts on mathematics and reading to retain federal funding, there is less time (and money) for other subjects.

In light of recent educational reforms, I would argue that we currently have three competing models of education: one student-centered and two forms of teacher-centered. Of these two latter forms, the older one is endorsed by those who believe it to be the best way to teach high culture and the liberal arts more generally. I will refer to this model as *aristocratic*. The second form, and one which reflects the modern capitalist push toward programs like NCLB, emphasizes skills for the workplace (like mathematics and reading) rather than "non-practical" subjects, i.e., the arts and the humanities. I will refer to this version of teacher-centered education as the *business model*.

The *Wilhelm Meister* novels address all three forms of education as well as the strengths and weaknesses of each. These two novels also demonstrate that the most successful form of education necessarily has to be a hybrid model that incorporates aspects of all three. One cannot give students full control of their educational paths, because they will be led easily astray by their own desires, lack of self-knowledge, and limited perspective (namely a predominantly solipsistic one). Nor can one let business concerns dominate education, because one will lose the appreciation of beauty and the arts, the facility to adapt in a dynamically changing world, and the ability to question the desirability of new science and business directions. Finally, although aristocratic forms of government were already on the wane in Goethe's time, the novels teach that we still stand to gain from an older understanding of the worth of the arts. In this sense, Goethe, much like his contemporary Tocqueville, warned that the growing democratic movement had to be tempered with some aristocratic impulses, especially in the arts and education, if it were to flourish.

For the *Apprenticeship*, Wilhelm's relationship to his close friend, the businessman Werner, not only becomes a means to track Wilhelm's dynamic education, but it also serves as a discussion point for the proper balance between the arts and commerce. For the *Journeyman Years*, the overt discussions of education, especially in respect to the Pedagogical Province, further illustrate the desirability of striking the right balance between business and the arts at the institutional level.

The first novel thus outlines the consequences of certain pedagogical methodologies for the individual. The second, in turn, examines those same issues on a larger, institutional scale. Key to both is finding the right balance among contrary pulls so that the individual emerges with as much freedom as possible while also being a productive citizen in some way.

WILHELM MEISTER'S APPRENTICESHIP

In the first novel, *Wilhelm Meister's Apprenticeship* (1795–6), we hear a great deal about the protagonist's childhood and his experiences as a young man. Wilhelm is the son of a successful merchant. From childhood on, he has felt the pull of the arts. He loves the puppet theater, writes poetry and plays, and disdains the realm of commerce. His father would like nothing more than to have his son follow in his footsteps and finds his aesthetic interests a waste of time. Early in the novel, Wilhelm plans to run away with an actress, become an actor, and found a new German national theater. Shortly before implementing this plan, he discovers evidence that his lover is having an affair and suffers a serious illness as a result. He refuses all contact with her and upon recovery, gives up all artistic endeavors and devotes himself for a time to the family mercantile concerns. During a business trip, he becomes involved with several actors, gets drawn into their company, and indeed becomes not only an author for them but also their financial backer (rather freely using his father's funds). Along the way, he takes two strange characters under his wing: an androgynous child acrobat named Mignon and a long-robed and bearded harpist. (In the end, Mignon turns out to be the daughter born from an incestuous relationship between the harpist, who at one time was a monk, and his sister.) After a short stint as an actor where Wilhelm performs the lead in *Hamlet* to acclaim (but only because his character so resembles Hamlet's that he plays himself), he discovers that his wanderings and various false starts have been overseen all along by a mysterious Tower Society, whose members are planning social and political reforms in Europe and in America. He also discovers that he has a son, Felix, by the actress whom he abandoned. At the novel's end, he leaves his acting ambitions behind and is to marry Natalie, a paragon of feminine virtue, successful educator, and the sister of one of the aristocratic members of the Tower Society.

In the *Apprenticeship*, we are presented with three opposing views of education: student-centered (Wilhelm's beginning stance), teacher-centered and business focused (Werner), and teacher-centered and aristocratic (the Abbé, Natalie, the Marchese). In many ways, the novel ultimately pits aristocratic values (honor, noble bearing, love and support of the high arts) against middle-class ones (hard work, creation of capital, family values, and a growing democratic tendency) within the context of educational principles.

The arts versus commerce

One of Wilhelm's most important relationships throughout the *Apprenticeship* is with Werner, the son of his father's business partner. What is notable about their friendship is that it illustrates the desirability of equilibrium in one's life as well as the consequences when it is not achieved. Wilhelm begins the novel in an imbalanced state. He values the arts but not commerce. His friend, Werner, in contrast, initially sees the value of both commerce and the liberal arts. By the end, however, they wind up in opposing states, Wilhelm with a balanced perspective and Werner with a completely imbalanced one. By studying these contrasts, the novel illustrates that there is nothing inherently wrong with having either an artistic or a commercial bent. Both are necessary for a society to flourish to the fullest. The problems arise if education does not serve to balance those inclinations against others or at least to recognize the need to have both.

Early in the novel, when Wilhelm and Werner frequently interact, the narrator characterizes their relationship according to the principle of compensation. Each is imbalanced in a particular way. Wilhelm is too enthusiastic, while Werner too coolly rational. Once Wilhelm decides upon a project with his heart, he cannot tolerate any rational argument against it. As a boy, Wilhelm put on puppet productions; Werner profited monetarily from them by providing the necessary materials. Wilhelm believes (much like Werther) that whatever he emotively feels is right.[7] For example, he does not learn from the failure of his dramatic, childhood productions. Although he is mortified as a child when he invites an audience for a play for which he has neglected to write a script or to rehearse, as an adult he still believes that his enthusiasm will be enough to enable him to reform the German stage. Werner, in contrast, suffers from the opposite fault. By the end of the novel, he sees the whole world through the rational, calculating realm of business, where almost every endeavor is measured by the profits that are to be accrued.

Notably, the friendship of the two men, when frequently together, serves to soften their extremes:

> Werner was one of those who, having settled into a particular mode of existence, are usually taken to be cold, because they never flare up quickly or visibly. His relationship with Wilhelm was one of continual conflict, which, however, brought them ever closer together, for despite their different attitudes, *each of them profited by the other*. Werner gave himself credit for being able to restrain in some degree Wilhelm's lively, but occasionally over-enthusiastic, spirit, and Wilhelm, for his part, had a sense of real triumph when in the heat of his emotion he was able to carry his sober-minded friend with him. The one tried himself out on the other, they saw each other almost every day, and one could have said that their desire to discover each other through their conversations was only increased by the impossibility of making themselves mutually understood. Basically, however, they were both good men, and both working toward the same goal, separately and together, and yet never able to understand why the one could not reduce the other to his way of thinking. (emphasis added, 9: 32)[8]

---

[7] For a comparison of Werther and Wilhelm in terms or their respective relationship to art, see von Molnár.

[8] Werner war einer von den geprüften, in ihrem Dasein bestimmten Leuten, die man gewöhnlich kalte Leute zu nennen pflegt, weil sie bei Anlässen weder schnell noch sichtlich auflodern; auch war sein Umgang mit Wilhelmen ein anhaltender Zwist, wodurch sich ihre Liebe aber nur desto fester knüpfte: denn ungeachtet ihrer verschiedenen Denkungsart fand jeder seine Rechnung bei dem andern. Werner tat sich darauf etwas zugute, daß er dem vortrefflichen, obgleich gelegentlich ausschweifenden Geist Wilhelms mitunter Zügel und Gebiß anzulegen schien, und Wilhelm fühlte oft einen herrlichen Triumph, wenn er seinen bedächtlichen Freund in warmer Aufwallung mit sich fortnahm. So übte sich einer an dem andern, sie wurden gewohnt sich täglich zu sehen, und man hätte sagen sollen, das Verlangen einander zu finden, sich mit einander zu besprechen, sei durch die Unmöglichkeit, einander verständlich zu werden, vermehrt worden. Im Grunde aber gingen sie doch, weil sie beide gute Menschen waren, neben einander, mit einander nach Einem Ziel, und konnten niemals

The nature of their friendship is one of opposites, and although each makes some headway with the other, neither ever believes that he has been completely successful because each believes that he is right in his own extreme view. The right balance, as the narrator leads us to understand, lies somewhere in the middle. One of the lines of progression for this novel becomes the process of how Wilhelm finds equilibrium from within himself as opposed to finding it in reaction to others. By the novel's end, not only has he realized the usefulness and experience-broadening aspects of business, but he also wishes to do something practical himself without, however, abandoning his appreciation for the arts. His education ultimately serves to find a dynamic balance between the aristocratic realm of art and the more practical world of business. Werner's endpoint, however, is quite different from Wilhelm's. Once Wilhelm's countervailing influence is gone, Werner becomes totally consumed with business and even more limited than before.

One can perhaps best track the changes in both men and their progress and regress by analyzing one of the novel's most important recurring images: the personified and contrasting visual images of commerce and art. As an adolescent, Wilhelm writes a poem in which he portrays the beautiful goddess of theater trumping a pathetic, miserly image of commerce:

I remember writing a poem . . . in which the Muse of Tragedy and another female figure representing Commerce were struggling for possession of my worthy self . . . How timid was my portrayal of the old housewife with her keys and distaff, spectacles on her nose, always busy and bustling, quarrelsome and domestic, petty and pompous! How pitiful my account of those who had to submit to her and perform their menial duties in the sweat of the brow.

And how different the other figure! What a vision for an oppressed spirit! Noble of stature, she was in every ounce of her being and behavior the true daughter of freedom. Her sense of herself gave her dignity and pride. Her garments suited her perfectly, the wide folds of her dress moved like echoes of the graceful movements of a divine creature. What a contrast between the two! . . . The altercations between these two females were heated, their speeches, in the usual black-and-white of a fourteen-year-old, suitably contrasted. The old woman talked like one who had to pick up and save every pin, and the other as though she were distributing kingdoms. The warnings and threats of the old woman were treated with scorn; I turned my back on the riches she promised me, and

begreifen, warum denn keiner den andern auf seine Gesinnung reduzieren könne. (FA 1, 9: 413) naked and disinherited, I gave myself to the muse who lent me her golden veil to cover my nakedness. (9: 15)[9]

References to this poem arise at least four different times: 1) when Wilhelm rather proudly tells his lover, the actress Marianne, about the poem; 2) when the reader hears Werner's assessment of it; 3) when Wilhelm realizes his childish mischaracterization of both the arts and commerce within it; and 4) when Werner is depicted in a manner reminiscent of the goddess of commerce.

Although Wilhelm makes a gesture to distance himself from the poem of his youth (calling it "the black and white" perspective of a fourteen-year-old), he is still nevertheless quite self-satisfied with the point of view expressed in it. He tells the story in part to show his long-term commitment to the arts and to fortify his own convictions to join the theater now as an adult. The fact that he plans to found a new national theater (although he has at this point never profession-ally acted a day in his life or been in any way part of a theater), echoes his childish enthusiasm and the failed puppet theater. Now, as in his adolescence, he does not want to give business any credit and sees all of the advantages on the side of the arts, which, he believes, can spring up on their own without attention to the more practical side of things.

---

[9] Ich erinnere mich noch eines Gedichtes, das sich unter meinen Papieren finden muß, in welchem die Muse der tragischen Dichtkunst und eine andere Frauengestalt, in der ich das Gewerbe personifiziert hatte, sich um meine werte Person recht wacker zanken. Die Erfindung ist gemein, und ich erinnere mich nicht, ob die Verse etwas taugen; aber Ihr sollt es sehen, um der Furcht, des Abscheues, der Liebe und der Leidenschaft willen, die darin herrschen. Wie ängstlich hatte ich die alte Hausmutter geschildert mit dem Rocken im Gürtel, mit Schlüsseln an der Seite, Brillen auf der Nase, immer fleißig, immer in Unruhe, zänkisch und haushältisch, kleinlich und beschwerlich! Wie kümmerlich beschrieb ich den Zustand dessen, der sich unter ihrer Rute bücken und sein knechtisches Tagewerk im Schweiße des Angesichtes verdienen sollte!

Wie anders trat jene dagegen auf! Welche Erscheinung ward sie dem bekümmerten Herzen! Herrlich gebildet, in ihrem Wesen und Betragen als eine Tochter der Freiheit anzusehen. Das Gefühl ihrer selbst gab ihr Würde ohne Stolz; ihre Kleider ziemten ihr, sie umhüllten jedes Glied, ohne es zu zwängen, und die reichlichen Falten des Stoffes wiederholten, wie ein tausendfaches Echo, die reizenden Bewegungen der Göttlichen. Welch ein Kontrast! Und auf welche Seite sich mein Herz wandte, kannst du leicht denken. Auch war nichts vergessen, um meine Muse kenntlich zu machen. Kronen und Dolche, Ketten und Masken, wie sie mir meine Vorgänger überliefert hatten, waren ihr auch hier zugeteilt. Der Wettstreit war heftig, die Reden beider Personen kontrastierten gehörig, da man im vierzehnten Jahre gewöhnlich das Schwarze und Weiße recht nah an einander zu malen pflegt. Die Alte redete, wie es einer Person geziemt, die eine Stecknadel aufhebt, und jene, wie eine, die Königreiche verschenkt. Die warnenden Drohungen der Alten wurden verschmäht; ich sah die mir versprochenen Reichtümer schon mit dem Rücken an: enterbt und nackt übergab ich mich der Muse, die mir ihren goldnen Schleier zuwarf und meine Blöße bedeckte. (FA 1, 9: 383–4)

Wilhelm, thus, is very one-sided, and according to Goethe's theory of compensation, this one-sidedness limits the freedom of his choices and actions. Wilhelm's blunders through most of the novel (from his false conclusion about his lover's infidelity to his unfounded belief in his own acting ability) stem from a passionate nature that he has not yet learned to check with his more rational or practical side. In essence, Wilhelm cripples his own opportunities and delays the beginning of his real life by unreflectively following his childhood dreams. Had he trusted the right people, listened to their sage advice, and reflected more upon his own shortcomings and those of others, he would have attained much earlier the place of enlightenment that he finally achieves. Of course, it is through the experience of these blunderings that he eventually learns, but it is important to keep in mind that even while he is learning from his experiences, they are not occurring haphazardly. The Tower Society has been carefully monitoring his every action and preventing him from going too far astray. Thus, while his passions and the experience that he gains by following them give him a significant part of his education, the Tower Society serves as a reminder that all could have ended quite differently but for their checks on Wilhelm's decisions.

The poem cited above serves not only as a window to Wilhelm's soul, but also to that of his friend, Werner. At this point in the novel, Werner shows a much broader perspective on the world than Wilhelm. His comments on the poem even begin in a measured way when he finds the "verses pretty enough," and he gives good advice when he tells Wilhelm to travel as a means of expanding his mind. His comments also caricature the perspective of a businessman and point to some of the exaggerated tendencies that will evolve as he grows older and is away from Wilhelm's influence:

> I well remember your personification of commerce as a miserable, shriveled up old witch. You must have filched that portrait from some old junk shop. At the time you had no idea what the world of business is really like. The mind of a true businessman is more wide-ranging than that of all other men — has to be so. What an overview we gain by the orderly fashion in which we conduct business. It permits us to survey the whole without being confused by the parts. What tremendous advantages accrue to the businessman by double bookkeeping. This is one of the finest inventions of the human mind, and every serious manager should introduce it into his business. (9: 18) [10]

[10] Ich erinnere mich noch deines personifizierten Gewerbes, deiner zusammenge-

Werner rightly recognizes Wilhelm's tunnel vision. Wilhelm has had no experience in business and therefore does not really know what it entails or what its strengths and weaknesses really are. Wilhelm's own particular passions have resulted in a false image. However lopsided Werner's own enthusiasms for business ultimately may be, he wisely encourages education, in this case travel and interactions with a variety of different types of people, as a means of improving oneself. Werner tries to impress Wilhelm with the notion that education and experience, not blind enthusiasms, should inform one's perspective. The passage serves not only to show Wilhelm's shortcomings but Werner's as well. Double-bookkeeping is extraordinarily useful, but it is an overstatement to see it as "one of the finest inventions of the human mind." This perspective, i.e., one that weighs the benefits of business alone in evaluating the world around him, will be one that becomes more marked as Werner grows older.

Although Werner himself thus suffers from a one-sided nature, he is at least intellectually aware at this point in his life that one should strive for balance. Once Wilhelm has felt himself betrayed by his lover and decides to abandon his aesthetic side, he burns almost all of his creative writing projects and promises never to engage in the arts again. Werner calls such a position "extreme" and "insisted that it was ridiculous to abandon a talent he had exercised with pleasure and some skill . . . There were always those dull hours that could be filled up in this way, and something would gradually emerge that would give pleasure to us and to others" (9: 44).[11] In other words, although Werner places a great deal of emphasis on the life of commerce, he sees how important the liberal arts are to one's leisure life. He tries to persuade Wilhelm to reconcile the opposing forces within his soul. He

---

schrumpften erbärmlichen Sybille. Du magst das Bild in irgend einem elenden Kramladen aufgeschnappt haben. Von der Handlung hattest du damals keinen Begriff; ich wüßte nicht, wessen Geist ausgebreiteter wäre, ausgebreiteter sein müßte, als der Geist eines echten Handelsmannes. Welchen Überblick verschafft uns nicht die Ordnung, in der wir unsere Geschäfte führen! Sie läßt uns jederzeit das Ganze überschauen, ohne daß wir nötig hätten, uns durch das Einzelne verwirren zu lassen. Welche Vorteile gewährt die doppelte Buchhaltung dem Kaufmanne! Es ist eine der schönsten Erfindungen des menschlichen Geistes, und ein jeder guter Haushalter sollte sie in seiner Wirtschaft einführen. (FA 1, 9: 388–9)

[11] Werner behauptete, es sei nicht vernünftig, ein Talent, zu dem man nur einigermaßen Neigung und Geschick habe, deswegen, weil man es niemals in der größten Vollkommenheit ausüben werde, ganz aufzugeben. Es finde sich ja so manche leere Zeit, die man dadurch ausfüllen und nach und nach etwas hervorbringen könne, wodurch wir uns und andern ein Vergnügen bereiten. (FA 1, 9: 434)

would like to see Wilhelm find a moderate stance between his interests and business duties.[12]

Werner's advice about the educational nature of travel does get borne out. Wilhelm learns a great deal about life and people from his travels, especially when he tries to view the world as a businessman. We can measure how far Wilhelm has come when he himself returns to the images of his youthful poem and recognizes his own lack of perspective. In preparing a fictitious travelogue for his father's benefit, Wilhelm is surprised at how much he learns. He becomes a better observer of the world around him and understands some of his father's and Werner's earlier advice. He learns the satisfaction of attempting to "mediate commercial interests and human needs." This new-found balance in perspective even gives him pause about whether to embark on an acting career.

> "Well," he said to himself, "here you are having to choose again between those two women who haunted your thoughts when you were young. The one does not look so paltry now, and the other not so splendid as she did. An inner voice impels you to follow one or the other, and there are valid external reasons for choosing either." (9: 165)[13]

These reflections occur about halfway through the novel. Wilhelm here demonstrates that he has profited by his education and has begun to see the world in a more balanced way. The active, commercial life is not so scorned, nor is the artistic life so elevated. At this point, he has not yet reached complete equilibrium with himself but is at least thinking about it until he gets confused both by the news of his father's death and the receipt of a letter from Werner (9: 171). This letter so praises the bourgeois, commercial lifestyle that Wilhelm appears to join the troupe of actors as an act of rebellion that goes against his better judgment. However far he has already come, he still needs further enlightenment before he reaches greater equilibrium.

---

[12] Mein Freund, versetzte Werner nach einigem Nachdenken, ich habe schon oft bedauert, daß du das, was du so lebhaft fühlst, mit Gewalt aus deiner Seele zu verbannen strebst. Ich müßte mich sehr irren, wenn du nicht besser tätest, dir selbst einigermaßen nachzugeben, als dich durch die Widersprüche eines so harten Entsagens aufzureiben, und dir mit der Einen unschuldigen Freude den Genuß aller übrigen zu entziehen. (FA 1, 9: 437)

[13] Da steh ich nun, sagte er zu sich selbst, abermals am Scheidewege zwischen den beiden Frauen, die mir in meiner Jugend erschienen. Die eine sieht nicht mehr so kümmerlich aus, wie damals, und die andere nicht so prächtig. Der einen wie der andern zu folgen fühlst du eine Art von innern Beruf, und von beiden Seiten sind die äußern Anlässe stark genug; es scheint dir unmöglich dich zu entscheiden . . . (FA 1, 9: 641)

The process of Wilhelm's education is a slow one. It is only toward the end of the novel, on the day he discovers he is a parent, that he is finally ready to use his education to be a well-rounded person: "On this day, the happiest of his entire life, his own education seemed also to be beginning anew: he felt the need to inform himself, while being required to inform another" (9: 305).[14] Wilhelm has finally broken free of placing his own self and desires at the center of his educational formation, but rather has an outward goal: the concerns and well-being of another person. Such outward concerns integrate Wilhelm into society in a way new to him: "for along with the feeling of a father he had acquired the virtues of a solid citizen" (9: 307).[15] Strikingly, this revelatory moment is juxtaposed with Wilhelm's reunion with Werner. Their meeting marks the changes of both. Werner finds Wilhelm to have improved for the better — he is "taller, stronger, more upright, more cultivated in manner and more pleasant in behavior" (9: 305).[16] He even finds Wilhelm to be more restrained. Werner, in contrast, has changed in a very different, negative way. In fact, his physical description is quite reminiscent of Wilhelm's earlier portrait of commerce:

> The impression that Werner made on him was by no means so favorable. The good fellow seemed to have regressed rather than advanced. He was much thinner, his pointed face seemed sharper, and his nose longer, he was bald, his voice was loud and strident and his flat chest, drooping shoulders and pallid cheeks showed quite clearly that this was a sickly creature with a mania for work. (9: 305)[17]

Werner's physical regression mirrors his interior, spiritual one. Upon first meeting his friend after many years, Werner sees him in terms of commodity and is not bothered by his own sickly appearance because

---

[14] An diesem Tage, dem vergnügtesten seines Lebens schien auch seine eigne Bildung erst anzufangen, er fühlte die Notwendigkeit sich zu belehren, indem er zu lehren aufgefordert ward. (FA 1, 9: 877)

[15] . . . mit dem Gefühl des Vaters hatte er auch alle Tugenden eines Bürgers erworben. (FA 1, 9: 881)

[16] . . . größer, stärker, gerader, in seinem Wesen gebildeter und in seinem Betragen angenehmer geworden. (FA 1, 9: 877)

[17] Es fehlte viel, daß Werner einen gleich vorteilhaften Eindruck auf Wilhelmen gemacht haben sollte. Der gute Mann schien eher zurück als vorwärts gegangen zu sein. Er war viel magerer, als ehemals, sein spitzes Gesicht schien feiner, seine Nase länger zu sein, seine Stirn und sein Scheitel waren von Haaren entblößt, seine Stimme hell, heftig und schreiend, und seine eingedruckte Brust, seine vorfallenden Schultern, seine farblosen Wangen ließen keinen Zweifel übrig, daß ein arbeitsamer Hypochondriste gegenwärtig sei. (FA 1, 9: 877–8)

he has made a "mint of money." At one time Werner advocated involv-ing oneself with the arts as a leisure activity. He now spends every evening playing cards. The relationship of each friend to the external world has also markedly changed. Wilhelm belongs to a group who hopes to institute tax reforms to benefit a greater number of individu-als. Werner gives no thought to the duty of paying taxes or its proper social function, but only does so out of blind habit and a necessary cost of doing business, i.e., he gives no thoughts to the social benefit to others of this tax. Wilhelm's gaze has expanded to consider the well-being of others. Werner's view has contracted to become more solipsistic. Even Werner admits that Wilhelm's circuitous path in the end was profitable (10: 349).

Why have the two friends, once close, evolved in such different ways? Wilhelm's experiences throughout the novel enable him to grow as an individual and to learn to temper his selfish ways. He learns finally to see for himself the consequences of an imbalanced character. Whereas contact with Wilhelm was once a positive mediating force, Werner has now become more one-sided than ever before. It is important here to be clear. The problem is *not* that Werner engages in business. Many mem-bers of the Tower Society do so as well, and even Wilhelm has come to see that business serves as a means to an end. The problem in Werner's case is that there is no mediating or balancing force against his desire to make money. His education in this sense has failed him, and his sickly external appearance mirrors the narrowness of his point of view.

Wilhelm has succeeded in his developmental endeavors because he has learned to see himself — his virtues and his faults — in the correct perspective. In so doing, he is neither like his childish, solipsistic self, nor is he the wasted image of commerce that Werner represents. As a key member of the Tower Society, Jarno, tells Wilhelm:

> When a man makes his first entry into the world, it is good that he has a high opinion of himself, believes he can acquire many excellent qualities, and there-fore endeavors to do everything; but when his development has reached a certain stage, it is advantageous for him to lose himself in a larger whole, learn to live for others, and forget himself in dutiful activities for others. Only then will he come to know himself, for activity makes us compare ourselves with others. (9: 301)[18]

---

[18] Es ist gut, daß der Mensch, der erst in die Welt tritt, viel von sich halte, daß er sich viele Vorzüge zu erwerben denke, daß er alles möglich zu machen suche; aber wenn seine Bildung auf einem gewissen Grade steht, dann ist es vorteilhaft, wenn er sich in einer größern

The question now becomes, how does one balance in the right way the claims of commerce and the arts so that neither side becomes a caricature? In other words, how can a society that is largely focused on capitalist productivity and wealth find a balance that includes leisure and the arts? Time and again, the source for that balance is found in aristocratic virtues, albeit ones that themselves have been balanced against bourgeois counterparts. The aristocrats may be the ones who best understand the arts and traditional values, but they can only survive in the newly democratizing world if they too are willing to make changes in their views and ways of life. Thus, while the Society is founded by aristocrats by birth, they seek people of merit to join their ranks no matter what their class or birth. Their proposed colony in the New World (America) as well as communities in the Old World (Europe) will welcome anyone as long as he or she contributes in some way to the good of society. In these novels, Goethe thus experiments with a type of idealized individual who exhibits "hybrid" characteristics: love of the arts and honor inculcated through an aristocratic perspective, and love of activity and productivity gained though middle-class values.

Aristocratic education and the arts

Two characters in the novel are primarily associated with education: Natalie, Wilhelm's future wife, and the Abbé, who is the leading figure of the Tower Society and who has supervised the education of four aristocratic children, including Natalie.

Natalie believes in an openly interventionist educational system. It is also teacher-centered in the traditional sense, in that it is based upon principles that need to be applied and inculcated. It is the job of the teacher to provide that which the student lacks and to do so transparently:

> If someone does not provide help when it is needed, he will to my mind, never be of any help. If he does not come up with advice immediately, he will never provide any. It seems to me of the utmost importance to enunciate certain principles and inculcate these into children — principles that will give their lives some stability. I would almost be inclined to say that it is better to err because of principles than to do so from arbitrariness of nature, and my observation of human beings tells

Masse verlieren lernt, wenn er lernt um anderer willen zu leben, und seiner selbst in einer pflichtmäßigen Tätigkeit zu vergessen. Da lernt er erst sich selbst kennen, denn das Handeln eigentlich vergleicht uns mit andern. (FA 1, 9: 871)

me that there is always some gap in their nature which can only be filled by a principle expressly communicated to them. (9: 323)[19]

Her approach is teacher-centered in that she believes in providing hierarchically based knowledge to the students and that rather than having the students determine their course of study, the teacher should always direct it.

Natalie's pedagogical principles are based upon the principle of compensation and take into account specific deficits of her individual charges. Education is to fill whatever gaps exist in an individual. Wilhelm in choosing Natalie as his wife shows that his own education has taught him the value of her outlook, one which is based upon always supplying that which is needed. As her brother jokes (and which actually comes to pass), she will not "marry until some bride or other is missing, and you, with your customary generosity, will provide yourself as a supplement to someone's existence" (9: 346).[20] The novel provides many reasons to trust in Natalie's version of education.[21]

One possible argument against accepting Natalie's pedagogical approach is that it seems opposed to that of the Abbé, who is, after all, the mastermind of the whole Tower enterprise. On the surface, the Abbé's method gives the initial impression that he favors a student-centered approach where the individual should follow his or her own instincts.[22] A close examination of the Abbé's own words, however,

---

[19] Wer nicht im Augenblick hilft, scheint mir nie zu helfen, wer nicht im Augenblicke Rat gibt, nie zu raten. Eben so nötig scheint es mir gewisse Gesetze auszusprechen, und den Kindern einzuschärfen, die dem Leben einen gewissen Halt geben. Ja, ich möchte beinah behaupten: es sei besser nach Regeln zu irren, als zu irren, wenn uns die Willkür unserer Natur hin und her treibt, und wie ich die Menschen sehe, scheint mir in ihrer Natur immer eine Lücke zu bleiben, die nur durch ein entschieden ausgesprochenes Gesetz ausgefüllt werden kann. (FA 1, 9: 907)

[20] Ich glaube Du heiratest nicht eher, als bis einmal irgendwo eine Braut fehlt, und Du gibst Dich alsdann, nach Deiner gewohnten Gutherzigkeit, auch als Supplement irgend einer Existenz hin. (FA 1, 9: 946)

[21] Many of the other characters, especially those who are perceived in a positive light, praise her methods. Theresa and Jarno, for example, both endorse her methods and praise what emerges. The first chapter of the *Journeyman Years* further reinforces Wilhelm's allegiance to her principles. He informs the reader that he has been an integral part in creating new rules that stress external, easily teachable principles (10: 100–1).

[22] There are many ironies associated with the educational issues in the *Apprenticeship*. The Abbé, who has been supervising in large part the rather mysterious educational process of several of the characters, does not seem to be that successful. Wilhelm believes that he would have appeared less foolish had he experienced more direct intervention on the part of the Society. A closer look at the text, especially the Abbé's own words on education, however, demonstrates that his approach is not as hands-off, as student-centered as Wilhelm may believe, and that the very part of his philosophy that once allowed more student control may very well

indicates his affinity with central aspects of Natalie's pedagogical principles and places him firmly in the teacher-centered camp.

The Abbé professes a very global educational perspective in which the theory of compensation plays a central role. He particularly stresses the necessity of balancing the useful and the practical against the superfluous and the aesthetic:

> All men make up mankind and all forces together make up the world. These are often in conflict with each other, and while trying to destroy each other they are held together and reproduced by Nature. From the faintest active urge of the animal to the most highly developed activity of the mind, from the stammering delight of the child to the superlative expression of bards and orators, from the first scuffles of boys to those vast undertakings by which whole countries are defended or conquered, from the most meager desire and most fleeting attraction to the most violent passions and deepest involvements, from the clearest sense of physical presence to the dimmest intimations and hopes of distant spiritual promise — all this, and much else besides, lies in the human spirit, waiting to be developed, and not just in one of us, but in all of us. Every aptitude is significant and should be developed. One man cultivates the beautiful and another what is useful, but only the combination of both constitutes the true man. Usefulness cultivates itself, for it is cultivated by the general mass of people, and no one can do without it; but beauty must be expressly cultivated for few people embody it and many need it. (9: 339)[23]

have undergone some changes over the years as a result of his own experience. Three of the Abbé's four charges have distinct character flaws: the Countess gets lost in superstitious follies because of her superficial education, Friedrich remains largely a clown, and Lothario, aptly named, gets into scrape after scrape for not being able to control his libido, and even comes close to being killed because of it. Of the four siblings, Wilhelm's future wife, Natalie, has suffered the least under the Abbé's system. She herself claims that this is because the Abbé has allowed her to pursue her own pedagogical model — one that appears to be directly opposed to his own. Most importantly, she also suggests that the Abbé, in light of his experiences with her siblings, may have changed his mind about his pedagogical approach (9: 319). In the case of Wilhelm, he later realizes that he has not been left to struggle on his own as much as he believes. At every important juncture in his life, he has interacted with members from the Tower, who have insured that he did not go too far astray: Jarno directs Wilhelm's taste by having him read Shakespeare, he is not allowed to stay too long with the troupe of actors, he is assured of the paternity of his son, etc.

[23] Nur alle Menschen machen die Menschheit aus, nur alle Kräfte zusammengenommen die Welt. Diese sind unter sich oft im Widerstreit, und indem sie sich zu zerstören suchen, hält sie die Natur zusammen, und bringt sie wieder hervor. Von dem geringsten tierischen Handwerkstriebe, bis zur höchsten Ausübung der geistigsten Kunst, vom Lallen und Jauchzen des Kindes, bis zur trefflichsten Äußerung des Redners und Sängers, vom ersten Balgen der Knaben bis zu den ungeheuren Anstalten, wodurch Länder erhalten und erobert werden, vom leichtesten Wohlwollen und der flüchtigsten Liebe, bis zur heftigsten Leidenschaft und zum ernstesten Bunde, von dem reinsten Gefühl der sinnlichen Gegenwart bis zu den leisesten

I have quoted this passage in full because it encapsulates so many of the themes already discussed. All human beings, as all of nature's entities, have particular propensities that seek to dominate the individual. At the same time, however, these propensities strive against opposing ones. Together, they create a comprehensive whole. In some instances, such as the friendship between Werner and Wilhelm, that whole is not achieved by one person, but through a community. One person contributes imagination, passion and the arts while the other contributes pragmatism and commercial productivity. Such an understanding of balance is amenable to a democratic view. Different people contribute different attributes and by working together they can create a balanced whole. Such a view also explains why the Tower Society accepts individuals with drastically different talents and perspectives. The one requirement for admission is that everyone contributes to the good of the whole in some way.

The passage above also demonstrates a hierarchical understanding of compensation on at least two different levels. First, in rare instances, a single human being appears capable of finding such balance on his or her own. Jarno, at least, believes that the Abbé has achieved this goal. Most people are interested in discrete fields or topics and lack the breadth of focus of the Abbé, who "is interested in everything, takes pleasure in acknowledging and furthering everything" (9: 338). He therefore does not suffer under the limitations of most individuals who have to find a counterweight through others. Wilhelm also appears to be on his way toward achieving this balance and perhaps therefore is worthy of being the hero of both novels after all. As discussed below, his medical training in the *Journeyman Years* closely coincides with the pursuit of art. So, too, does his liberal, general education, including his love of Shakespeare, serve him in a variety of encounters along his journey toward perfecting himself and finding a useful role in society.

Second, and more importantly, the Abbé's discussion clearly stakes out a hierarchical position of the aesthetic over the useful. Everyone can be useful, but very few can be artists. Because art is so central for our lives, one must be sure to foster its development. When we recall the case of Werner, a successful businessman with no personal use for

Ahndungen und Hoffnungen der entferntesten geistigen Zukunft, alles das und weit mehr liegt im Menschen, und muß ausgebildet werden; aber nicht in Einem, sondern in vielen. Jede Anlage ist wichtig, und sie muß entwickelt werden. Wenn einer nur das Schöne, der andere nur das Nützliche befördert, so machen beide zusammen erst einen Menschen aus. Das Nützliche befördert sich selbst, denn die Menge bringt es hervor, und alle könnens nicht entbehren; das Schöne muß befördert werden, denn wenige stellens dar, und viele bedürfens. (FA 1, 9: 932–3)

the arts, we see the dangers of which the Abbé here warns. In a democratic society, where the masses or the majority rule, usefulness will take
care of itself, but one needs to be mindful of maintaining art, something that very few can understand and even fewer can practise. (It is
interesting to note in this context that Congress expressly excluded any
stimulus money for museums.)

The Abbé in another important passage expounds on what this
principle of compensation means for both the arts and for an understanding of educational goals. It is quite clear from this passage that
he is on the more conservative side of the philosophical fence when
he lambastes relativism and suggests that it is a weakness to see things
from the perspective of ill-educated or self-taught students:

> People tend to believe that the faculty of appreciating art develops as naturally as
> the tongue or the palate, and they judge a work of art as they do food. They do
> not understand that a different type of culture is required to attain a true appre-
> ciation of art. What I find most difficult is the separation a man must achieve
> within himself if he is ever to attain self-cultivation. That is why we encounter so
> many one-sided cultures, each of which presumes to speak for all. (9: 351)[24]

In general, the Abbé is saying that it is not good enough for someone to
say that a piece of art is good because they like it. One will never be able
to understand it unless one can transcend a simple, emotional reaction
to it. An appreciation for higher culture does not evolve on its own.
People need to be trained and taught by experts rather than be led by
their own feelings and emotions. The only way that individuals can eventually understand art is if they learn to go outside themselves, i.e., to see
their initial perspectives ironically and gain new perspectives as a result.
In other words, the goal of education is to enable one to view oneself
and one's own ideas from multiple perspectives. The Abbé explains:

> When a person sets himself a goal of manifold activity or experience, he must
> be capable of developing manifold organs in himself which are, in a manner of
> speaking, independent of each other. Anyone who aims at acting or experiencing

---

[24] . . . die Menschen glauben, die Organe, ein Kunstwerk zu genießen, bildeten sich eben
so von selbst aus, wie die Zunge und der Gaum, man urteile über ein Kunstwerk, wie über
eine Speise, und man begreift nicht, was für einer andern Kultur es bedarf, um sich zum
wahren Kunstgenusse zu erheben. Das schwerste finde ich die Art von Absonderung, die der
Mensch in sich selbst bewirken muß, wenn er sich überhaupt bilden will, deswegen finden
wir so viel einseitige Kulturen, wovon doch jede sich anmaßt über das Ganze abzusprechen.
(FA 1, 9: 954)

with his total self, or tries to embrace everything outside himself into one total experience, will spend his time in constantly unfulfilled striving. How difficult it is to do what may seem so natural, to consider a fine statue or a superb painting in and for itself, music as music, acting as acting, a building for its own proportions and permanence! Nowadays most people treat finished works of art as if they were soft clay. The finished marble shall modify its shape according to their inclinations, their opinions and whims, the firmly established building expand or contract; a painting shall offer instruction, a play be morally uplifting, everything become something else. But because most people are themselves without form, since they cannot give a shape to their own self, their personality, they labor away at depriving objects of their form, so that everything shall become the same loose and flabby substance as themselves. They reduce everything to what they term "effects," to the notion that everything is relative; and so the only things that are not relative are nonsense and bad taste which, in the end, predominate as absolutes. (9: 351)[25]

If Werner demonstrates the shortcomings of someone who is entirely rational, then the Abbé's speech above addresses the shortcomings of those who would see everything through their own, narrow, emotional perspective, i.e., from the perspective of an untaught student. Rather than letting themselves be educated by a work of art, such individuals try to impose their own ill-formed sensibilities upon it. The Abbé's underlying aesthetic assumption is that works of art have a universal, independent existence that one learns to comprehend through education and that enables individuals to elevate themselves by studying art on its own terms. The Abbé quite clearly is against modern relativism

[25] . . . sobald der Mensch an mannigfaltige Tätigkeit oder mannigfaltigen Genuß Anspruch macht, so muß er auch fähig sein mannigfaltige Organe an sich gleichsam unabhängig von einander auszubilden. Wer alles und jedes in seiner ganzen Menschheit tun oder genießen will, wer alles außer sich zu einer solchen Art von Genuß verknüpfen will, der wird seine Zeit nur mit einem ewig unbefriedigten Streben hinbringen. Wie schwer ist es, was so natürlich scheint, eine gute Natur, ein treffliches Gemälde an und für sich zu beschauen, den Gesang um des Gesangs willen zu vernehmen, den Schauspieler im Schauspieler zu bewundern, sich eines Gebäudes um seiner eigenen Harmonie und seiner Dauer willen zu erfreuen. Nun sieht man aber meist nur die Menschen die entscheidendsten Werke der Kunst geradezu behandeln, als wenn es ein weicher Ton wäre. Nach ihren Neigungen, Meinungen und Grillen soll sich der gebildete Marmor sogleich wieder ummodeln, das festgemauerte Gebäude sich ausdehnen oder zusammenziehen, ein Gemälde soll lehren, ein Schauspiel bessern und alles soll alles werden. Eigentlich aber weil die meisten Menschen selbst formlos sind, weil sie sich und ihrem Wesen selbst keine Gestalt geben können, so arbeiten sie den Gegenständen ihre Gestalt zu nehmen, damit ja alles loser und lockrer Stoff werde, wozu sie auch gehören. Alles reduzieren sie zuletzt auf den sogenannten Effekt, alles ist relativ, und so wird auch alles relativ, außer dem Unsinn und der Abgeschmacktheit, die denn auch ganz absolut regiert. (FA 1, 9: 954–5)

where everyone assumes that artworks have no real meaning, but are subject to individual interpretations. He certainly believes that there are better and worse ways to interpret a work of art, and the worst way is to see it as a mirror of an unreflective self. It is, however, very important to note that the Abbé is not arguing that artworks have moral roles, but that indeed, those that try to turn art into a bully pulpit are among those who treat art in an instrumental manner. Art is for art's sake, and not for the promotion of religious or moral values.

The Abbé is very concerned about the future of the arts and education in the modern world. His remarks focus on the role of the observers, the audience. His interlocutor, the Marchese, adds a further dimension to the discussion by focusing upon the creators of works of arts, the artists themselves. In particular, he fears the changes that modernity will wrest upon them and worries about the coolly calculating side of modern artists. He predicts that in the future, artists will become much more concerned about popularity and commercial success than about the quality of the works. In short, whereas artists were once considered to have focused their energies on creating works of art that elevate themselves and others and are created from an inspiration from within, the Marchese fears they are now more concerned with reacting to the public rather than with informing it. He views the modern artist as a panderer who wishes to please and profit rather than to excel and elevate. He warns that if artists are not fostered and protected, they will sell out, and the quality of art will be affected:

> It is not easy to contemplate what part circumstances have to play in an artist's activity, and the endless demands an outstanding genius, a person of remarkable talent, has to make on himself, and the immense effort he must expend on his training and development. If external conditions do little for him, if he concludes that the world is easily satisfied and only desires a pleasing and comforting illusion, it would be surprising if convenience and self-satisfaction did not commit him to mediocrity, and it would be strange if he did not prefer to acquire money and praise by producing fashionable wares than by pursuing a course that will more or less result in impoverishment and martyrdom. Therefore the artists of our age are always offering instead of giving. They always aim at attracting rather than satisfying. Everything is suggested with no solid foundation and no proper execution. One only needs to spend a short while quietly at a gallery, observing what works of art appeal to the multitude, which of them are praised and which are ignored, to lose all joy in the present age and have little hope for the future. (9: 351)[26]

---

[26] . . . es läßt sich nicht leicht denken und übersehen, was die Umstände für den Künstler tun

The Marchese contrasts the artist from earlier times as one who thought more about what he did and as a consequence "established principles and elucidated for oneself and others the reasons why this or that should be done" (9: 350),[27] with the artist of the modern age who places public acclaim and profit above the principles of his art. Art therefore becomes a much more commercial endeavor, marketed rather than supported.

Of course, it is no accident that these words come from a nobleman, from that class which was dying out and from the one that had traditionally fostered and supported the arts. And while the Abbé is supportive of the general democratization of society, he nevertheless wishes to have special protection for the arts. In this, his and the Marchese's concerns presage and coincide with those of Tocqueville on the subject of art within democracies. According to Tocqueville, democracies "will cultivate the arts that serve to render life easy in preference to those whose object is to adorn it. They will habitually prefer the useful to the beautiful and they will require that the beautiful should be useful" (2: 50). His observations thus echo the Abbé's in the belief that modernity will have to struggle to find ways to support beautiful, superfluous objects. Tocqueville explains that democratic propensities are likely to break down quality on two different scores. First, the guild system is not encouraged in democratic societies because of its aristocratic principles. Production is not free but has extreme quality controls, and admission to the guilds is highly selective. The products that emerge as a result, he argues, are of a higher quality than those produced on another model, because the artists do not just have to please themselves but they also must please the other members of their organization who in turn enforce high standards.

müssen, und dann sind bei dem größten Genie, bei dem entscheidensten Talente noch immer die Forderungen unendlich, die er an sich selbst zu machen hat, unsäglich der Fleiß, der zu seiner Ausbildung nötig ist. Wenn nun die Umstände wenig für ihn tun, wenn er bemerkt, daß die Welt sehr leicht zu befriedigen ist, und selbst nur einen leichten, gefälligen, behaglichen Schein begehrt; so wäre es zu verwundern, wenn nicht Bequemlichkeit und Eigenliebe ihn bei dem Mittelmäßigen fest hielten, es wäre seltsam, wenn er nicht lieber für Modewaren Geld und Lob eintauschen, als den rechten Weg wählen sollte, der ihn mehr oder weniger zu einem kümmerlichen Märtyrertum führt. Deswegen bieten die Künstler unserer Zeit nur immer an, um niemals zu geben. Sie wollen immer reizen, um niemals zu befriedigen; alles ist nur angedeutet, und man findet nirgends Grund noch Ausführung. Man darf aber auch nur eine Zeit lang ruhig in einer Galerie verweilen, und beobachten, nach welchen Kunstwerken sich die Menge zieht, welche gepriesen und welche vernachlässigt werden, so hat man wenig Lust an der Gegenwart, und für die Zukunft wenig Hoffnung. (FA 1, 9: 953–4)

[27] ... Grundsätze aufzustellen, und die Ursachen, warum dieses oder jenes zu tun sei, sich selbst und andern deutlich zu machen. (FA 1, 9: 953)

Second, because the clientele is aristocratic, they expect to purchase goods of high quality for the high price that they pay. The middle class in democracies, in stark contrast, expect to pay low prices for their goods, but are less upset when the quality is not so high:

> The aristocrats naturally derive from their superior and hereditary position a taste for what is extremely well made and lasting. This affects the general way of thinking in the nation in relation to the arts. It often occurs among such a people that even the peasant will rather go without the objects he covets than procure them in a state of imperfection. In aristocracies then, the handicraftsmen work for only a limited number of fastidious customers; the profit they hope to make depends principally on the perfection of their workmanship.
>
> Such is no longer the case when, all privileges being abolished, ranks are intermingled and men are forever rising or sinking in the social scale . . . there is always in democracies a large number of men whose fortune is on the increase, but whose desires grow much faster than their fortunes . . . Such men are eager to find some short cut to these gratifications, already almost within their reach . . . [T]he result is that in democracies there is always a multitude of persons whose wants are above their means and who are very willing to take up with imperfect satisfaction rather than abandon the object of their desires altogether. The artisan readily understands these passions, for he himself partakes in them. In an aristocracy he would seek to sell his workmanship at a high price to few; he now conceives that the more expeditious way of getting rich is to sell them at a low price to all . . . When none but the wealthy had watches, they were almost all very good ones; few are now made that are worth much, but everybody has one in his pocket. Thus the democratic principle not only tends to direct the human mind to the useful arts, but it induces the artisan to produce with great rapidity many imperfect commodities, and the consumer to content himself with these commodities. (2: 51–2)

Although Tocqueville here is discussing the more practical arts, he observes that the same principles apply to the fine arts (2: 53–3).[28] As a result, he observes that the arts of the past served to elevate, while

---

[28] The arts and handicrafts are closely connected in the *Journeyman Years* as well: "art and technique always balance one another, and, closely related as they are, always incline toward each other, so that art cannot decline without turning into commendable handicraft, handicraft cannot rise without becoming artistic" (10: 326). Hieran schloß sich die Betrachtung daß es eben schön sei zu bemerken, wie Kunst und Technik sich immer gleichsam die Waage halten, und so nah verwandt immer eine zu der andern sich hinneigt, so daß die Kunst nicht sinken kann ohne in löbliches Handwerk überzugehen, das Handwerk sich nicht steigern ohne kunstreich zu werden. (FA 1, 10: 608)

those of his own day tend to trivialize; the former focused on the spirit;
the latter upon the material:

> The painters of the Renaissance generally sought far above themselves, and
> away from their own time, for mighty subjects which left to their imagination an
> unbounded range. Our painters often employ their talents in the exact imitation
> of the details of private life, which they have always before their eyes; and they
> are forever copying trivial objects, the originals of which are only too abundant
> in nature. (2: 54–5)

Of course, aesthetic tastes and artistic styles change with the time, and
one would not expect to find agreement across historical periods and
geographical locations about what constitutes great art. What is noteworthy in Tocqueville's observations, and here he very much echoes
what Goethe's characters say above, is that standards and quality of
craftsmanship suffer in modernity largely because of mass culture and
market forces. Tocqueville, of course, found very much to praise in
America and wrote his book in part from the perspective of wanting
to alert people about the dangers of democracies so that they might
better enjoy their vast potential. One finds a similar strand of thought
in Goethe's novel as well. America represents a land of hope for the
characters who wish to create a new society that blends the best of the
Old and New Worlds. While the Tower Society is generally ruled by
aristocrats, these aristocrats have been democratized. They no longer
want to exert their old privileges but seek to establish more equitable
societies. Similarly, Society members from the other classes realize
the advantages to aristocracy. Wilhelm throughout the novel praises
aristocrats for their ability to think more freely and their support of
the arts. The Tower Society thus represents a community where the
principle of compensation is at play: the old regime is modified by the
newer bourgeois class and vice versa in order to find the right balance
in the changing times. The aristocrats get as much "bourgeoisied" as
the bourgeoisie get "aristocraticized." The interclass marriages thus are
symbolic of the blending of values.

STUDENT-CENTERED AND TEACHER-CENTERED CLASSROOMS

One of the main issues in *Wilhelm Meister's Apprenticeship* is how the arts
should be incorporated into society through education. The characters
of the novel hope to establish utopic communities by fostering the arts

alongside more bourgeois, money-making, or practical activities. If we return to contemporary educational models, we see that the dominant educational systems, whether student-centered or teacher-centered, do not follow the dynamic patterns suggested by Goethe's characters, and as a consequence serve ultimately to undermine the arts.

Progressive, student-centered models

Each opposing methodology — student-centered and teacher-centered — claims to have the students' best interest at heart.[29] Progressives would argue that their approach takes the entire child into account (i.e., by caring about self-esteem and other emotional concerns), that teacher-centered approaches bore the students and hence make it more difficult for them to learn, and that students will retain knowledge better if they have actively participated in its accumulation. Moreover, its overall democratic perspective is reflective of the values of our society, where everyone is valued, no matter how great or small their level of contribution or intelligence. Lest, however, my readers believe that such methodologies are reserved for the "softer" subjects in the humanities, several years ago when attending a conference for university administrators, I participated in a workshop taught by an engineering professor who was advocating this approach in the applied sciences as well. Similarly, after I published a piece in *Slate* that

---

[29] See Chall, who succinctly summarizes the basic differences between student-centered and teacher-centered instruction: "teacher-centered education is concerned primarily with academic learning, while student-centered education focuses more on student development and motivation" (11). Wilga Rivers sees the common thread of the myriad of student-centered approaches as being that teachers care more for the social well-being of the student than for what he or she learns: "The beliefs they embody have persisted, as a constantly surfacing underground, wherever teachers have cared more deeply about their students than about their subject matter" (65). The implication here, of course, is that teachers who place the emphasis upon teaching subject matter over the nurturing of the student's self-esteem do not care for their students. Each camp also argues that the priorities of the other are wrong and that its methodologies harm the students. Dewey's teacher, G. Stanley Hall, queries: "What shall it profit a child to gain the world of knowledge and lose his own health? Cramming and over-schooling have impaired many a feeble mind, for which as the proverb says, nothing is so dangerous as ideas too large for it" (quoted in Chall 43). Others who favor teacher-centered approaches argue just as strenuously that such approaches are:

> a peculiar self-defeating version of democracy [that] somehow made it possible for [new-curriculum proponents] to assert that immature, insecure, nervous, retarded slow learners from poor cultural environments were in no sense inferior to more mature, secure, confident, gifted children from better cultural environments. This verbal genuflection before democracy seems to have enabled them to conceal from themselves that they were, with breathtaking certainty, writing off the majority of the nation's children as being more or less uneducable. (Stevenson and Stigler, cited in Chall 22)

addressed some of the problems to both approaches, I heard from professors outside of the humanities (including engineering) who were horrified at the growth of student-centered learning in the applied classroom. There are, after all, tangible consequences if students are not properly taught to design bridges or high-rises according to the standards of the field.

Taken to its extreme, this methodology supports the notion that everyone should have the same education, from geniuses to those who are academically challenged. For example, the demand that developmentally disabled students have the "right" to a college experience is an outgrowth of this philosophy. Note that it is not that they have the right to be educated, but rather that they have the "right" to attend any university. For example, in a November 5, 2006 *New York Times* piece, Kaufman describes the "wave of cognitively challenged students who are demanding and gaining a place on campuses nationwide" (24). The students discussed in this article have "childish intellectual limitations," yet because of the premium placed upon equality of rights in life or social experiences, these students are being more widely admitted in regular college classrooms although they do not have the capabilities to do the work. Thus, in its extreme form, education is not about accruing knowledge but about the opportunity for everyone to have the same social experience.

One of the main problems with Wilhelm's early education was that it was highly solipsistic. He did not believe that he needed any checks on his desires, and he believed to have chosen the right path in large part simply because he liked it. So, too, do student-centered approaches in education emphasize the desires and uneducated perspectives of the students. In student-centered classrooms, teachers are no longer called "teachers," but rather "resource persons," "architects," or "facilitators." Likewise, students are no longer called "students," as this emphasizes their roles as passive receptacles, but rather "learners," "builders," and "co-workers."[30] Educators who advocate student-centered approaches set almost no limits to the power that students can have in the classroom. They often determine the direction that lessons take, what materials should be taught, and how they should be taught. They are encouraged also to grade their own work as well as that of their peers. Participation, self-esteem, and social well-being are valued over gains in specific skills or the achievement of certain benchmarks.

As discussed earlier in the context of teaching English grammar,

---

[30] For illustrations of the use of this kind of language, see Lee and VanPatten.

many aspects of high culture are considered politically tainted: grammar has operated as an oppressive tool of a patriarchal hierarchy and to refuse to teach it will liberate our students and society. Similar issues are quite prevalent in the foreign language classroom. How one teaches a language very much depends upon what one wants the student to be able to accomplish. The methodology will be quite different if our main goal is for students to read classic literary texts or if we want them to be able to converse on everyday topics with ease.

Currently, a student-centered mode of teaching, called the communicative approach, is the most popular methodology in the foreign language classroom in this country. It is the most popular for two reasons: 1) it coincides with the academy's rejection of high culture; and 2) it is easier to master and consequently less intimidating for the student.[31] In this approach, grammar structures are downplayed, as is reading, but instead students are encouraged from the very first day of class to speak in the target language without too much concern about the grammar. In the communicative approach, students spend much more time working in groups or in partner activities than interacting with the instructor. They thus are more active and participatory during class, but what is being said is not as monitored as would be in a more traditional, grammar- or reading-centered approach.

When I first started teaching at my university about fourteen years ago, I was told by the director of the language program at that time not to take points off for grammatical mistakes because this would inhibit the students' desire to communicate. Such an approach is an extreme one, but not one that is unheard of. I was also forbidden to use red ink in grading student papers, as this was considered to have a traumatic effect. Green was the recommended color. I must admit that the students at the University of Illinois at Chicago (UIC), in contrast to those at the University of Chicago — where I had first taught beginning language courses as a graduate student and where at that time a much more traditional approach was favored — did indeed speak more freely and were much less inhibited. Their listening comprehension was also probably higher. What they said, however, was much less precise and at times much less comprehensible than those students who had been trained in more traditional approaches (although the response time of

---

[31] This latter point, moreover, has a dual effect: it supports a methodology that holds student self-esteem in higher regard than knowledge and is consequently much more likely to attract students to take the course. Since colleges are more and more supporting departments according to the "tuition dollars" they bring in, there is almost no choice but to teach in this way.

those traditionally trained would certainly have been longer and more labored). The UIC students' reading comprehension was also considerably lower. When I taught basic language classes as a graduate student at the University of Chicago in the early 1990s, students were reading complex literary short stories in the beginning of the second year of language instruction. Students, albeit with difficulty, were able to read these texts because the thrust of the instruction was on the ability to learn the tools for reading. Nor can these differences be accounted for by the disparate student bodies. When I was an undergraduate student at the University of Oregon (which also had a program at that time that had a traditional emphasis on grammar and reading), we read Kafka's *Metamorphosis* at the end of the second year and Thomas Mann's *Death in Venice* at the beginning of the third. With students who have learned German by the communicative method, I would not give them either text until a much more advanced stage.

These examples do not mean that collaborative learning is bad or that only one model of instruction is effective. It is the case, however, that a political decision is being made for the students about what kind of education they will have. The communicative classroom by definition downplays high culture. Its goal is to teach communication, not literature. Perhaps the biggest indictment against student-centered teaching is that rather than being rooted in democracy, it is really rooted in paternalism. The educator does not teach the student to gain as much knowledge as possible, but seeks to limit the student to the kind of knowledge or experiences deemed appropriate. What Rousseau clearly knew, but what proponents of student-centered instruction seem to have forgotten, is that the preceptor always really is in charge. Rousseau's educational methodologies simply create the illusion that the child is in control:

> Let your pupil always believe he is the master, and let it always be you who are. There is not subjection so perfect as that which keeps the appearance of freedom. Thus the will itself is made captive. The poor child who knows nothing, who can do nothing, who has no learning, is he not at your mercy? Do you not dispose, with respect to him of everything which surrounds him? Are you not the master of affecting him as you please? Are not his labors, his games, his pleasures, his pains, all in your hands without his knowing it? Doubtless he ought to do only what he wants; but he ought to want only what you want him to do. He ought not to make a step without your having foreseen it; he ought not to open his mouth without your knowing what he is going to say. (120)

In the end, Rousseau's system is anything but democratic, as it functions according to a noble lie. The student believes himself or herself to be in control, whereas in reality the teacher controls everything. Of course, Rousseau argues that such manipulative control is for the student's and society's happiness. After all, Rousseau's pupil, Emile, is being raised with a political agenda in mind: Rousseau is trying to raise a man who will be a good (according to Rousseau's views) citizen.[32] If however, one is evaluating teaching methodologies according to political aims, I would argue that Rousseau's model is even more hierarchical and auto-cratic than classical, teacher-centered models. In the student-centered model, teachers not only hold back some of the knowledge that they may have because they fear that it might socially or emotionally harm their students, but the whole methodological premise is that of decep-tion. Everyone knows who is in charge in a teacher-centered classroom and why they are there. In a student-centered classroom, the goal of the teacher is to make the students believe that they are in charge.

Of course, one could argue that if students learn more under a particular approach, then this kind of deception might not matter as much. However, if one truly believes, as many scholars do who advocate student-centered instruction, that educational methodolo-gies are related to political realities, then they are endorsing a kind of paternalism that I would argue is more extreme in being covert. Why do we need to pretend with adult students that they are in charge and we are simply facilitators? Students, of course, know that teachers know more than they do, and it has been my own experience that many crave traditional instruction. In language classes, they want to be taught grammar, in seminars they want to be given background lectures because they are old enough and mature enough to learn without being patronized.[33]

One might think that a way to solve this debate is to give students a test to see which methodology works best. Pedagogy experts on both sides will argue strenuously for the superiority of their approaches.

---

[32] It is here interesting to note in passing that Rousseau's ultimate aims in his political works have been fiercely debated. One group sees his politics as ensuring a kind of demo-cratic governance and the other argues that his politics amount to a benevolent tyranny, where the people only believe themselves to be in control.

[33] It is ironic to see that those who claim not to be able to "teach" students, but to "facilitate" their learning, are quick enough to correct opinions that disagree with their approach. Students, for example, who expect the teacher to impart knowledge, need to be "reoriented": facilitators "must change students' expectations of what happens inside the language classroom so that students know how to become 'competent members' of the class" (Lee and VanPatten 17).

Given, however, that each side has a different educational goal (e.g., communication versus reading) how does one determine — outside of the politics of the original choice — which test to take?[34] Experts on both sides, especially those who engage in educational issues on the primary level, will argue that the tests given to the students are already tainted by the philosophy of those writing them. For example, if students in a progressive classroom do not perform well on a reading or mathematics test, the test will be faulted for the emphasis that it places on knowledge rather than on social skills. Others will argue for the supremacy of their methods in the face of data. Chall, for example, cites several examples of educators who persist in student-centered approaches although the data show that reading levels and mathematical skills decline in these classrooms, especially for students who are economically at risk (48–53, 62–8, 139). Such teachers appear to reject the teacher-centered approach because of their deep-seated beliefs in the benefits to be accrued by more natural and more democratic approaches, even though these practices, as Chall argues, "may have brought about problems as great or greater than the practices and ideas they were designed to replace" (134). James Traub similarly argues in *The New York Times Education Life* (July 20, 2008): "And so it is probably safe to say that ideology has done as much to retard the rise of scientifically based research as the skittishness of researchers themselves. The pattern of traditional teaching methods faring better in rigorous comparisons than more open-ended ones, and then of the

---

[34] Many teachers see these educational methodologies as being related to and analogous to political ones, and indeed, one can see how these political concerns can even take precedence over having content-based knowledge as goals for education. Chall, for example, sees it as the primary goal of the progressive movement to change society: "Overall, though, most of those who worked toward the new student-centered education agreed that the first objective of education was to transform, through the schools, both individuals and society — to make both ever more humane, creative, and democratic." As we saw above, the authors of the 1974 NCTE resolution wanted to pursue democratic principles even if it meant that the principles harmed today's students, for the hoped-for trade-off of a better tomorrow. At best, one can say that they were idealists who hoped to change society so that one day all dialects and forms of expression would be accepted. At worst, they could be seen as (albeit unconsciously) pursuing a policy that was even more hierarchical than the models that they were seeking to replace. America, moreover, has a history of this kind of tension. Intellectuals have wanted to be both above the masses while simultaneously desiring to be one with them. For example, Leon Fink in his *Progressive Intellectuals* observes that this was an acute problem for many of the progressives: "From the beginning, therefore, the American intellectual had chosen a paradoxical vocation: a social critic committeed at once to identification with the whole of the people and an elitist whose own mores and life situation would prove somewhat alienating from the very public he or she had chosen to serve" (5).

open-ended ones flourishing nevertheless, has repeated itself many times over" ("Does It Work," 24).

If we now turn to the more traditional, results-based methodology, we can begin to see where the extremes of this position will lead us, especially in the absence of a liberal education. Whatever the problems that student-centered teaching has produced, we are now fast learning the negative effects of an extreme, business-modeled, teacher-centered approach as well.

Business, teacher-centered approaches

Traditionalists would argue that the educational crisis in America today is a result of the softer educational approaches of the progressives. One can readily see why such a backlash would occur. If teachers are no longer teaching grammar or mathematics in a way in which the answers and not only the process count, then one worries about how students will function in the real world. Conservatives point to the poor performance of students in grade and high schools and believe that caring for self-esteem has come at the cost of reading and writing. As a remedy, those who support this perspective are often in favor of standardized tests. The initial bipartisan support of NCLB is perhaps an indication of how poorly the electorate perceives educational standards in the country. The Act is largely seen as the first step toward better preparing our students for the workforce. The idea behind this legislation is to make educators accountable. Federal funding is dependent upon improvement of test scores.

The critics of the Act have been many and various, most faulting it for not including sufficient funding and allowing states to set their own benchmarks. The legislation, however, has had another unintentional, yet serious, impact on educational subject matter. Courses that are not evaluated by the tests, e.g., music, the arts, etc., have been cut back to pay for intensified efforts on those courses that are tested, or to pay for the mandated tutoring for failing schools. In other words, the number of subjects taught has greatly narrowed. So, too, has creativity been limited. First, this occurs because teachers now face greater pressures to teach for tests, which understandably are quite narrow in scope. Second, it occurs because the types of courses that focus on the more creative side of human nature have been eliminated, and the tests themselves reward the formulaic rather than the creative. However one may wish to argue for the necessity of this on the primary or secondary levels, the Bush Administration put similar pressures upon universities. It favored and hoped to implement, for example, enforced standardized tests for the students of any college that received federal aid. While it remains to be seen what approach the Obama Administration will favor, in view of the fact that NCLB is considered a bipartisan Act, it would be surprising to see a serious break with it. The recent stimulus money for schools is linked to "measurable progress," and the Obama Administration's initial support of NCLB has led critics, such as Diane Ravitch, to proclaim that "Obama has given Bush a third term in education policy." She further ironically queries whether the current Secretary of Education, Arne Duncan, is "Margaret Spellings in drag" <http://blogs.edweek.org/edweek/Bridging-Differences/2009/02/is_arne_duncan_really_margaret.html>.

In recent years the pressures for "accountability" in higher education have increased because tuition costs have risen more quickly than has the cost of living. In short, as I discuss in greater detail below, legislation on higher education could severely narrow the scope of what will be taught at universities at the undergraduate level. Students, especially in state schools and community colleges which rely heavily on federal funding, may soon no longer have the opportunity to take a wide array of courses covering literature and the arts, and they too will of necessity be taught in ways to pass tests rather than to challenge themselves and be creative.

Many polls demonstrate the public dissatisfaction with the current primary and secondary school systems in this country. In addition, levels of proficiency, measured by such tools as SATs and other standardized tests, have declined over the last several decades. Schools are in crisis, and as the United States National Commission on Excellence in Education declared in the 1980s, we are "A Nation at Risk." The published report of this committee proclaims, "If an unfriendly foreign power had attempted to impose on America the mediocre educational performance that exists today, we might well have viewed it as an act of war. As it stands, we have allowed this to happen to ourselves" (5).

The focus of this report, as of many of the subsequent Republican-generated ones, is the lack of preparedness of our graduates, whether high school or college, for the growing complexity of demands in a modern workplace. This focus on employability is to a certain extent not only understandable, but realistic: a major reason why people go to school is to insure their livelihood. However, a close look at the philosophy behind such proposed educational reforms reveals a much more troubling aspect to the emphasis on business. Prominent conservative educational reformers, such as Louis V. Gerstner, argue that if schools are to be successful, they need to be run as businesses. Thus whereas in a liberal school, the teacher is a facilitator or resource person, in a conservative model, the teacher becomes a corporate manager. As Gerstner, *et al.* explain:

> Making the teacher a manager of instruction is more than a change in titles; it is a profound change in the way teachers work and in the way they should be paid and regarded. A manager orchestrates work effort, bringing together technology (physical capital) and people (human capital) to produce a product or service. In this case, the outcome is learning. The manager creates the environment in which learning can occur. The manager establishes incentives and disincentives, offers rewards and penalties to motivate workers. In many firms, in fact, the manager is not only the key actor, but is accountable for results. (246)

It is quite striking to note that in this business model, students are not the customer but a portion of the product. When schools are asked to think as entrepreneurs: "What would I do if I could do anything that I wanted, subject only to one constraint: meeting customer requirements" (xi), they are not being asked to place the needs of students first but those of business as well as the well-being of society as a whole. The question is therefore, "What kind of education do the clients, i.e., the prospective employers, the government, local community etc. want?" and not "What kind of education best benefits the student?"

Nor are such statements isolated. Gerstner's brand of advocacy to run schools like business is a red thread through many seminal Republican educational documents. If we take a close look at *A Nation at Risk*, we find that this document sees well-educated students primarily as a desirable product for the good of something else. Note, for example, that intelligence is here compared to the commodity of blue jeans:

> Knowledge, learning, information, and skilled intelligence are the new raw materials of international commerce and are today spreading throughout the world as vigorously as miracle drugs, synthetic fertilizers, and blue jeans did earlier. If only to keep and improve on the slim competitive edge we still retain in world markets, we must dedicate ourselves to the reform of our educational system for the benefit of all — old and young alike, affluent and poor, majority and minority. Learning is the indispensable investment required for success in the "information age" we are entering.

George W. Bush's first Secretary of Education, Rod Paige, in introducing NCLB, reiterated the economic findings of *A Nation at Risk*. He returned to this document to claim "we have acknowledged the

importance of our education system to our economy. Now we acknowledge its importance to our national security, and to the strength of
our democracy itself . . . We promise to leave no student behind. And
in return, this nation may ask our young people to use their skills and
knowledge to defend our citizens, to contribute to our economy, to
rebuild our communities and to strengthen our democracy" (Strategic
Plan 2002–07, Secretary's Statement). Here, Secretary Paige goes one
step further than his predecessors. While still promoting the notion
that educated students are a product to be used to promote economic
well-being, he further places upon these students the responsibility
to pay back society for the education that they have received. Note,
again, that the ultimate goal of education is to serve the good of the
community rather than the individual, and that a very particular "good"
is being emphasized.

On the surface, such statements may seem benign — after all, don't
we all want to be "productive" members of society? — but the philosophical shift contained within them is radical and has a number of
troubling aspects. First and foremost, by emphasizing the good of a
collective, this model emulates political models such as communism
and fascism, which do clearly value the good of the whole (no matter
how corrupt) over the good of the individual. The student becomes a
means to an end. This country, as most democracies, was founded upon
the heightened importance of the individual. Yet, we are proposing
educational models that teach the complete opposite, and this change
may be seen in other aspects of our society. It is no coincidence, I would
argue, that since 9/11 basic aspects of the Constitution that are meant
to protect individual rights have been attacked. Individuals have been
tortured and held without charge and without trial because the Bush
Administration argued that it did so to protect the larger population
of the country. Again, as Posner would have it, the Constitution is not
a suicide pact (see Chapter 1, note 47).

Second, a business is measured according to its profits, its outcome
assessments. A product either meets a current need and sells or it
does not. Current markets determine current products. Education,
however, ought to be a very different enterprise. First, its "outcome"
is not necessarily immediate or easily measured. The very best aspects
of an education — from critical thinking to aesthetic appreciation
— often mature and develop with age and cannot be measured on a
standardized test. One can to some degree measure a student's ability
to organize ideas or write clearly, but how does one measure the truly
significant moments in education, the moments of transformation

when a student says things like, "this text makes me re-evaluate the direction that I am going," or "this poem articulates a feeling that I have never really understood before," or "this discussion helped me to understand why I believe this position is important?" A further problem is that the market is largely about the present, the demands and desires of the here and now, whereas a good education gives one a grounding for whatever may happen in the future. If we concentrate on particular skills that are in demand now, what guarantee do students have that these skills will still be in demand in ten years' time?

By focusing so narrowly on the demands of the business world, we are actually narrowing the educational field so that students will be less likely to adapt when they need to. For example, I would argue that it is a good thing to learn any foreign language. It allows students entry into another culture, trains their mind, teaches them grammar, and comparisons between the two languages and cultures often enlighten students on their own culture. Twenty years ago, there were not many economic or political reasons to learn Chinese or Arabic. Now there are profound reasons for speaking both. It takes years to master a language, and if we focus only on the here and now, we will miss many rich and strategic opportunities. As Houston argues, teaching students to pass tests will make them less able to function in a business setting:

> The reality is that anyone in business will tell you that successful workers in the new global economy must have skills of collaboration, ingenuity, problem solving, comfort with ambiguity, and a dozen other things — none of which are tested for and subsequently taught as a result of NCLB. (745)

Third, in light of recent corporate scandals from Enron to AIG, from mortgage lenders to hedge funders, we should pause before embracing business models for our schools. It is not simply a question of greed, although the desire to accumulate vast amounts of wealth certainly fueled many of these scandals and has left the public wondering if free-market capitalism should be left to run by itself without more regulations. More than that, businesses like to have uniformity — to the extent that some even mandate "dress-down Fridays." They want to have team players. They want to have people who can work together and not people who rock the boat. Whistle-blowers are an anathema to the corporate culture, yet they are exactly what businesses often need. Students educated according to corporate models will not have the independence of thought, the originality, the insight, or even the courage to face down "big brother." Nor were the corporate scandals simply caused by a lack of accountability, although the rules of accountability (and accounting!) will certainly grow more teeth in light of the scandals. Many of these corporations and banks simply lied and falsified reports in order to continue business as usual.

One could even argue that many states have similarly started to "cook the books," so to speak, in light of NCLB. Since schools have a lot of discretion in how they test (including such factors as re-testing or excluding low-performance students from the tests), the results can be quite unreliable (e.g., see Guilfoyle 10). Darling-Hammond cites an example at a school in Texas where scores went through the roof:

> In a large Texas city, for example, scores soared while tens of thousands of students — mostly African-American and Latino — disappeared from school. Educators reported that exclusionary policies were used to hold back, suspend, expel or counsel out students in order to boost test scores. Overall, fewer than 40 percent of African-American and Latino students graduated. (2)

Schools, like the corporate world, at times play with the data to get the results that they need, despite grave consequences.

What is perhaps the greatest threat emanating from standardized tests that NCLB encourages is that the focus of education is upon "products" that can be measured (basic skills such as reading comprehension, business mathematics, etc.) rather than on those aspects of education that cannot. Thus, as a result, what used to form the core of education (literature, music, foreign languages, and even history) is no longer emphasized in the classroom since it is not part of the tests. When I was attending an Illinois educational summit years ago, I heard people argue for including the subject of history in NCLB-type examinations. They were worried that unless history were tested, it would no longer be taught. This anecdote is supported by research. Darling-Hammond argues that the focus on testing takes valuable funds away from other programs: "on a test score game that appears to be narrowing the curriculum, uprooting successful programs and pushing low-achieving students out of many schools" (2). Spohn also argues that because much of funding today is grant based, it had become much harder after NCLB to obtain funding for art programs than for math programs (8). Lori Meyer agrees that there is less and less funding for art programs, since the majority of states do not include them in their accountability system (35). Guilfoyle cites Margaret Spellings' motto of "What gets measured gets done" to argue that what does not get measured does not get done: "such subjects as history, art, civics, music, and physical education as well as intangibles like school culture and student health and well-being" (9). Of special note is that schools in lower-income areas will, as a result, have even less access to arts and music programs. This will be detrimental to the school's overall performance, as studies have shown that music and arts programs have beneficial effects to overall learning (Darling-Hammond 1 and Meyer 35).

Our contemporary hybrid form of educational methodologies seems to appropriate what is worst in the student- and teacher-centered approaches. Although Goethe's novels address the weaknesses of both approaches, they also propose a different hybrid solution than the one that we have adopted today. Both novels make the case that a practical and useful education does not need to be a soul-deadening one, and that the arts can and should flourish alongside business and trades. Goethe's novels on the one hand serve as an apt illustration for the significant cost for those who lack a liberal education, eschew hierarchy within educational systems, or completely disregard individual inclinations. Goethe's novels, however, also present positive models which are both aristocratic (in that the liberal arts serve as the basis for one's education) and bourgeois (in that one's education needs to have practical roots as well). Divorce one perspective from the other, however, and one has a stunted personality and limited potential in life and work. Only the combination of the two allows for a productive balance. It is therefore no accident that the Tower Society, the controlling force of the novels, is mostly comprised of aristocrats who support reforms favorable to the growing middle class and that Wilhelm, the son of a middle-class merchant, is readily accepted by the Tower because of his contributions in the realm of imagination and creativity.[35]

WILHELM MEISTER'S JOURNEYMAN YEARS: HYBRID MODEL OF EDUCATION

As in the case of Evangelicals and secular spiritualists, the left and the right appear to have radically different goals, but upon close examination, they seem to share more than one might at first expect. In the case of education, conservatives and liberals, albeit from different perspectives, threaten education and to some extent undermine their self-proclaimed goals. Those on the left are creating an even more paternalistic and limited society than the one they wish to prevent,

---

[35] Here, I follow Ammerlahn who argues that Wilhelm provides the needed perspective on the arts and creativity to the largely practical society.

and those on the right are creating an "end product" which will be less prepared for a changing, dynamic world than ever before. Both groups fail, I would argue, because both, whether consciously or not, eliminate the liberal arts from the curriculum. In another sense, however, both groups are also right in pursuing some of their goals. We should respect and foster the individuality of students (as the left emphasizes), and we should likewise educate them in a way that will make them functioning, productive members of society (as the right argues). *Wilhelm Meister's Journeyman Years* provides at least one model for how one can successfully combine the two methodologies without some of the negative consequences that we are facing in today's educational models.

The second novel, *Wilhelm Meisters Journeyman Years*, takes up where the *Apprenticeship* left off. Because of a new and partially self-imposed regimen of renunciation, Wilhelm has left Natalie for a time to travel alone with his son. The entire novel is episodic. This is in part because Wilhelm is bound by rules that only allow him to spend three nights in the same location, and his frequent change of place leads to new contacts with stories of their own, often relayed in the form of novellas. Whereas the first novel focuses primarily upon the impact of education upon one individual, Wilhelm, the second one spends a greater amount of time looking at education on an institutional level. The reader thus glimpses educational systems for surgeons and different trades (including mining, weaving, and carpentry). If *Wilhelm Meister's Journeyman Years* can be said to have a center, it is the Pedagogical Province where Wilhelm decides to send his son to be educated. The question of education opens the novel and indeed consumes a large part of it. How is Wilhelm to educate his son? What role does liberal education have in the modern world? What is the best system of education?

Surprisingly, Jarno (now called Montan), to whom Wilhelm turns time and again for advice throughout both novels, denounces the liberal arts. For him, "the day for specialization has come; fortunate is he who comprehends this and labors in this spirit for himself and others" (10: 118).[36] Whereas Wilhelm tries to defend a multifaceted education (vielseitige Bildung) as granting a more liberal and liberated view of the world than an education overly focused on trade (Ich möchte aber doch . . . meinem Sohn einen freieren Blick über die Welt verschaffen, als ein beschränktes Handwerk zu geben vermag (FA 1, 10: 297).), Jarno is caustically dismissive: 'Why all the fuss? . . . Let him read the

---

[36] Ja es ist jetzo die Zeit der Einseitigkeiten; wohl dem, der es begreift, für sich und andere in diesem Sinne wirkt. (FA 1, 10: 295)

newspapers like any philistine and drink coffee like any old woman."[37] For Wilhelm it is a matter of how human beings will relate to the world, how they will interact with others, and how they will have the psychic resources to deal with the changing world once they grow up:

> Confine a man as you wish; the time will still come when he will gaze about him in his epoch; and how can he comprehend it if he does not know at least something of what has gone before? And would he not enter every spice shop with astonishment if had no concept of the countries from which these indispensable rarities have made their way to him. (10: 119)[38]

For Jarno, who wants to develop new communities in America and reform old ones in Europe, "to restrict oneself to a *single* craft is the best thing" (10: 118, emphasis in German original).[39] He therefore tries passionately to convince his friend Wilhelm of what is to be gained in the Old World as well as the New from a focus on technical skills.

Once again, we can see the principle of compensation at work in the novel. The man advocating technical skill is pitted against the man "who had always sought treasures in the human heart alone" (10: 119).[40] I contend that Wilhelm is the hero of the novel because he is able to find the right balance between his liberal education and the specialization of his chosen career. He thus represents for Goethe the best that modern education can provide: a person who has been broadened by his educational experiences, who allows them to inform his work in the best possible sense, and whose career even benefits by them. Goethe's educational model therefore is not an aristocratic one, where one learns the classics simply to learn them, but rather a middle-class model where traditional education is aligned with a professional one. Jarno's one-sided position is discredited, as was Werner's in the first novel. In many ways, Jarno is worse than Werner. Werner, even when completely governed by his love and quest for money, still recognizes

[37] Wozu die Umstände? . . . lese er die Zeitungen wie jeder Philister, und trinke Kaffee wie jede alte Frau. (FA 1, 10: 297)

[38] Man umgrenze den Menschen wie man wolle, so schaut er doch zuletzt in seiner Zeit umher, und wie kann er die begreifen, wenn er nicht einigermaßen weiß, was vorhergegangen ist. Und müßte er nicht mit Erstaunen in jeden Gewürzladen eintreten, wenn er keinen Begriff von den Ländern hätte, woher diese unentbehrlichen Seltsamkeiten bis zu ihm gekommen sind? (FA 1, 10: 297)

[39] Sich auf *ein* Handwerk zu beschränken ist das beste. (FA 1, 10: 295, emphasis in original)

[40] . . . der immer nur im menschlichen Herzen den wahren Schatz gesucht. (FA 1, 10: 296)

some of the advantages of the course of life that Wilhelm has taken. Jarno repudiates that which has benefited him. He has been given a liberal education and indeed even benefits by it on the lonely mountainside where he has decided to pursue his newly chosen career. His liberal education, his previous exposure to literature and philosophy, enable him to live a reflective and full intellectual life even in solitude. He has decided to specialize out of his own free will and with the full benefits of his education. In seeking to deny this good to others, he very much resembles those professors who renounce the teaching of high culture to their students, but who themselves have benefited from it and who merrily attend the opera and classical concerts without a pang of conscience or acknowledgment of their inconsistencies.

The Pedagogical Province
Wilhelm decides to send his son to the Pedagogical Province in large part because of a recommendation of a wise old man, who in the novel acts as a repository for people's goods and secrets. He explains to Wilhelm his educational philosophy and how the school's practical approach is aligned with it:

> All living, all activity, all art must be preceded by technical skill, which can be acquired only through limitation. To know one thing properly and be adept at it results in higher cultivation than half-competence in a hundred different fields. Where I am sending you all the fields of endeavor have been divided up. The pupil is tested at each step; thus the true bent of his nature can be ascertained, even though he may be turned from his path by competing desires. Wise men subtly help the boy find what suits him best. They shorten the detours by which we all too gladly tend to stray from our true calling. (10: 197)[41]

This short passage serves as an excellent introduction to the school as well as the pedagogical philosophy of both novels. First and foremost, the student is not given a one-size-fits-all education, but he (the school is only for boys) is carefully evaluated, and his education depends upon

---

[41] Allem Leben, allem Tun, aller Kunst muß das Handwerk vorausgehen, welches nur in der Beschränkung erworben wird. Eines recht wissen und ausüben gibt höhere Bildung als Halbheit im Hundertfältigen. Da wo ich Sie hinweise hat man alle Tätigkeiten gesondert; geprüft werden die Zöglinge auf jedem Schritt; dabei erkennt man wo seine Natur eigentlich hinstrebt, ob er sich gleich mit zerstreuten Wünschen bald da bald dorthin wendet. Weise Männer lassen den Knaben unter der Hand dasjenige finden was ihm gemäß ist, sie verkürzen die Umwege, durch welche der Mensch von seiner Bestimmung, nur allzugefällig, abirren mag. (FA 1, 10: 413)

his individual strengths. The first principle of the school is to examine the particular tendencies of the individual before determining a course of study. In this sense, the school very much values the talents and abilities of the individual and accordingly seeks to place him within the best course of study given his inclinations. The school maintains different "districts" in which various arts and skills are taught, from farming and animal husbandry to music and sculpting. When Wilhelm visits the school, this principle of fostering the individual strengths of the students emerges time and again. For example, the school frowns upon uniforms and instead lets the boys select their own color and cuts of clothing to allow them to express themselves. After being placed within a branch of learning, the boys are still monitored to insure that they have been correctly placed. Indeed, the first words of explanation from the heads of the school focus upon this aspect of its philosophy: "Well-born, healthy children . . . bring a great deal with them. Nature has endowed each of them with whatever he would need for time and duration. Our duty is to develop these things, though often they develop better on their own" (10: 203).[42]

At first glance, these words may indicate a Rousseauian model of education. The children are formed by nature and perhaps could develop their talents in particular fields better on their own than by the intervention of authorities. But however much the school's principles revolve around fashioning an educational program according to the inclinations of its students, one very quickly realizes how central hierarchy and tradition are to its philosophy as well. Once the school has determined the particular inclinations of its students, the best way to insure that these are properly fostered is to balance them against certain kinds of rules and limitations. Throughout the entire process, we witness time and again how the principle of compensation is in effect: personal inclinations are balanced against training, individual freedom against respect for others, and practical knowledge against liberal education. These principles become clearer by turning to the details of the text.

Reverence

Wilhelm is quite surprised to learn that the main thrust of the Pedagogical Province is to teach students reverence (Ehrfurcht).

---

[42] "Wohlgeborne, gesunde Kinder," versetzten jene, "bringen viel mit; die Natur hat jedem alles gegeben, was er für Zeit und Dauer nötig hätte, dieses zu entwickeln ist unsere Pflicht, öfters entwickelt sich's besser von selbst." (FA 1, 10: 420)

According to the school, this is the one thing that almost everyone
needs to be taught: "But there is one thing that no one brings with him
in the world, and it is this on which everything depends and by which
man becomes human in the full sense" (10: 203).[43] The notion of
reverence becomes central for education because without it, students
will never respect those above them (their teachers, authority figures),
revere nature for what it gives and what it causes one to suffer, or form
friendships. Students are taught these "reverences" in the order above
and adopt a posture that will indicate to those around them at which
level they currently stand. As one of the school officials explains:

> You have seen three sets of gestures, and we teach a threefold reverence, which
> reaches its greatest strength and effectiveness only when it flows as one and forms
> a whole. The first is reverence for that which is above us. That gesture, the arms
> crossed over the chest and a joyful gaze toward the sky is what we require of
> young children, thereby demanding they testify that there is a God above who is
> reflected and manifested in their parents, teachers, and superiors. The second:
> reverence for that which is beneath us. The hands held behind the back, bound,
> as it were, and the lowered smiling glance say that one must regard the earth
> carefully and serenely; it affords nourishment, it furnishes unutterable delights,
> but it also produces disproportionate suffering. If someone suffers bodily injury,
> by his own doing or innocently, if others deliberately or inadvertently injure him,
> if the indifference of the earth inflicts some suffering upon him, let him consider
> it well, for this sort of peril remains with him his whole life long. But we liberate
> our pupil from this position as quickly as possible, as soon as we are certain that
> the lesson of this stage has had sufficient effect. Then we call upon him to take
> courage, to turn to his comrades and be guided by them. Now he stands up
> straight and bold, but not in selfish isolation; only in alliance with others like
> him does he form a front against the world. (10: 203–4)[44]

---

[43] Aber eins bringt niemand mit auf die Welt, und doch ist es das, worauf alles ankommt,
damit der Mensch nach allen Seiten zu ein Mensch sei. (FA 1, 10: 420)

[44] Dreierlei Gebärde habt Ihr gesehen, und wir überliefern eine dreifache Ehrfurcht,
die wenn sie zusammenfließt und ein Ganzes bildet, erst ihre höchste Kraft und Wirkung
erreicht. Das erste ist Ehrfurcht vor dem was über uns ist. Jene Gebärde, die Arme kreuzweis
über die Brust, einen freudigen Blick gen Himmel, das ist was wir unmündigen Kindern
auflegen und zugleich das Zeugnis von ihnen verlangen, daß ein Gott da droben sei, der
sich in Eltern, Lehrern, Vorgesetzten abbildet und offenbart. Das zweite, Ehrfurcht vor
dem was unter uns ist. Die auf den Rücken gefalteten, gleichsam gebundenen Hände, der
gesenkte, lächelnde Blick sagen, daß man die Erde wohl und heiter zu betrachten habe; sie
gibt Gelegenheit zur Nahrung; sie gewährt unsägliche Freuden; aber unverhältnismäßige
Leiden bringt sie. Wenn einer sich körperlich beschädigte, verschuldend oder unschuldig,
wenn ihn andere vorsätzlich oder zufällig verletzten, wenn das irdische Willenlose ihm ein
Leid zufügte, das bedenk' er wohl: denn solche Gefahr begleitet ihn sein Leben lang. Aber

These rules, however, are not meant to be arbitrary impositions of authority, but are seen as a means to greater liberty once the student has matured. According to the pedagogues, reverence implies a mastery of the self, a willingness to learn to impose certain limitations on oneself to gain greater freedoms: "To be fearful is easy, but painful; to cultivate reverence is difficult, but comfortable . . . When a person lets himself be governed by reverence, he preserves his honor in paying honor; he is not at odds with himself, as in the other case [fear]" (10: 204).[45] Part of learning reverence is to learn respect in order to free oneself — to learn to understand oneself as limited in comparison with others in order eventually to elevate oneself. The three reverences rely upon and define one another: "From the three reverences springs the highest reverence, reverence for oneself, and the others are born once again from this latter, so that the individual can only arrive at the highest attainment of which he is capable, so that he may view himself the finest thing that God and Nature have produced, yes, so that he can remain at this height without being dragged back again to a common level by presumptuousness and self-centeredness" (10: 205).[46]

In this sense, the imposition of hierarchical principles (of revering those above, those beneath, and eventually those equal to ourselves) leads to a greater ultimate liberation for the individual. It is a process of ennobling that begins with a willingness to recognize something higher than oneself. This process very much echoes the tradition of a liberal education. One is taught to respect books and traditions, but with the aim of analyzing and challenging those same traditions once one has gained an understanding of them. As one of the novel's aphorisms illustrates: "Old foundations are to be honored, but we must not give up our right to lay new foundations" (10: 305).[47] One does not need

---

aus dieser Stellung befreien wir unsern Zögling baldmöglichst, sogleich wenn wir überzeugt sind, daß die Lehre dieses Grads genugsam auf ihn gewirkt habe; dann aber heißen wir ihn sich ermannen, gegen Kameraden gewendet nach ihnen sich richten. Nun steht er strack und kühn, nicht etwa selbstisch vereinzelt; nur in Verbindung mit seines Gleichen macht er Fronte gegen die Welt. (FA 1, 10: 420–1)

[45] Sich zu fürchten ist leicht, aber beschwerlich, Ehrfurcht zu hegen ist schwer, aber bequem . . . Bei der Ehrfurcht, die der Mensch in sich walten läßt, kann er, indem er Ehre gibt, seine Ehre behalten, er ist nicht mit sich selbst veruneint wie in jenem Fall [Furcht] (FA 1, 10: 421–2)

[46] . . . aus diesen drei Ehrfurchten entspringt die oberste Ehrfurcht, die Ehrfurcht vor sich selbst, und jene entwickeln sich abermals aus dieser, so daß der Mensch zum Höchsten gelangt, was er zu erreichen fähig ist, daß er sich selbst für das Beste halten darf was Gott und Natur hervorgebracht haben, ja, daß er auf dieser Höhe verweilen kann, ohne durch Dünkel und Selbstheit wieder in's Gemeine gezogen zu werden. (FA 1, 10: 423)

[47] Altes Fundament ehrt man, darf aber das Recht nicht aufgeben, irgendwo wieder einmal von vorn zu gründen. (FA 1, 10: 574)

to remain in the past, but one needs to build upon it. Nor does one need to obey all the rules as one goes forward, but one does need to understand their purpose before changing them.

This notion of limiting one's freedom of expression or one's desires through structure and rules serves as one of the leitmotifs of the novel as well as throughout many of Goethe's other works. In one of his most famous poems, "Nature and Art," the poet describes the relationship of freedom, art, and limits:

Nature, it seems, must always clash with Art,
And yet, before we know it, both are one;
I too have learned: Their enmity is none,
Since each compels me, and in equal part.

Hard, honest work counts most! And once we start
To measure out the hours and never shun
Art's daily labor till our task is done,
Freely again may Nature move the heart.

So too all growth and ripening of the mind (Bildung):
To the pure heights of ultimate consummation
In vain the unbound spirit seeks to flee.

Who seeks great gain leaves easy gain behind.
None proves a master but by limitation
And only law can give us liberty. (1: 165)[48]

---

[48] Natur und Kunst sie scheinen sich zu fliehen,
Und haben sich, eh' man es denkt, gefunden;
Der Widerwille ist auch mir verschwunden,
Und beide scheinen gleich mich anzuziehen.

Es gilt wohl nur ein redliches Bemühen!
Und wenn wir erst in abgemess'nen Stunden
Mit Geist und Fleiß uns an die Kunst gebunden,
Mag frei Natur im Herzen wieder glühen

So ist's mit aller Bildung auch beschaffen:
Vergebens werden ungebundne Geister
Nach der Vollendung reiner Höhe streben.

Wer Großes will muß sich zusammenraffen;
In der Beschränkung zeigt sich erst der Meister,
Und das Gesetz nur kann uns Freiheit geben. (FA 1, 2: 838–9)

This poem addresses the poet's creative process. It describes the necessary balance between inspiration and hard work that results in the creation of a work of art. Allowing one's inclinations to run free without some kind of check upon them would not lead to a good work of art and would impede the very goal of the artist. This same principle of balance is, according to the poem, behind any formation or education (so too all growth and ripening of the mind). While the opposing forces of free inspiration and hard work initially seem to be in competition, the creative process flourishes only in the tension between the two. The language of this poem mirrors the wise old man's observations on education (10: 197). The same word, "Beschränkung," is used for limits in both cases, as is the term "Bildung" for the end process of education/formation. According to the poem, free spirits, i.e., those who do not impose some restraints on their inclinations, will never reach the artistic heights of those who do. Moreover, if freedom is the ultimate goal of an individual, that too must be gained through the imposition of restraints.

One can see how lack of inhibitions can be destructive. *The Sorrows of Young Werther* begins and ends with Werther's desire for self-gratification. The protagonist, as we saw in the last chapter, refused to respect any rule or authority whether grammar, class, rules of law, or religion. The consequences of his extreme narcissism are also extreme. He dies isolated and disconnected from society in one of the goriest of suicides. Wilhelm Meister himself, it is true, was mired in mistakes that largely stemmed from his lack of understanding of his own self and his desire to indulge his childhood desire. It is only at the point at which he recognizes the demands of another — his son — that Wilhelm leaves his apprenticeship behind. The Pedagogical Province in its approach to passion and inclination sets an example that is diametrically opposed to that of Werther or even that of the young Wilhelm.

Through the example of reverence, one can begin to see how much the Province's approach to education differs from a student-centered one. The first lessons that need to be learned are precisely those that place the student in a larger, hierarchical context. This is not a school that validates the students no matter what they do for fear of harming their self-esteem, but rather one that believes that a true sense of one's worth can only arise if one has been trained first to respect those above and around us. Reverence cannot stem from self-indulgence or self-centeredness but from hard work and education. At the same time, however, the ultimate goal of education is quite different than one that sees the student instrumentally, i.e., as a certain kind of product for the greater good of society. Although the student learns a trade or profession, the main goal of education is his own well-being.

Balancing the democratic against the aristocratic

The dynamic relationship between freedom and limits will become clearer if we turn to some of the actual discussions of educational policy in the "classrooms" of the Province, i.e., the regions where certain crafts, trades, and arts are taught. Here, we see examples of how the principle of compensation is at the heart of the school. No matter what the individual inclination of the student, he is taught other subjects to round out his education. Most especially, no matter how practical the inclination of the students, all are taught the liberal arts, especially music. In this respect, the Province's relationships with traditions and formal rules and structures are quite telling and are overtly linked to the principles of reverence outlined above. The pedagogues take their methodological cues from musical training: "Would the musician allow a student to pluck the strings wildly, or to invent intervals at his own whim and pleasure?"[49] Just as in music firm principles have to be taught and followed before one can engage in one's own creative attempts, so too in the other fields "nothing is left to the free will of the learner" (nichts der Willkür des Lernenden zu überlassen sei, FA 1, 10: 521):

> But the greatest justification for our strict demands and our insistence on definite rules is this: that it is precisely the genius, the person with inborn talent, who grasps them most promptly and obeys them most willingly. Only the mediocre talent wishes to enthrone his limited individuality in the place of the absolute and gloss over his bungling by pretending it represents ungovernable originality and independence. But we do not allow this sort of thing: we guard our students from all those missteps by which a good portion of life, and sometimes an entire life, can be thrown into confusion and fragmented.
>
> We like best dealing with the genius, for this sort is always blessed with the ability to recognize promptly what is good for him. He understands that art is called art precisely because it is not Nature. He is able to respect even what one might call the conventional; for what does this mean other than that the most outstanding men have agreed to consider as best that which is essential, indispensable. And is this standard not always conducive to happiness?
>
> Here, as elsewhere in our realm, the task of the teacher is greatly aided by the three forms of reverence, and by their signs, which have been introduced and

---

[49] Würde der Musiker einem Schüler vergönnen wild auf den Saiten herumzugreifen, oder sich gar Intervalle nach eigner Lust und Belieben zu erfinden? (FA 1, 10: 521).

impressed on the pupils, with slight modifications according to the prevailing activity. (10: 271)[50]

The school by no means has a soft approach to learning. However much the individual inclinations of the students are studied to insure that they are properly tracked in their education, the desires of the students are not taken into account within the curriculum, and indeed, they play no role in forming the direction of instruction. By implementing the rules described above, the pedagogues wish first to educate the genius, who will best recognize the rules and by acknowledging them, respect those who have gone before him. Only the genius will then have the right to make his own rules because he is the only one who will thoroughly understand them. Second, the emphasis on hierarchy prevents mediocre talents from wasting their time and from burdening others with their bad products. For example, in the musical district of the school, no one is allowed to practice within earshot of others. In learning one's instrument, one has to respect those around one as well as the traditions that have led up to its playing.

Several of the novel's aphorisms support an interpretation that education needs to be hierarchical for the good of the individual *and* the good of the many. Culture and art, accordingly, should not be sacrificed to the natural and ill-formed desires of the students:

> Though born a rational being, man needs much education, whether gradually imparted by the care of his parents and teachers, by gentle example, or revealed by stern experience. Likewise a *potential* artist is born, but not an *accomplished* one . . .

---

[50] Was uns aber zu strengen Forderungen, zu entschiedenen Gesetzen am meisten berechtigt, ist: daß gerade das Genie, das angeborne Talent sie am ersten begreift, ihnen den willigsten Gehorsam leistet. Nur das Halbvermögen wünschte gern seine beschränkte Besonderheit an die Stelle des unbedingten Ganzen zu setzen, und seine falschen Griffe, unter Vorwand einer unbezwinglichen Originalität und Selbstständigkeit, zu beschönigen. Das lassen wir aber nicht gelten, sondern hüten unsere Schüler vor allen Mißtritten, wodurch ein großer Teil des Lebens, ja manchmal das ganze Leben verwirrt und zerpflückt wird.

Mit dem Genie haben wir am liebsten zu tun, denn dieses wird eben von dem guten Geiste beseelt, bald zu erkennen was ihm nutz ist. Es begreift, daß Kunst eben darum Kunst heiße, weil sie nicht Natur ist. Es bequemt sich zum Respekt, sogar vor dem was man konventionell nennen könnte: denn was ist dieses anders, als daß die vorzüglichsten Menschen übereinkamen, das Notwendige, das Unerläßliche für das Beste zu halten; und gereicht es nicht überall zum Glück?

Zur großen Erleichterung für die Lehrer sind auch hier, wie überall bei uns, die drei Ehrfurchten und ihre Zeichen, mit einiger Abänderung, der Natur des obwaltenden Geschäfts gemäß, eingeführt und eingeprägt. (FA 1, 10: 522)

> Unless he is inclined to learn from more highly trained artists of past and
> present days what he lacks in order to be a true artist, a false notion of preserv-
> ing originality will lead him to look over his own shoulder. For not only what we
> are born with, but also whatever we can acquire belongs to us, and we are those
> things. (10: 297, emphasis in original)[51]

The novel returns again and again to the notion that desires need
to be restrained and that impulses need to be taught if the best in
people is to emerge. Potential needs hard work and structure if it is
to be realized. It should not be coddled and praised. "Unrestrained
activity, of whatever kind, leads at last to bankruptcy" and "Everything
that liberates the mind without giving us more self-mastery is harmful"
are but two of the numerous aphorisms that reflect this principle of
the school.[52] Indeed, as discussed below, Wilhelm's own decision to
become a surgeon reflects this position and demonstrates how far he
has come from wanting to establish a theater and act before he had
had any professional experience.

The concept of restraint plays a key issue in both *Wilhelm Meister*
novels. Indeed, the second novel has as its subtitle, "The Renunciants"
(*Die Entsagenden*). I have already discussed above Wilhelm's regret
that his education was not supervised with a more heavy hand. He
has come to embrace the notion that imposing rules and obligations
and learning skills by mechanical means is an effective beginning for
students unclear about their own inclinations and unable to control
their desires. With such an evaluation of his own educational experience, it comes as no surprise that Wilhelm is so willing to take his son
to the Pedagogical Province. According to the old man, the Province,
albeit quite subtly, closely monitors, controls, and guides the desires of
the charges. In other words, the "detours" that Wilhelm, for example,
underwent promise to be "shortened" for his son.

---

[51] Der zur Vernunft geborene Mensch bedarf noch großer Bildung, sie mag sich ihm
nun durch Sorgfalt der Eltern und Erzieher, durch friedliches Beispiel, oder durch strenge
Erfahrung nach und nach offenbaren. Ebenso wird zwar der *angehende* Künstler, aber nicht
der *vollendete* geboren . . .
   Ist er nun nicht geneigt von höher ausgebildeten Künstlern der Vor- und Mitzeit das
zu lernen was ihm fehlt um eigentlicher Künstler zu sein, so wird er im falschen Begriff von
bewahrter Originalität hinter sich selbst zurückbleiben; denn nicht allein das was mit uns
geboren ist, sondern auch das was wir erwerben können, gehört uns an und wir sind es. (FA 1,
10:561–2, emphasis in original)
[52] Unbedingte Tätigkeit, von welcher Art sie sei, macht zuletzt bankerott (FA 1, 10:
560). Alles was unsern Geist befreit, ohne uns die Herrschaft über uns selbst zu geben, ist
verderblich (FA 1, 10: 567).

Liberal education

The importance of a liberal education is highlighted in the novel in several ways. We see how knowledge of literature and music is important in Felix's education and in his future career. We also see how Wilhelm's time spent in acting and reading literature in the first novel leads to both practical and social benefits in the second. In both cases, the principle of compensation accounts for how one proclivity is balanced against its opposite to create a well-rounded and productive human being.

As a boy, Wilhelm's son Felix is enamored of horses and seems to be a natural horseman. The school recognizes this inclination and fosters it, but also counters it by others. First, following its principles of instilling respect for rules and traditions, Felix has to learn about caring for all animals and farming before he can focus on horses. He also has to do all of the messy work with all barnyard animals as well as the hard labor of the field. Although he has a difficult time in the probationary period, he manages to overcome these unpleasant tasks by reminding himself of the future rewards.

Wilhelm is quite pleased to see how his son has turned out: he encounters a well-built, healthy, and witty youth. He wonders how the rather restricted agricultural education has been balanced out to achieve this well-rounded whole in his own son. He wishes to "learn in what other areas the pupils are trained, lest, engaged in such wild and rather crude occupations as feeding and rearing animals, they should themselves become wild animals" (10: 268).[53] The answer is perhaps surprising. Students who spend time with animals and on the farm are taught the language arts. Wilhelm was "very glad to hear that precisely this violent and apparently rough vocation was linked with that most refined of studies: the practice and cultivation of language" (10: 268).[54] To keep students balanced, they are taught not only foreign languages, but also the music associated with the language of their choice. Although all of the students are also taught to sing right away, those such as Felix who are involved with agriculture delve into the arts and culture of foreign languages in some depth. As the boy's educational supervisor explains: "Activity and industry are much more

---

[53] . . . wünscht zu erfahren worin man die Zöglinge sonst noch zu üben pflege, um zu verhindern daß bei so wilder, gewissermaßen roher Beschäftigung, Tiere nährend und erziehend, der Jüngling nicht selbst zum Tiere verwildere. (FA 1, 10: 517)

[54] Und so war es ihm dann sehr lieb zu vernehmen daß gerade mit dieser gewaltsam und rauhscheinenden Bestimmung die zarteste von der Welt verknüpft sei, Sprachübung und Sprachbildung. (FA 1, 10: 517)

compatible with sustained study than is generally believed" (10: 269).[55] Felix, as a result, is able to sing Italian songs "with delicacy and feeling, during the tedious stretches of his herdsman's life" (10: 269).[56]

Felix's education, on the one hand, speaks to the advantages of a liberal education. Although his career training is not culturally refined, his subsequent education in the language arts insures that his thoughts do not remain with the animals. One means by which we can perhaps judge his success is that the woman of his dreams, Hersilie, who is well educated and aristocratic, is charmed by him. To her, he describes his studies and his pleasures, and she finds his entreaties earnest and appealing. Although she clearly is physically attracted to him, his "sweet and flattering words" contribute in no small degree to making him lovable in her eyes (10: 415).

While Felix's love of the Italian language and culture has the very elevated result of enriching his life, it also has very practical uses. He is a capable player in the capitalist world of trade, because he can directly interact with those who wish to buy his wares. Language study is thus important to "conduct bargaining and selling with the utmost ease" (10: 268).[57] An education in the liberal arts is simultaneously life-enriching as well as profit-inducing for the student. There is no contradiction here between the need to specialize (agriculture and horsemanship) and the need for a broad education. Liberal education balances out specialized training, and ultimately aids the individual in the very endeavor in which he is being trained.

Wilhelm's own circuitous education can be seen as following a parallel track. Although he decides to train and specialize as a surgeon, in the end, it is his background and appreciation for the arts that enable him to become a humane one. In other words, whereas Jarno complains that the liberal arts serve no purpose, Wilhelm's and his son's stories show the life-enriching and practical aspects of a liberal education. If the arts are to survive in the modern world, according to the Marchese and the Abbé, they must be consciously fostered. The examples of Wilhelm and Felix further demonstrate that the arts are not just for aristocrats, but are central to one's life enrichment as well as to one's career in any class or social stratum.

---

[55] Lebenstätigkeit und Tüchtigkeit ist mit auslangendem Unterricht weit verträglicher als man denkt. (FA 1, 10: 519)

[56] . . . in der Langeweile des Hüterlebens, gar manches Lied zierlich und gefühlvoll vortragen hören. (FA 1, 10: 519)

[57] . . . bei'm Feilschen und Markten aber alle Bequemlichkeit finden mag. (FA 1, 10: 518)

The novel thus on the one hand is highly traditional in its support of the arts. It argues for old-fashioned training of artists and for rigorous attention to the rules and standards that have gone before. On the other hand, the expansion of the liberal arts to include the middle class is much more radically modern, especially since the argument in their favor is not purely "art for art's sake," but rather art for art's sake and for business's sake.

In many ways, Wilhelm's trajectory is unorthodox. He first vacillates between the worlds of business and theater only to settle on the socially (for Goethe's time) less elevated position of a surgeon. He credits the liberal arts, however, for his success in his profession. Wilhelm's study of the human body in the context of the stage has given him an edge in the knowledge of the human form. A good actor, a good director must have a very precise understanding of the instrument of the body, and this knowledge has assisted Wilhelm in his studies: "And so I was sufficiently prepared to pay steady attention to the anatomical lectures that taught the external features in detail" (10: 322).[58] As with any liberal education, one can never predict which of its aspects will be useful, but in this case it is quite notable that that which Jarno was despairingly critical of in Wilhelm — that he had no talent as an actor — actually comes to serve him once he decides to be a surgeon. Thus, like his son who learns languages first for his edification, but who then later uses them in his career, so too have Wilhelm's earlier experiences as an artist contributed to his progress as a surgeon.

Wilhelm next outlines how his liberal education, guided by his heart (i.e., his emotional side), enables him to circumnavigate a very unpleasant aspect of his training: dissection. It is quite clear from the narrative that Wilhelm believes that dissection has two problems. First, it causes the surgeon to objectify the body too much, i.e., he loses part of his humanity as he becomes inured to the mechanics of dealing with the body. Second, the process of obtaining the bodies is often heartless, if not downright illegal. Families of criminals, suicides, or sufferers of mental illness had no say in what happened to the bodies of their loved ones. Even with such "harsh laws" (harte Gesetze), bodies were still in such demand that families "had to fear for the dearly departed. Not age, not dignity, neither high nor low was safe in its resting place."[59]

---

[58] . . . und auf diese Weise war ich vorbereitet genug, dem anatomischen Vortrag der die äußern Teile näher kennen lehrte eine folgerechte Aufmerksamkeit zu schenken. (FA 1, 10: 601)

[59] . . . daß man auch sogar für die friedlichen Gräber geliebter Abgeschiedener zu fürchten

(It was not that long ago in the USA that similar means were openly used and even Alistair Cooke's body parts were used without consent in 2006.[60]) Wilhelm is quite critical of the "unnatural scientific hunger which demands to be satisfied by fair means or foul" and questions whether in medical experimentation the ends really justify the means (10: 323).[61] Wilhelm's own background and training further render him incapable of not caring where the bodies come from. Indeed, when it is his turn to dissect the corpse of a beautiful woman who had committed suicide and whose family had tried to claim the body in vain, he cannot go through with "the dubious task." In addition to the troubling ethical considerations of operating on a body so acquired, Wilhelm's appreciation of her beauty prevents him from treating her simply as an object of study: "his reluctance to mutilate this magnificent product of nature any further struggled with the demands which any man striving for knowledge must place on himself, and which everyone else in the room was busy satisfying" (323).[62] Whether one agrees with Wilhelm's position or not, he adds a dimension to the discussion about the objectification of bodies and the ethics of medical practices thanks to his background in the liberal arts. His education thus poses questions about the accepted practices of society.

In spite of his ethical and aesthetic objections to the methods of training, Wilhelm does not give up his desire to be a surgeon. Rather, he seeks to find alternative means to acquire knowledge through the arts. In this sense, he is quite a different character than Faust. Faust tries to conquer the world only after poetry (Helen of Troy and Euphorion) has become dead to him. Wilhelm tries to find means through art to both save his soul and progress in his scientific studies. He refuses to desecrate nature when an artistic model can be used in its stead. Wilhelm learns his necessary anatomical lessons by working with anatomically correct models of the human body. In this, Wilhelm

habe. Kein Alter, keine Würde, weder Hohes noch Niedriges war in seiner Ruhestätte mehr sicher. (FA 1, 10: 601)

[60] Zuger notes that "barely a century ago American medical schools were helping themselves to alumni of the local poorhouse for some of their teaching material and paying grave robbers for the rest. Only with a 1968 federal act did a nationwide system of voluntary donation bring uniformity to the process" (D5).

[61] In solchen Augenblicken entsteht eine Art von unnatürlichem wissenschaftlichem Hunger, welcher nach der widerwärtigsten Befriedigung wie nach dem Anmutigsten und Notwendigsten zu begehren aufregt. (FA 1, 10: 602)

[62] Der Widerwille dieses herrliche Naturerzeugnis noch weiter zu entstellen stritt mit der Aufforderung, welche der wissensbegierige Mann an sich zu machen hat und welcher sämtliche Umhersitzende Genüge leisteten. (FA 1, 10: 602)

follows Goethe's own real-life efforts to promote the study of anatomy not through human bodies but through crafted reproductions. (Today, similar debates are ongoing about the extent to which virtual technology "obviates our need for dead bodies, as some anatomy courses move from real dissection to its virtual counterpart — clean and odor-free, in crystal-clear focus with infinite zoom." Zuger D5) Within the novel, Wilhelm is pleased to work with the replicas, first because they spare him from the dismay and disgust of working with human bodies, and second because the replicas are in themselves artistic objects. The carver is a man who "was going begging because the saints and martyrs that he was accustomed to carving were no longer in demand" (325).[63] The religious artist becomes an artist to serve science, but this is all done while preserving the dignity of the human body. Similarly, the man overseeing the whole replica project had wanted to be an artist, but because his era demanded that the body be clothed in fig leaves or animal skins (10: 326), decided to use his talents for science rather than stay in a field where he could no longer express the true beauty of the body. Thus, in a world where Jarno would like to see pure and narrow specializations, one sees example after example of how the liberal arts serve particular purposes that benefit the individual as well as society. They do not stand in the way of progress, but help to insure that it retains its humanity.

The pedagogical model in the *Journeyman Years* is to foster education that includes both practical training and liberal arts education — one that trains as well as edifies. Goethe predicted that if human beings were truly to flourish, especially in a technologically advanced and chaotically capitalist world, they would need an education that was dynamic and included an appreciation of the arts. It is no accident that some of the members of the secret society turn their sights to America in order to capitalize on the vast possibilities of commerce and economic development, whereas others return from there repulsed by the colonialist actions and seek to re-embrace the culture of Europe instead: "this priceless culture, born thousands of years ago, which had grown, expanded, been diminished, oppressed but never entirely suppressed, which had drawn new breath, revived, and continued to generate boundless activity" (10: 150).[64]

---

[63] . . . dessen Kunst nach Brode ging, indem die Heiligen und Märtyrer die er zu schnitzen gewohnt war, keinen Abgang mehr fanden. (FA 1, 10: 605)

[64] . . . diese unschätzbare Kultur seit mehreren tausend Jahren entsprungen, gewachsen, augebreitet, gedämpft, gedrückt, nie ganz erdrückt, wieder aufatmend, sich neu belebend und nach wie vor in unendlichen Tätigkeiten hervortretend. (FA 1, 10: 343)

CONCLUSION

This book by no means claims to exhaust the topics that are relevant today. One could examine many issues within Goethe's works, such as theories of gender, the contrasts between the cultures of the West and the East, or even the concept of world literature. One could also turn to *Elective Affinities* (1809) to analyze issues regarding family structures, creativity, and procreation. In many ways, this novel, by focusing upon issues of productivity and creativity within the framework of a dissolving and more fluid family structure, could prompt us to consider some of the consequences of our current family structures and reproductive dilemmas. For Goethe's novel, creativity breaks down at the same time that procreativity does. What happens within a microcosm when people stop being productive, either through creative endeavors or through procreation?

In each of these cases, as in the ones that I have been examining in more detail within my book, the principle of compensation suggests that we must always consider the consequences of the gains that we seek. Whenever Goethe presents a particular benefit for his characters, there is almost certainly a significant cost to it. The promises of commerce and technology, as his protagonist Faust illustrates, may provide jobs for millions but come at the price of aesthetics, justice, and a sense of individual value. Piracy and theft from weaker sovereignties are the basis for the jobs that Faust so gleefully foresees. Nor is there room for beauty or individualism in the new world order. Faust resents the rustic, charming house of Baucis and Philemon in part because it signals his lack of control. The death of this couple also demonstrates the extent to which the ends can come to justify the means: human lives are sacrificed for job opportunities, eminent domain over the preservation of older, more hospitable ways. Lawrence Summers' suggestion about exporting pollution to developing countries (see Chapter 1) is but one example of how this system operates today.

If Faust, however, represents the excesses of eliminating concerns for nature, art, and the individual, then Werther demonstrates the dangers of an excessive worship of the self. Werther believes that passions are so true and bring one so close to God that one does not need rules. Sentimentalism in effect comes to destroy justice and art as much as does Faust's capitalist drive. Werther, too, justifies murder. He would gladly see the farmhand go free for his crime of passion because he has loved so intensely. If all standards ought to be eliminated in favor of the heart (and Werther's rejection of hierarchy touches many spheres, including justice, religion, social mores, art, grammar, politics, and work product), his suicide leaves open the question of whether an individual can really bear the loneliness and destruction of community that accompanies such rejection and whether a society based primarily upon passion would even be desirable. Moreover, Werther's stated goal (Lotte's and Albert's well-being) for his suicide is at direct odds with the effects of it. When the novel closes, it is unclear whether Lotte or her marriage will survive. As I have argued in Chapter 2, a related form of cross-purposes is evident in two, seemingly disparate groups in America today. Religious fundamentalists and secular spiritualists may believe that they are bringing about a better way of life for themselves and others by their rejection of education in favor of individual piety and individual pursuit of happiness respectively, but here, too, one must question whether each is not accelerating the destruction of that which they most want to save. Recent sexual scandals involving Evangelical conservatives (Mark Sanford, John Ensign) show how shaky it can be to build a political base around individual moral purity, while liberal educators, in consciously deciding not to teach students grammar and high culture wind up limiting their students' opportunities more than standards-based education ever could.

Within the *Wilhelm Meister* novels, we quite literally see a battle between competing concerns and the costs of both. To a great extent, Wilhelm's education is about learning to balance extremes so that the consequences of one's decisions are moderated. The first of the two novels, *Wilhelm Meister's Apprenticeship,* has as one of its leitmotifs the struggle between a sentimentalized character, the Werther-like, young Wilhelm, and the hard-nosed, rational businessman, Werner. Each character struggles to persuade the other of the superiority of his position, but the novel suggests that a balance between the two should be attempted. Wilhelm damages a great many lives and even comes close to losing his own because he follows his heart and openly disregards reason, business, and family. Wilhelm finally comes to appreciate the need for balance, and he does so almost at the very moment at which we see the negative consequences of following a purely business model in life. When Werner appears to Wilhelm, his exclusive pursuit of business is reflected in his physical appearance: he is stooped and aged before his time; his interests greatly narrowed in scope. Wilhelm gains in nobility as he gains balance; Werner loses all appeal in his single-minded pursuit of money.

The second of Goethe's *Wilhelm Meister* novels continues many of the themes of the first one, but in the *Journeyman Years* the question of education is broadened beyond the concerns of Wilhelm's personal development to that of the proper role of institutionalized education. As in the first novel, the focus on being a productive member of society is contrasted with the pursuit of one's own individual inclinations. In the end, the novel suggests a hybrid model of education, where standards and discrete knowledge are constantly balanced against an individual's ability. Liberal education is the cornerstone of this balance because it enriches the individual's mind and elevates him or her above the most banal aspects of how one makes a living. Wilhelm is a more moral surgeon because of his education, and Felix's mind will rise above the stable because of knowledge of music and foreign culture. Today's educational practices in America, however, reject the notion of liberal education either because of its connection to hierarchical political forms (as the liberals would argue) or because it cannot be tested in the same way (as especially the conservatives would like to see) as those rudimentary skills needed in business.

I believe the main function of Goethe's principle of compensation is to show that struggles and gains are never value-free and are constantly in flux and hence require re-evaluation at every major turning point. Situations change, as does the main thrust of certain ages. We are currently undergoing a self-examination in light of an economic meltdown. What new controls do we need on banking and business? Did a failure in our educational system contribute to this meltdown? Will we be better or worse off with a universalized health care system? Should we be rationing health care?

Goethe's principle of compensation does not provide us with a formula to follow, but challenges us to be aware that there will be costs for whatever decisions we make. In many ways, the main lesson from studying the principle is that one needs to be ready and able to change in light of such analyses. One of the maxims from *Wilhelm Meister's Journeyman Years* describes the fundamental principle of nature as being one characterized by flux:

The fundamental property of the living entity: to divide, to unite, to dissolve in the universal, to persist in its particularity, to metamorphose, to assert its specificity, and since anything alive can manifest itself under thousands of conditions, to emerge and disappear, to solidify and to melt, to freeze and to flow, to expand and contract. Since all these processes are taking place in the same moment, anything and everything can occur at the same time. Origination and extinction, creation and destruction, birth and death, joy and sorrow — everything interacts, in equal sense and equal measure, for which reason even the most particular event always appears as the image and likeness of the universal. (10: 308)[1]

The maxim addresses a variety of polarities pitted against one another that are in constant interplay. Nature seems characterized by perpetual motion and change. The principle of compensation is a means for Goethe of tracking and describing those changes for entities at particular moments in time. And while one may discuss a specific advantage or disadvantage at a given moment within the story of any individual, the key for any entity is to remain in motion. Just as Faust's two souls impel him throughout most of the play, so too does Goethe characterize all of nature as engaging in dynamic interactions that keep it productive and active. Goethe, after all, believed in his own immortality because he could never imagine that a being as active as himself would cease activity after death.

If we return to the three main protagonists discussed in this work, each in the end has a different relationship toward motion and balance. I would argue that Wilhelm is the most successful because he embraces the dynamism of compensation to seek balance. He remains in movement throughout both novels and dynamically changes in light of his experiences and mistakes. Both Faust and Werther ultimately choose stasis. Wilhelm, moreover, unlike Faust, never forgets the arts and consequently utilizes science in a humane way. Wilhelm may abandon his earlier dreams of the theater, but he does not then seek to destroy the theater or repudiate the literary arts. He instead takes advantage of what he has learned from them. Faust's desire to forget his humanity (his earlier love of Gretchen) and to obliterate nature

---

[1] Grundeigenschaft der lebendigen Einheit: sich zu trennen, sich zu vereinen, sich in's Allgemeine zu ergehen, im Besondern zu verharren, sich zu verwandeln, sich zu spezifizieren, und wie das Lebendige unter tausend Bedingungen sich dartun mag, hervorzutreten und zu verschwinden, zu solideszieren und zu schmelzen, zu erstarren und zu fließen, sich auszudehnen und sich zusammen zu ziehen. Weil nun alle diese Wirkungen im gleichen Zeitmoment zugleich vorgehen, so kann alles und jedes zu gleicher Zeit eintreten. Entstehen und Vergehen, Schaffen und Vernichten, Geburt und Tod, Freud und Leid, alles wirkt durch einander, in gleichem Sinn und gleicher Maße, deswegen denn auch das Besonderste, das sich ereignet, immer als Bild und Gleichnis des Allgemeinsten auftritt. (FA 1, 10: 577–8)

and poetry ultimately leads to his death and his inability to act in the future.

If Faust embraces a kind of stasis rooted in the world of capitalism, i.e., he is willing to die once he can imagine millions of people working on his land, then Werther represents a stasis of a very different kind. Werther realizes on a conscious level that he indulges a sick heart, but he is incapable of changing his ways. His failure to be productive, whether in his attempts to create artistic objects or to hold down a job, becomes symptomatic of the larger problem. He so fosters his emotional, imaginative side that he slowly divorces himself from society and finally commits suicide. Wilhelm's character in the beginning is very similar to Werther's. He, however, unlike Werther, progresses beyond this stage to become a productive (and seemingly happy) member of society. And while the world around Wilhelm is changing and presents many problems and challenges, Wilhelm, rather than retreating from it and finally rejecting it altogether, actively attempts, on his own and through the Tower Society, to improve the world. To return to the Lord's views in the Prolog of *Faust*, if human beings are allowed to err as long as they strive, then Wilhelm, unlike Faust and Werther, seems poised to continue this journey.

WORKS CITED

Ammerlahn, Hellmut. "The Marriage of Artist Novel and *Bildungsroman*: Goethe's *Wilhelm Meister*, a Paradigm in Disguise." *German Life and Letters* 59.1 (2006): 25–46.

Anstett, Jean-Jacques. "Werthers religiöse Krise." *Études Germaniques* 4 (1949): 121–8. Quoted here from translated reprint: *Goethes Werther. Kritik und Forschung.* Ed. Hans Peter Herrmann. Wege der Forschung 607. Darmstadt: Wissenschaftliche Buchgesellschaft, 1994. 163–73.

Aquinas, Thomas. *Summa Contra Gentiles.* Trans. Charles J. O'Neil. Notre Dame: University of Notre Dame Press, 1975 [1955–7].

Aristotle. *The Complete Works of Aristotle: The Revised Oxford Translation.* Ed. Jonathan Barnes. Bollingen Series 71: 2. Princeton, NJ: Princeton University Press, 1984.

Armstrong, John. *Love, Life, Goethe: Lessons of the Imagination from the Great German Poet.* New York: Farrar, Straus and Giroux, 2007.

"Art & Yoga for Spiritual Renewal Classes & Workshops 2009." *Awakening Arts.* Winter 2008. July 4, 2008. <http://www.awakearts.com/schedule.html>.

Atkins, Stuart. "Irony and Ambiguity in the Final Scene of Goethe's Faust." *Stuart Atkins: Essay on Goethe.* Eds. Jane K. Brown and Thomas P. Saine. Columbia, SC: Camden House, 1995. 277–92.

——. "J. C. Lavater and Goethe: Problems of Psychology and Theology in *Die Leiden des jungen Werthers.*" *PMLA* 63 (1948): 520–76.

Bahr, Ehrhard. *The Novel as Archive: The Genesis, Reception, and Criticism of Goethe's Wilhelm Meisters Wanderjahre.* Columbia, SC: Camden House, 1998.

Barnouw, Jeffrey. "Faust and the Ethos of Technology." *Interpreting Goethe's Faust Today.* Eds. Jane K. Brown, *et al.* Columbia, SC: Camden House, 1994. 29–42.

Baumgartner, Alexander. *Göthe: Sein Leben und seine Werke.* 3 vols. Freiburg: Herder'sche Verlagshandlung, 1882. Quoted here from the second, expanded 1885 edition.

Benedictine Sisters of Perpetual Adoration. *Confession: Its Fruitful Practice.* Rockford: Tan Books, 2000.

Benjamin, Walter. *Gesammelte Schriften.* 12 vols. Eds. Rolf Tiedemann and Hermann Schweppenhäuser. Frankfurt: Suhrkamp, 1980.

Bennett, Benjamin. *Goethe's Theory of Poetry: Faust and the Regeneration of Language.* Ithaca: Cornell University Press, 1986.

Berman, Marshall. *All That Is Solid Melts into Air: The Experience of Modernity.* 1982. New York: Penguin, 1988.

Bernstein, J. M., ed. *Classic and Romantic German Aesthetics.* Cambridge Texts in the History of Philosophy. Cambridge/New York: Cambridge University Press, 2003.

Binswanger, Hans Christoph. *Money and Magic: A Critique of the Modern Economy in the Light of Goethe's Faust.* Trans. J. E. Harrison. Chicago: University of Chicago Press, 1994. [1985]

Blessin, Stefan. *Goethes Romane: Aufbruch in die Moderne.* 1979. Paderborn: Ferdinand Schöningh, 1996.

Bloom, Allan. *Closing of the American Mind: How Higher Education Has Failed Democracy.* New York: Simon and Schuster, 1987.

——. "Introduction." *Emile or On Education. Jean-Jacques Rousseau.* Trans. Allan Bloom. New York: Basic Books, 1979.

Böhm, Wilhelm. *Goethe's Faust in neuer Deutung: Ein Kommentar für unsere Zeit.* Cologne: Verlag E. A. Seemann, 1949.

"Book Shop." Kripalu Center for Yoga and Health. 2009. July 4, 2008. <http://www.kripalu.org/shop/shop/Book/>.

Borromeo, Charles, ed. *The Catechism of the Council of Trent.* Trans. John A. McHugh and Charles J. Callan. 15th Printing. Rockford: Tan Books and Publishers, 1982.

Boyle, Nicholas. *Goethe: The Poet and the Age.* Vol. 1. Oxford: Clarendon Press, 1991.

Brooks, David. *Bobos in Paradise: The New Upper Class and How They Got There.* New York: Simon and Schuster, 2000.

Brown, Jane K. "When Is Conservative Modern?: or, Why Bother with Goethe?" *Modern Language Studies* 31.1 (2001): 35–43.

——. *Goethe's Faust: The German Tragedy.* Ithaca: Cornell University Press, 1986.

Brown, Jane K., and Thomas P. Saine, eds. *Stuart Atkins: Essays on Goethe.* Columbia, SC: Camden House, 1995.

Bullitt, Margaret M. "A Socialist Faust?" *Comparative Literature* 32.2 (1980): 184–95.

Burwick, Roswitha. "Goethe's *Werther* and Mary Shelley's *Frankenstein.*" *The Wordsworth Circle* 24 (1993): 47–52.

Carlyle, Thomas. *Critical and Miscellaneous Essays: Collected and Republished.* 4 vols. Boston: Houghton, Mifflin and Co., nd.

Chall, Jeanne S. *The Academic Achievement Challenge: What Really Works in the Classroom?* New York: Guilford Press, 2000.

Chiarloni, Anna. "Goethe und der Pietismus: Erinnerung und Verdrängung." *Goethe Jahrbuch* 106 (1989): 133–59.

Clausen, Bettina, and Harro Segebrecht. "Technik und Naturbeherrschung im Konflikt: Zur Entzerrung einiger Bilder auch über Kleist und Goethe." *Technik in der Literatur.* Ed. Harro Segeberg. Frankfurt am Main: Suhrkamp, 1987. 33–50.

Clinton, Hillary Rodham. *It Takes a Village: and Other Lessons Children Teach Us.* New York: Simon and Schuster, 1996.

Cohen, Patricia. "On Campus, the '60s Begin to Fade as Liberal Professors Retire." *The New York Times.* July 3, 2008, late ed.: A16.

Collins, Kenneth J. *The Evangelical Moment: The Promise of an American Religion.* Grand Rapids, MI: Baker Academic, 2005.

Curran, Jane V. *Goethe's Wilhelm Meister's Apprenticeship: A Reader's Commentary.*

Studies in German Literature, Linguistics, and Culture. Rochester, NY: Camden House, 2002.

"Current Dance Events." *The Dance Sources Project.* Ed. Steven Malkus. July 4, 2008. <http://pages.prodigy.net/stevenmalkus1/currentevents.htm>.

Daly, Peter M., *et al.*, eds. *Why Weimar?: Questioning the Legacy of Weimar from Goethe to 1999.* McGill European Studies 5. New York: Peter Lang, 2003.

Darling-Hammond, Linda. "Evaluating *No Child Left Behind.*" *Nation* 284.20 (May 21, 2007): 11–18.

Dohm, Burkhard. "Radikalpietistin und 'schöne Seele': Susanna Katharina von Klettenberg." *Goethe und der Pietismus.* Eds. Hans-Georg Kemper and Hans Schneider. Hallesche Forschungen 6. Tübingen: Niemeyer Verlag, 2001. 111–33.

Dowd, Maureen. "Disgorge, Wall Street Fat Cats." *The New York Times.* February 1, 2009, late ed.: WK11.

Dworkin, Ronald M. "Is Wealth a Value?" *Journal of Legal Studies* 9.2 (March 1980): 191–226.

Dye, Robert Ellis. "Man and God in Goethe's *Werther.*" *Symposium* 29 (1975): 314–29.

"Eden East Yoga Information." *Eden East Yoga Studio.* July 4, 2008. <http://www. edeneastyogastudio.com/yoga-info.htm>.

Eibl, Karl. "Zur Bedeutung der Wette im Faust." *Goethe-Jahrbuch* 116 (1999): 271–80.

Emerson, Ralph Waldo. *The Collected Works of Ralph Waldo Emerson.* Eds. Slater, Joseph, Alfred R. Ferguson and Jean Ferguson Carr. Cambridge, MA/ London: Harvard University Press, 1979.

Fink, Leon. *Progressive Intellectuals and the Dilemmas of Democratic Commitment.* Cambridge, MA: Harvard University Press, 1997.

Flitner, Wilhelm. *Goethe im Spätwerk: Glaube, Weltsicht, Ethos.* Paderborn: F. Schöningh, 1983.

Foster, Andrea L. "Illinois Plans to Draw 70,000 Students to Distance Education by 2018." *Chronicle of Higher Education.* April 27, 2007: A50.

Gentleman's Magazine. "Ms Glover Obituary." November 1784. np, [London?], nd.

Gerstner, Louis V. Jr., Roger D. Semerad, Denis Philip Doyle, and William B. Johnston. *Reinventing Education: Entrepreneurship in America's Public Schools.* New York: Dutton, 1994.

"Global Yoga Journeys — Murren Information." *Global Yoga Journeys.* October 30, 2009. <http://www.globalyogajourneys.com/hiking.html>.

Goethe, Johann Wolfgang von. *Sämtliche Werke: Briefe, Tagebücher und Gespräche.* Ed. Dieter Borchmeyer, *et al.* Frankfurt am Main: Deutscher Klassiker Verlag, 1985–99.

——. *Goethe's Collected Works.* 12 vols. New York: Suhrkamp, 1983–89.

——. *Anhang an Goethes Werke: Abtheilung für Gespräche.* Ed. Woldemar Freiherr von Biedermann. Vol. 10: *Nachträge, 1775–1832.* F. W. v. Biedermann, Leipzig, 1896.

Graefe, Johanna. "Die Religion in den 'Leiden des jungen Werther': Eine Untersuchung auf Grund des Wortbestandes." *Goethe* 20 (1958): 72–98.

Gray, Ronald. *Goethe: A Critical Introduction.* London: Cambridge University Press, 1967.

Greeley, Andrew, and Michael Hout. *The Truth about Conservative Christians: What They Think and What They Believe.* Chicago: University of Chicago Press, 2006.

Guilfoyle, Christy. "NCLB: Is There Life Beyond Testing?" *Educational Leadership* 64.3 (November 2006): 8–13.

Hatch, Nathan O. *The Democratization of American Christianity.* New Haven: Yale University Press, 1989.

Herrmann, Hans Peter. *Goethes 'Werther': Kritik und Forschung.* Wege der Forschung 607. Darmstadt: Wissenschaftliche Buchgesellschaft, 1994.

Hoelzel, Alfred. "The Conclusion of Goethe's *Faust*: Ambivalence and Ambiguity." *German Quarterly* 55.1 (1982): 1–12.

Hoever, Hugo H. *St Joseph Catholic Manual.* New York: Catholic Book Publishing Co., 1956.

Houston, Paul D. "The Seven Deadly Sins of *No Child Left Behind.*" *Phi Delta Kappan* 88.10 (June 2007): 744–8.

Hunter, James Davison. *American Evangelicalism: Conservative Religion and the Quandary of Modernity.* New Brunswick, NJ: Rutgers University Press, 1983.

"I Am the Decisive Element." *Yoga to the People.* 2008. July 4, 2008. <http://www.yogatothepeople.com/stories/decisive-element.html>.

"Inspiring Quotes and Poems." *Stretchways.* July 4, 2008. <http://www.stretchways.com/FifthStab5/Poems.html>.

Jasper, Willi. "Faust and the Germans." *Why Weimar? Questioning the Legacy of Weimar from Goethe to 1999.* Ed. Peter M. Daly, *et al.* McGill European Studies 5. New York: Peter Lang, 2003. 179–88.

Kahn, Ludwig W. *Literatur und Glaubenskrise.* Sprache und Literatur 17. Stuttgart: W. Kohlhammer Verlag, 1964.

Kaufman, Leslie. "Just a Normal Girl." *The New York Times Education Life.* November 5, 2006, late ed., sec. 4: 24+.

Kemper, Hans-Georg, and Hans Schneider, eds. *Goethe und der Pietismus.* Hallesche Forschungen 6. Tübingen: Niemeyer Verlag, 2001.

Kemper, Hans-Georg. "'Göttergleich.' Zur Genese der Genie-Religion aus pietistischem und hermetischem 'Geist.'" *Goethe und der Pietismus.* Eds. Hans-Georg Kemper and Hans Schneider. Tübingen: Niemeyer Verlag, 2001. 171–208.

Klett, Ada M. *Der Streit um 'Faust II' seit 1900.* Jenaer germanistische Forschungen 33. Ed. A. Leitzmann. Jena: Frommann [W. Biedermann], 1939.

Kostovski, Ilja. *Dostoevsky and Goethe: Two Devils, Two Geniuses: A Study of the Demonic in Their Work.* Trans. Donald Hitchcock. New York: Revisionist Press, 1974.

Kowalik, Jill Anne. "Pietist Grief, *Empfindsamkeit*, and Werther." *Goethe Yearbook* 9 (1999): 77–130.

Kripal, Jeffrey J. "From Emerson to Esalen: America's Religion of No Religion." *Chronicle of Higher Education.* April 13, 2007: B6–B8.

Kristol, Irving. "The Feminization of the Democrats." January 1, 2000. *AEI Online.* September 9, 1996. <http://www.aei.org/publications/pubID.6930/pub_detail.asp>.

Lamport, F. J. "Goethe's *Faust*: A Cautionary Tale?" *Forum for Modern Language Studies* 35 (1999): 193–206.

Lee, James F., and Bill VanPatten. *Making Communicative Language Teaching Happen.* The McGraw-Hill foreign language professional series. Directions for language learning and teaching 1. New York: McGraw-Hill, 1995.

"Let Them Eat Pollution." *The Economist.* February 8, 1992: 66.

Livingstone, Angela. "The Meaning of Faust in Pasternak's Poetry." *The European Foundations of Russian Modernism.* Ed. Peter I. Barta. Lewiston, NY: E. Mellen Press, 1991. 165–88.

Long, Roderick. "Xenophon on Law and Violence." *Strike the Root.* April 30, 2009. <http://www.strike-the-root.com/4/long/long5.html>.

Lukács, Georg. *Goethe and His Age.* Trans. Robert Anchor. New York: Grosset and Dunlap, 1968.

Mandelkow, Karl Robert. *Goethe in Deutschland I: Rezeptionsgeschichte eines Klassikers (1733–1918).* München: C. H. Beck, 1980.

Mann, Thomas. "Goethes *Werther.*" *Stockholmer Gesamtausgabe der Werke von Thomas Mann.* Frankfurt am Main: S. Fischer Verlag, 1953. Cited here from Herrmann.

Marglin, Stephen A. *The Dismal Science: How Thinking Like an Economist Undermines Community.* Cambridge, MA: Harvard University Press, 2008.

McCarthy, John A. *Remapping Reality: Chaos and Creativity in Science and Literature. Goethe. Nietzsche. Grass.* Internationale Forschungen zur allgemeinen und vergleichenden Literaturwissenschaft 97. Amsterdam: Rodopi, 2006.

Meyer, Lori. "The Complete Curriculum: Ensuring a Place for the Arts in America's Schools." *Arts Education Policy Review* 106.3 (January–February 2005): 35–9.

Michéa, René. "Les notions de "cœur" et d'"âme" dans *Werther.*" *Études Germaniques* 23 (1968): 1–11. Cited here from Herrmann.

Miller, J. Hillis. *Ariadne's Thread: Story Lines.* New Haven: Yale University Press, 1992.

Molnár, Géza von. "Wilhelm Meister's Apprenticeship as an Alternative to Werther's Fate." *Goethe Proceedings: Essays Commemorating the Goethe Sesquicentennial at the University of California, Davis.* Studies in German Literature, Linguistics, and Culture 12. Ed. Clifford A. Bernd, *et al.* Columbia, SC: Camden House, 1984. 77–91.

Muenzer, Clark S. *Figures of Identity: Goethe's Novels and the Enigmatic Self.* The Penn State Series in German Literature. University Park: Pennsylvania State University Press, 1984.

Müller, Klaus-Detlef. "Commentary and Notes." *Johann Wolfgang von Goethe. Sämtliche Werke: Briefe, Tagebücher und Gespräche.* Ed. Dieter Borchmeyer, *et al.* Vol. 1.14. Frankfurt: Deutscher Klassiker Verlag, 1986.

National Council of Teachers of English. "Resolution on the Students' Right to their Own Language." <http://www.ncte.org/positions/statements/righttoownlanguage>.

Noyes, John K. "Goethe on Cosmopolitanism and Colonialism: Bildung and the Dialectic of Critical Mobility." *Eighteenth-Century Studies* 39 (2006): 443–62.

Orwin, Clifford. "Moist Eyes: Political Tears from Rousseau to Clinton." 1997. *AIE.* January 1, 2000. American Enterprise Institute for Public Policy Research. Bradley Lecture Series. <http://www.aei.org/speech/18967>.

Paige, Rod. "Secretary's Statement." United States Department of Education.

Strategic Plan 2002–2007. February 2002. <www.ed.gov/about/reports/strat/plan2002–07/plan.pdf>

Peterson, Farmer John, and Angelic Organic. *Farmer John's Cookbook: The Real Dirt on Vegetables.* Layton, UT: Gibbs Smith, 2006.

Pinson, Koppel S. *Pietism as a Factor in the Rise of German Nationalism.* Studies in History, Economics, and Public Law 398. New York: Octagon Books, 1968 [1934].

Purdy, Daniel. *The Tyranny of Elegance: Consumer Cosmopolitanism in the Era of Goethe.* Baltimore: Johns Hopkins University Press, 1998.

Ravitch, Diane. "Is Arne Duncan Really Margaret Spellings in Drag?" February 24, 2009. *Education Week.* Ed. Jeanne McCann. April 25, 2009. <http://blogs.edweek.org/edweek/Bridging- Differences/2009/02/is_arne_duncan_really_margaret.html>.

Reiss, Hans. *Goethe's Novels.* New York: St. Martin's Press, 1969.

Richards, Robert J. *The Romantic Conception of Life: Science and Philosophy in the Age of Goethe.* Science and Its Conceptual Foundations. Chicago: University of Chicago Press, 2002.

Rigby, Catherine E. *Topographies of the Sacred: The Poetics of Place in European Romanticism.* Under the Sign of Nature. Charlottesville: University of Virginia Press, 2004.

Rivers, Wilga M. *Communicating Naturally in a Second Language: Theory and Practice in Language Teaching.* Cambridge/New York: Cambridge University Press, 1983.

Rousseau, Jean-Jacques. *Emile or On Education.* Trans. Allan Bloom. New York: Basic Books, 1979.

——. "Essay on the Origin of Languages." *On the Origin of Language. Jean-Jacques Rousseau. Johann Gottfried Herder.* Trans. with afterwords by John H. Moran and Alexander Gode. Chicago: University of Chicago Press, 1986.

——. "Essay on the Origin of Inequality." (*Second Discourse.*) Ed. and trans. Victor Gourevitch. New York: Perennial Library, 1986.

Sauder, Gerhard. "Der junge Goethe und das religiöse Denken des 18. Jahrhunderts." *Goethe-Jahrbuch* 112 (1995): 97–110.

Saul, Nicholas. "The Motif of Baptism in Three Eighteenth-Century Novels: Secularization or Sacralization?" *German Life and Letters* 39.2 (1986): 107–33.

Schlegel, Friedrich. "Athenaeum Fragments." *Classic and Romantic German Aesthetics.* Cambridge Texts in the History of Philosophy. Ed. J. M. Bernstein. Cambridge/New York: Cambridge University Press, 2003.

——. "On Goethe's Meister." *Classic and Romantic German Aesthetics.* Cambridge Texts in the History of Philosophy. Ed. J. M. Bernstein. Cambridge/New York: Cambridge University Press, 2003.

Schmidt, Leigh Eric. *Restless Souls: The Making of American Spirituality.* San Francisco: Harper San Francisco, 2005.

Schöffler, Herbert. "*Die Leiden des jungen Werther.* Ihr geistesgeschichtlicher Hintergrund." *Deutscher Geist im 18. Jahrhundert* (1956): 155–81. Quoted from the reprinted version in: *Goethes Werther: Kritik und Forschung.* Ed. Hans Peter Herrmann. Darmstadt: Wissenschaftliche Buchgesellschaft, 1994. 58–87.

Schöne, Albrecht. *Faust: Kommentare.* Frankfurt: Deutscher Klassiker Verlag, 1994.

Schutjer, Karin. *Narrating Community after Kant: Schiller, Goethe, and Hölderlin.* Detroit: Wayne State University, 2001.

"Seekers, Then and Now." *Kripalu Center for Yoga and Health.* 2009. July 4, 2008. <http://www.kripalu.org/pdfs/kavi_book_prologue.pdf>.

Segebrecht, Harro. "Diagnose und Prognose des technischen Zeitalters im Schlußakt von Faust II." *Goethe-Jahrbuch* 114 (1997): 63–73.

Segrè, Gino. *Faust in Copenhagen: A Struggle for the Soul of Physics.* New York: Penguin Books, 2008.

Sepper, Dennis. *Goethe Contra Newton: Polemics and the Project for a New Science of Color.* Cambridge/New York: Cambridge University Press, 1988.

Serfaty, Viviane. *The Mirror and the Veil: An Overview of American Online Diaries and Blogs.* Amsterdam Monographs in American Studies 11. Amsterdam/New York: Rodopi, 2004.

Shakespeare, William. *The Riverside Shakespeare.* Ed. G. Blakemore Evans. Boston: Houghton Mifflin Co., 1974.

Soboth, Christian. "Willkommen und Abschied: Der junge Goethe und der Pietismus." *Goethe und der Pietismus.* Eds. Hans-Georg Kemper and Hans Schneider. Tübingen: Niemeyer Verlag, 2001. 209–30.

Spellings, Margaret. "Secretary Spellings' Prepared Remarks at the National Press Club: An Action Plan for Higher Education." United States Department of Education. September 26, 2006. <http://www.ed.gov/news/speeches/2006/09/09262006.html>.

Spengler, Oswald. *The Decline of the West.* Trans. Charles Francis Atkinson. 2 vols. New York: Alfred A. Knopf, 1937 [1926–28].

"Spirit Matters Retreats." *Spirit Matters.* Spring 2009. July 4, 2008. <http://www.spiritmatters.ca/Retreats/teachers/index.html>.

Spohn, Cydney. "Teacher Perspectives on *No Child Left Behind* and Arts Education: A Case Study." *Arts Education Policy Review* 109.4 (March–April 2008): 3–12.

Staiger, Emil. *Goethe.* 3 vols. Zurich: Artemis, 1960.

Steiner, Rudolf. *Anthroposophical Leading Thoughts.* 1904. Trans. Mary Adams and George Adams. SteinerBooks Anthroposophic Press. July 1, 2008. <http://www.steinerbooks.org/aboutrudolf.html>.

Swales, Martin. "Goethe's *Faust* and the Drama of European Modernity." *Publications of the English Goethe Society* 74 (2005): 83–94.

——. *Goethe: The Sorrows of Young Werther.* Landmarks of World Literature. Cambridge/New York: Cambridge University Press, 1987.

——. "The Character and Characterization of Faust." *A Companion to Goethe's Faust: Parts I and II.* Studies in German Literature, Linguistics, and Culture. Ed. Paul Bishop. Rochester, NY: Camden House, 2001. 28–55.

Sweeney, Douglas A. *The American Evangelical Story: A History of the Movement.* Grand Rapids: Baker Academic, 2005.

Tanner, Tony. *Adultery in the Novel. Contract and Transgression.* Baltimore: Johns Hopkins University Press, 1979.

Tantillo, Astrida Orle. "A New Reading of Werther as Goethe's Critique of Rousseau." *Orbis Litterarum: International Review of Literary Studies* 56.6 (2001): 443–65.

——. *The Will to Create: Goethe's Philosophy of Nature.* Pittsburgh: University of Pittsburgh Press, 2002.

——. "The Catholicism of Werther." *German Quarterly* 81 (2008): 408–23.

——. "Werther, Frankenstein, and Girardian Mediated Desire." *Studia Neophilologica* 80 (2008): 177–87.

——. "Damned to Heaven: The Tragedy of *Faust* Revisited." *Monatshefte* 99 (2007): 454–68.

——. "The Subjective Eye: Goethe's *Farbenlehre* and *Faust*" in *The Enlightened Eye: Goethe and Visual Culture.* Eds. Evelyn Moore and Patricia Simpson. Amsterdam: Editions Rodopi, 2007. 265–77.

——. "Reforming College: What Professors Don't Tell You." November 17, 2005. *Slate Magazine.* <http//www.slate.com/id/2130327/>

——. Review of John Armstrong's *Love, Life, Goethe: Lessons of the Imagination From the Great German Poet, Chicago Tribune,* Sunday Books Section (5) January 28, 2007.

Tocqueville, Alexis de. *Democracy in America.* The Henry Reeve Text as revised by Francis Bowen and Phillips Bradley. 2 vols. New York: Vintage Books, 1945.

"Transcendentalism." *Wikipedia.* April 26, 2009. <http://en.wikipedia.org/wiki/Transcendentalism>.

Traub, James. "*No Child Left Behind*; Does It Work?" *The New York Times Education Life.* November 10, 2002, late ed., sec. 4A: 24.

Trunz, Erich, ed. *Goethes Faust: Der Tragödie erster und zweiter Teil. Urfaust.* 16th ed. München: Beck Verlag, 1999 [1949].

United States National Commission on Excellence in Education. *A Nation at Risk: The Imperative for Educational Reform: A Report to the Nation and the Secretary of Education.* Washington, DC: The Commission: [Supt. of Docs., U.S. G.P.O. distributor], 1983.

Vaget, Hans Rudolf. "The GDR *Faust*: A Literary Autopsy." *Oxford German Studies* 24 (1995): 145–74.

Van Cromphout, Gustaaf. *Emerson's Modernity and the Example of Goethe.* Columbia: University of Missouri Press, 1990.

Van der Laan, James M. *Seeking Meaning for Goethe's Faust.* Continuum Literary Studies. London/New York: Continuum, 2007.

Viëtor, Karl. *Goethe, the Poet.* Trans. Moses Hadas. Cambridge: Harvard University Press, 1949.

Wilson, W. Daniel. "Young Goethe's Political Fantasies." *Literature of the Sturm und Drang.* Ed. David Hill. Camden House History on German Literature VI. Rochester: Camden House, 2003. 187–215.

Yurick, Sol. "Faust's Stages of Spiritual/Economic Growth and Takeoff into Transcendence." *Social Text* 17 (1987): 67–95.

Zabel, Hermann. "Goethes *Werther*; Eine weltliche Passionsgeschichte?" *Zeitschrift für Religions- und Geistesgeschichte* 24 (1972): 57–69.

Zeleny, Jeff, and Brian Knowlton. "Obama Wants to Expand Role of Religious Groups." *The New York Times.* July 2, 2008: A16+.

Zuger, Abigail, MD "Snapshots from the Days of Bare-Hands Anatomy." *The New York Times.* April 28, 2009, late ed., sec. D5.

INDEX

Philemon *see* Baucis and Philemon
philosophy 49, 60, 73, 79, 86, 89, 104,
    116, 121, 152, 162
  Aristotelian 10, 64
  conservative 141
  educational 125, 162–3
  Emerson 107, 110
  Goethe's natural 3–6, 15–16, 96n. 40
  liberal 11–13, 148
  Rousseauian 11, 16, 123–4
Phoenix University 65
Pietism
  elements in *Werther* 77–80, 84
  general priesthood in 75, 85
  Goethe's connection to 77
  history of 74–6, 102
  modern influences of 73–4, 76, 102,
    108–9
  role of women in 76
Pinson, Koppel S. 75
piracy 54, 177
plant organs 32–3, 109n. 53 *see also*
    Metamorphosis of Plants
Plato (428/427–348/347 BC) 10
Poetry and Truth (*Dichtung und Wahrheit*)
    86, 90–1, 99
polar tension 25n. 6, 31–2, 35
polarity *see also* compensation, principle
    of; eye
  in American society 70–1, 112
  in *Faust* 25–7, 31–2, 34–5, 37, 41
  natural 32, 180
  in plants 32
  and *Steigerung* 31–2
pollution 50–1, 177
populism 9, 104–5
Posner, Richard Allen, Judge 49–50,
    53, 156
postmodern perspectives 4, 18, 120
priestly orders 87 *see also* Catholicism,
    sacraments
Prolog in Heaven (*Prolog im Himmel*)
    23, 30–1, 33, 36, 63, 181
Protestantism 17, 43, 73, 75, 85–9,
    101, 105 *see also* Evangelicalism;
    Catholicism; Pietism;
    Reformation
  Lutheran 75, 90n. 27, 96
  sacraments 84n. 15, 86–7

Purdy, Daniel 71, 72n. 1
Puritanism 103

Ravitch, Diane 154
Realpolitik 53, 59
reason 7, 10–12, 26–7, 75–6, 79, 93,
    97n. 41, 101–2, 114, 117, 123, 178
Reformation 58, 75, 89
Reiss, Hans 85
relativism, aesthetic 141–2
Republican Party 58, 112, 154–5
reverence (*Ehrfurcht*) 163–5, 167–8
Rigby, Catherine E. 53
Romanticism
  poetry 22, 40
  science 39
rosary 93
Rousseau, Jean-Jacques (1712–78) 9,
    11–12, 16, 122–4, 150–1, 163
  Emile, or On Education 123, 151
  Second Discourse 12, 16
Rove, Karl 70, 74

St Francis de Sales, Doctor of the
    Church 91
Sanford, Mark, United States Senator
    178
SAT Reasoning Test (formerly
    Scholastic Aptitude Test) 154
Schmidt, Leigh Eric 106–7, 109–11
Schöffler, Herbert 85
Schubarth, Karl Ernst (1796–1860) 34
science
  ascendancy of 2, 16, 22–3, 29, 38–9,
    53, 65, 86n. 17, 126, 152
  hermetic 77
  objectivity in 11, 26, 174
  role of nature in 16, 31, 38–9, 59,
    78, 97
  and Romanticism 39
  in student-centered education
    147
  and trade 22
  vs. art 22, 65, 126, 175, 180
secularism 2–3, 15, 17, 58, 70, 73, 77,
    83–5, 93, 102–3, 109, 120, 159,
    178
self-expression 13, 82, 110, 112n. 58,
    116